social
limits
to growth

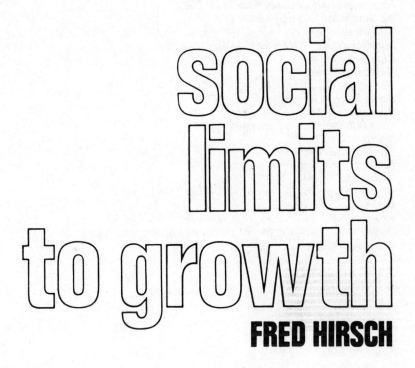

social limits to growth

FRED HIRSCH

A Twentieth Century Fund Study

Routledge & Kegan Paul
London and Henley

First published in Great Britain in 1977
by Routledge & Kegan Paul Ltd
39 Store Street,
London WC1E 7DD and
Broadway House,
Newtown Road,
Henley-on-Thames,
Oxon RG9 1EN
Reprinted 1977
First published as a paperback 1978
Reprinted 1978
Printed in Great Britain by
Lowe & Brydone Printers Ltd,
Thetford, Norfolk

ISBN 0 7100 8610 5 (c)
ISBN 0 7100 8711 X (p)

A TWENTIETH CENTURY FUND STUDY

The Twentieth Century Fund is an independent research foundation which undertakes policy studies of economic, political and social institutions and issues. The Fund was founded in 1919 and endowed by Edward A. Filene.

To Ruth, my collaborator

Preface

This book suggests that the current impasse on a number of key issues in the political economy of advanced nations is attributable in part to an outmoded perspective on the nature, and therefore the promise, of economic growth. The critique has some important immediate—mainly negative—implications for policy, and it opens up a wide range of consequential policy issues. It is for the reader to judge whether the theme developed here has sufficient validity and promise to justify the further analysis and inquiry called for by the approach put forward. Although the book has been a long time in the making—five years from first outline to final typescript—it represents little more than a starting point. It is devoted essentially to the frame in which the issues are seen and to the inferences for policy that follow and that need further investigation.

The support of the Twentieth Century Fund has made this book possible. The Fund financed my work from April 1972 until September 1974, while I was a research fellow at Nuffield College, Oxford. From its initial acceptance of the project through the slow journey to eventual completion, the Fund exercised unusual understanding and patience with the problems associated with a work of this kind. My appreciation for the support of the Fund, and particularly for that of its director, M. J. Rossant, therefore extends well beyond the conventional acknow.ledgment. I can only hope that the project has justified and not qualified the director's often expressed view that foundations should take chances.

Nuffield College provided the ideal environment for the work, and I express my warm thanks to the Warden and Fellows for offering me a research fellowship and for their hospitality and intellectual stimulus during my stay.

I have an unusually long list of individuals to thank for the personal help they gave me; presumably the extent of my indebtedness reflects the fact that I was immersing myself in a new branch of a subject. From the beginnings of the project, I have received invaluable guidance, stimulation, and criticism from Tibor Scitovsky. On a number of points, I doubt whether I have satisfied his exacting standards; yet, despite the usual disclaimer, he is in one sense responsible for the errors that follow, in that without his interest and continuing encouragement I am not sure that I would have persisted.

Another major acknowledgment is due Kenneth Boulding. His comments on the draft manuscript as a reader for the Fund contributed both general encouragement and much useful, constructive criticism. I am also grateful for comments and criticism of sections of the draft made at various stages by Brian Barry, John Flemming, John Goldthorpe, Richard Lecomber, Ian Little, Donald Moggridge, Mancur Olson, and Donald Winch; and by Walter Klein, Robert H. Nelson, and Peter Reuter of the Twentieth Century Fund staff, as well as two anonymous referees.

I am grateful to Arun Newell and Christopher Trinder for research assistance, to Stephen Carse for his work on checking of references, and to Theodore E. Young for editorial work. I am also grateful for the help given by my present secretary, Karen Kavanagh. As with my previous books, my wife, Ruth Hirsch, played a major part in the practical production process.

F.H.

Contents

Foreword by M. J. Rossant   xi

1 Introduction: The Argument in Brief   1

I *The Neglected Realm of Social Scarcity*
    2 A Duality in the Growth Potential   15
    3 The Material Economy
       and the Positional Economy   27
    4 The Ambiguity of Economic Output   55

II *The Commercialization Bias*
    5 The Economics of Bad Neighbors   71
    6 The New Commodity Fetishism   84
       Appendix   The Commercialization Effect:
               The Sexual Illustration   95
    7 A First Summary:
       The Hole in the Affluent Society   102

III *The Depleting Moral Legacy*
    8 An Overload on the Mixed Economy   117
    9 Political Keynesianism and the Managed Market   123
    10 The Moral Re-entry   137
    11 The Lost Legitimacy and the Distributional
        Compulsion   152

IV *Perspective and Conclusions*
    12 The Liberal Market as a Transition Case   161
    13 Inferences for Policy   178

    References   193
    Index   203

Foreword

Well over four years ago, Fred Hirsch approached the Twentieth Century Fund with a proposal for a study of growth in affluent economies. At a time when public debate was much more concerned with the warnings about the limits on growth put forth by the Club of Rome, the Board of Trustees of the Fund demonstrated considerable prescience in sponsoring Hirsch's project, which sought to deal with the very nature of growth. They decided that although the project might be risky, the risk was well worth taking, both because Hirsch himself was a thoughtful and elegant scholar and because he was attempting to deal with one of the fundamental, although largely ignored, problems of advanced societies, namely, the social problems that economic growth creates, especially for democracies.

This subject required wide reading, heated discussion with a variety of scholars, and much revising, always with the thought of paring the argument to its essentials. The project then had a long gestation period. In his thinking and subsequent writing, Hirsch rejected conventional analysis and facile solutions. The result is a significant contribution to the understanding of the economic growth process and its hazards in advanced societies.

It goes without saying that the Fund is delighted that this particular intellectual investment proved so rewarding. Speaking personally, it was a pleasure to work with so lively and original a thinker as Fred Hirsch, who also accepted critical comments with grace and humor. His work, of course, is all his, and he writes with eloquence and insight about the perplexing consequences of economic well being. His style and scholarship require careful reading, and he does not claim to have all the answers. But he deals with some of the most critical problems that confront us, and his message is of critical importance. Hirsch focuses, with brilliance and perceptiveness, on problems that will have to be resolved in a democratic context.

On behalf of the Trustees and the staff of the Fund, I want to express my appreciation for Hirsch's challenging analysis.

M. J. Rossant, Director
The Twentieth Century Fund

social limits to growth

1 Introduction: The Argument in Brief

This book tries to give an economist's answer to three questions.

(1) Why has economic advance become and remained so compelling a goal to all of us as individuals, even though it yields disappointing fruits when most, if not all of us, achieve it?

(2) Why has modern society become so concerned with distribution —with the division of the pie—when it is clear that the great majority of people can raise their living standards only through production of a larger pie?

(3) Why has the twentieth century seen a universal predominant trend toward collective provision and state regulation in economic areas at a time when individual freedom of action is especially extolled and is given unprecedented rein in noneconomic areas such as aesthetic and sexual standards?

Let us call these three issues (1) the paradox of affluence, (2) the distributional compulsion, and (3) the reluctant collectivism.

My major thesis is that these three issues are interrelated, and stem from a common source. This source is to be found in the nature of economic growth in advanced societies. The heart of the problem lies in the complexity and partial ambiguity of the concept of economic growth once the mass of the population has satisfied its main biological needs for life-sustaining food, shelter, and clothing. The traditional economic distinction between how much is produced, on what basis, and who gets it then becomes blurred. The issues of production, of individual versus collective provision, and of distribution then become intertwined.

This development marks a profound change. It is a change that economists in particular find difficult to accept because it has the appearance of scientific retrogression. Traditionally, the contribution of the economist to charting a way to economic progress has consisted largely of unscrambling the aspects of economic activity just mentioned—distinguishing between the share of the pie and its size, between the motivation of individual actions and their collective result. It was on these distinctions that the science of economics was launched by Adam Smith two centuries ago. Smith showed that pursuit by individuals in an uncoordinated way of their own interests could yet serve the interests of all and that the poor man in the rich community could live better than native kings.

The progress of economics has been devoted largely to developing and refining these insights, which has resulted in enormous advances in the quantification of economic phenomena. This quantification in turn supports not merely the claim of economics to primacy in the ranking of the social sciences but also its established primacy in the agenda of public policy. In the past generation, electoral politics throughout the industrial world, and beyond it, has been increasingly dominated by the big economic numbers—gross national product, personal disposable income, and the rate at which these indicators of material prosperity grow.

Yet in advanced societies, those in which the mass of the population has risen above merely life-sustaining consumption, the stage may now have been reached where the analytical framework that the economist has come to take for granted—but that the sociologist has long disputed—has become a hindrance in understanding some key contemporary problems. Confronting these problems in the framework of the traditional analytical separation leaves the answers in the air. The three broad questions listed at the outset—the paradox of affluence, the distributional compulsion, the reluctant collectivism—are puzzles or paradoxes when viewed in isolation. A clue to their resolution is to approach them as interconnected products of a neglected structural characteristic of modern economic growth. That is what this book tries to do.

I

The structural characteristic in question is that as the level of average consumption rises, an increasing portion of consumption takes on a social as well as an individual aspect. That is to say, the satisfaction that individuals derive from goods and services depends in increasing measure not only on their own consumption but on consumption by others as well.

To a hungry man, the satisfaction derived from a square meal is unaffected by the meals other people eat or, if he is hungry enough, by anything else they do. His meal is an entirely individual affair. In technical terms it is a pure private good. At the other extreme, the quality of the air that the modern citizen breathes in the center of a city depends almost entirely on what his fellow citizens contribute toward countering pollution, whether directly by public expenditure or indirectly through public regulation. Clean air in a metropolis is a social product. In technical terms, it is close to a pure public good.

These polar cases, however, are relatively few in number. It has recently become recognized by economists who specialize in these matters that the major part of consumption is neither purely private nor purely public. What is generally referred to as private or personal consumption is nonetheless affected in its essence—that is, in the satisfaction or utility it yields—by consumption of the same goods or services by others; and in that specific sense it can be said to contain a social element. Correspondingly, what is generally referred to as public consumption contains some of the characteristics of private goods, in the sense that its costs and benefits are or can be confined to a limited group.

The range of private consumption that contains a social element in the sense described is much wider than is generally recognized. In textbooks on economics, public goods are discussed in the context of goods and facilities that can be provided only, or most economically, on a collective basis, open to all and financed by all. City parks and streets and national defense are prominent examples. In addition, elements of public goods are recognized in side effects of private transactions such as pollution and congestion occurring in particular identifiable situations. But a more general public goods element can be attributed to a wide range of private expenditures. Thus the utility of expenditure on a given level of education as a means of access to the most sought after jobs will decline as more people attain that level of education. The value to me of my education depends not only on how much I have but also on how much the man ahead of me in the job line has. The satisfaction derived from an auto or a country cottage depends on the conditions in which they can be used, which will be strongly influenced by how many other people are using them. This factor, which is social in origin, may be a more important influence on my satisfaction than the characteristics of these items as "private" goods (on the speed of the auto, the spaciousness of the cottage, and so forth). Beyond some point that has long been surpassed in crowded industrial societies, conditions of use tend to deteriorate as use becomes more widespread.

Congestion is most apparent in its physical manifestation, in traffic jams. But traffic congestion can be seen as only a special case of the wider phenomenon of social congestion, which in turn is a major facet of social scarcity. Social scarcity is a central concept in this analysis. It expresses the idea that the good things of life are restricted not only by physical limitations of producing more of them but also by absorptive limits on their use. Where the social environment has a restricted capacity for extending use without quality deterioration, it imposes social limits to consumption. More specifically, the limit is imposed on satisfactions that depend not on the product or facility in isolation but on the surrounding conditions of use.

What precisely is *new* about this situation? The limits have always

4 / Introduction: The Argument in Brief

been there at some point, but they have not until recent times become obtrusive. That is the product, essentially, of past achievements in material growth not subject to social limits. In this sense, the concern with the limits to growth that has been voiced by and through the Club of Rome[1] is strikingly misplaced. It focuses on distant and uncertain physical limits and overlooks the immediate if less apocalyptic presence of social limits to growth.

So long as material privation is widespread, conquest of material scarcity is the dominant concern. As demands for purely private goods are increasingly satisfied, demands for goods and facilities with a public (social) character become increasingly active. These public demands make themselves felt through individual demands on the political system or through the market mechanism in the same way as do the demands for purely private goods. Individuals acquire both sets of goods without distinction, except where public goods are provided by public or collective action; even there, individuals may seek to increase their own share by private purchases.

These demands in themselves appear both legitimate and attainable. Why should the individual not spend his money on additional education as a means to a higher placed job, or on a second home in the country, if he prefers these pleasures to spending on a mink coat or whiskey or to a life of greater leisure? That question was being loudly voiced in the mid-1970s as part of a middle-class backlash in both Britain and the United States. It can be answered satisfactorily only by reference to the public goods or social content of the expenditures involved.

Considered in isolation, the individual's demand for education as a job entree, for an auto, for a country cottage, can be taken as genuinely individual wants, stemming from the individual's own preferences in the situation that confronts him. Acting alone, each individual seeks to make the best of his or her position. But satisfaction of these individual preferences itself alters the situation that faces others seeking to satisfy similar wants. A round of transactions to act out personal wants of this kind therefore leaves each individual with a worse bargain than was reckoned with when the transaction was undertaken, because the sum of such acts does not correspondingly improve the position of all individuals taken together. There is an "adding-up" problem. Opportunities for economic

[1] The Club of Rome is an informal international association, styling itself as an invisible college, which is best known for its "world model" representing the interconnections of resources, population, and environment in the mode of systems dynamics. The message, which received worldwide popular acclaim and widespread professional criticism, was contained in Donella H. Meadows, Dennis L. Meadows, Jørgen Randers, and William W. Behrens III, *The Limits to Growth*, A Report for the Club of Rome's Project on the Predicament of Mankind (London: Earth Island Limited, 1972).

advance, as they present themselves serially to one person after another, do not constitute equivalent opportunities for economic advance by all. What each of us can achieve, all cannot.

A break between individual and social opportunities may occur for a number of reasons; excessive pollution and congestion are the most commonly recognized results. A neglected general condition that produces this break is competition by people for place, rather than competition for performance. Advance in society is possible only by moving to a higher place among one's fellows, that is, by improving one's performance in relation to other people's performances. If everyone stands on tiptoe, no one sees better. Where social interaction of this kind is present, individual action is no longer a sure means of fulfilling individual choice: the preferred outcome may be attainable only through collective action. (We all agree explicitly or implicitly not to stand on tiptoe.) The familiar dichotomy between individual choice and collective provision or regulation then dissolves. Competition among isolated individuals in the free market entails hidden costs for others and ultimately for themselves. These costs are a deadweight cost for all and involve social waste, unless no preferable alternative method of allocation is available. But the same distortion may result from public provision where this responds to individual demands formulated without taking account of subsequent interactions.

A conspicuous example is provided in certain aspects of education. People possessing relatively high educational qualifications are seen to enjoy attractive professional and social opportunities. This situation induces a strong latent demand for access to such qualifications. Such demand may flow through the market, in the willingness of individuals to pay higher fees for educational services supplied by private institutions without public support. In our own times, the demand more often is directed to the state, to broaden access to the higher strata of the educational pyramid. The state is expected to foster equality of educational opportunity and perhaps also equality of educational outcome. But these concepts present a number of difficulties, some well known and some less so.

The concept of equal opportunity, or equality at the starting gate, is not much less question-begging when applied to education than when applied to life chances in general, the central ambiguity being which starting handicaps are to be removed. At the limit, the criterion of an equal start is an equal finish. Worse, equal outcome in education would be impeded not only by differences in individual talent and inclination; the concept also fails to allow for an important function education performs in modern society, that is, sorting or screening. In its own way education is a device for controlling social scarcity.

To the extent that education in fact functions so as to sort out those who can best survive and master an educational obstacle course, improved performance by some worsens the position of those who would otherwise be ahead. The "quality" of schooling, in effect, exists in two dimensions. There is an *absolute* dimension, in which quality is added by receptive students, good teachers, good facilities, and so on; but there is also a *relative* dimension, in which quality consists of the differential over the educational level attained by others. The enormous resistance induced in both the United States and Britain by public attempts to integrate previously inferior schools with previously superior schools cannot be fully understood without reference to both these aspects of educational quality. Even if complete assurance could be given that absolute quality would be fully preserved, the previous incumbents of the superior schools would still lose their edge. This loss in turn can be expected to induce them to demonstrate their proficiency in a tougher or longer course of study. To the extent that education is a screening device (a qualification that must be kept firmly in mind), then the possibility of general advance is an illusion.

What is possible for the single individual is not possible for all individuals—and would not be possible even if they all possessed equal talent. Individuals, whether shopping for educational advance in the market place or pushing for educational advance through political demands, do not see the break between individual and social opportunity; that is, they do not see that opportunities open to each person separately are not open to all. It follows that response to individual demands of this kind, whether in market processes or in public provision, cannot deliver the order.

Consumers, taken together, get a product they did not order; collectively, this result involves potential social waste. Consumers individually find that their access to socially scarce goods and facilities, where these are attainable even in part through market processes, is determined in accord not with absolute but with relative real income. The determining factor is the individual's position in the distribution of purchasing power. Frustration of individual expectations then results from both these characteristics: from social waste, which cuts into the level of welfare[2] available to all; and from an imposed hierarchy that confines socially scarce goods to those on the highest rungs of the distributional ladder, disappointing the expectations of those whose position is raised through a lift in the ladder as a whole.

So the distributional struggle returns, heightened rather than relieved by the dynamic process of growth. It is an exact reversal of what

[2] In the sense of some concept of ultimate consumer satisfaction, discussed in Chapter 4.

economists and present-day politicians have come to expect growth to deliver.

The compelling attraction of economic growth in its institutionalized modern form has been as a superior substitute for redistribution. Whereas the masses today could never get close to what the well-to-do have today, even by expropriating all of it, they can, in the conventional view, get most if not all the way there with patience in a not too distant tomorrow, through the magic of compound growth. But, as outlined above, once this growth brings mass consumption to the point where it causes problems of congestion in the widest sense—bluntly, where consumption or jobholding by others tends to crowd you out—then the key to personal welfare is again the ability to stay ahead of the crowd. Generalized growth then increases the crush.

Thus the frustration in affluence results from its very success in satisfying previously dominant material needs. This frustration is usually thought of as essentially a psychological phenomenon, a matter of our subjective internal assessment. What we previously had to struggle for now comes easily, so we appreciate it less. The analysis of this book fastens on a separate consequence of generalized material growth that is independent of any such psychological revaluation; it affects what individuals get as well as the satisfaction it brings them. What they get, in the growing sphere of social scarcity, depends to an increasing extent on their relative position in the economic hierarchy. Hence, the paradox of affluence. It embodies a distributional compulsion, which in turn leads to our reluctant collectivism.

These sources of frustration with the fruits of economic growth are concealed in the economist's standard categorization. Strictly speaking, our existing concept of economic output is appropriate only for truly private goods, having no element of interdependence between consumption by different individuals. The bedrock is valuation by individuals of goods and opportunities in the situation in which they find themselves. At any moment of time and for any one person, standing on tiptoe gives a better view, or at least prevents a worse one. Equally, getting ahead of the crowd is an effective and feasible means of improving one's welfare, a means available to any one individual. It yields a benefit, in this sense, and the measure of the benefit is what individuals pay to secure it. The individual benefit from the isolated action is clear-cut. The sum of benefits of all the actions taken together is nonetheless zero.

This reckoning, it should be emphasized, is still made on the measure of the individual's own valuation, the same valuation that imputes a positive benefit to the individual action. Since individual benefits of this kind simply do not add up, the connection between individual and aggregate advance is broken. Yet the modern concepts of economic output, and of growth in that output, are grounded on individual valuations and their addition. Individual preference is assumed to be revealed implicitly in market behavior—in the consumer's choice between products at their given market prices, in the worker's choice between jobs and between different opportunities of job training at the going rates of pay and conditions. If individual valuations do not add up, then the aggregated valuations based upon them become biased measures.

Unfortunately no better quantitative measure of economic output has yet been found. The need for a flanking set of social indicators is now widely accepted, at least in principle. The end product of such a system would be an integrated system of numbers comparable with the national income accounts. This objective is far from being realized. There is no social performance indicator that can be systematically calculated and easily understood.

The national accounts have been developed into an elaborate ground plan of the economy that is used for a large variety of purposes. The gross national product and its components are the best indicators of personal and national prosperity we have, if only because they are the only such indicators. They thereby maintain a strong hold on public attention. Inevitably, this attention has given its own validity to the analytical categorization which lies at the base of national accounting, as well as of the older, related economic concepts from which it grew. The products of the economics numbers factory enjoy a brisk demand; and the economic inducement to cater to effective demand is not suspended for economics itself. Nor are economists immune from the instinct of trade unionists; they too judge the social worth of their performance by the prosperity and prestige it brings to their craft.

The ambiguity in the concept of economic output pointed out here is of secondary or even negligible significance in making use of the conventional measures of national accounts for the formulation of official policy designed to regulate or stabilize the short-term performance of the economy. For comparisons of welfare over extended periods of time, in estimates of long-term economic growth, and in league tables of living standards among countries in different situations at a given period of time, national accounting measures are notoriously less suitable.

What is stressed here is a different limitation, one almost wholly neglected by economists: the problem of translating individual economic improvement into overall improvement. In the standard model of thinking, if the fruits of aggregate advance appear inadequate or disappointing, the deficiency merely reflects inadequate economic effort or excessive demands by individuals, or poor organization or inadequate capital equipment currently available to them. Too much has been expected too soon. This conceptual framework adopted by economists concerned with policy has penetrated the thinking, expectations, and performance criteria of politicians and electorates of all western countries. As a consequence, conventional wisdom thinks in terms of "excessive expectations." The populace wants it now. It cannot have it now. It is too impatient. The implication is that the gathering of the fruit must await exercise of the necessary virtues—essentially, effort and restraint. Yet for those aspects of individual welfare where the connection between individual and aggregate advancement does not exist, or is broken under the stress of widening access to limited availabilities, the established conceptual framework is invalid. Its application to ultimate consumer satisfaction in this sector operates as a frustration machine.

Thus to see total economic advance as individual advance writ large is to set up expectations that cannot be fulfilled, ever. It is not just a matter of scaling down demand and expectations that are extravagant in relation to effort by workers or to the availability of technology or the use made of it. This view has become the conventional one on problems of excess demand and inflation. The appropriate solution to the problem so conceived is simple, at least in principle: to adjust expectations down and/or performance up. The necessary adjustment is purely quantitative. If all put a little more into the pool and take a little less out for a while, then present expectations can in time be fulfilled. So runs the predominant message of politico-economic managers in the postwar generation. Only hold back a little, and the good things you rightly crave will come to you or, at least, to your children. The inflationary explosion of the early 1970s and the severe world recession that followed attempts to contain it have been widely interpreted in this vein—as a painful interruption in a progressive improvement in living standards that could be restored and sustained once the public was prevailed upon to exercise the necessary restraint.

It follows from this line of thought that the chief culprits responsible for derailing the train of technological advance are those institutions that inflate economic demands beyond the steady but limited growth in capacity to fulfill them. Trade unions exercising the bargaining power of their collective strength stand out as such culprits. It is the collective element in their activities—the mobilization of economic strength greater than the sum of the individual parts—that is seen to intrude on the balance and viability of an individualistic economy. The unquestioned premise of this approach is that competitive individualistic advance can ultimately deliver the goods. If it cannot, which participants in collective activity may instinctively feel and as the present analysis explicitly argues, then defensive collective expedients must be looked at in a new light.

To the extent that the mismatch between current expectations and resources is qualitative rather than quantitative, the restraint necessary would be not patience but stoicism, acceptance, and social cooperation— qualities that are out of key with our culture of individualistic advance.

Yet without such qualities, the traditional response by the public to the prospect of satisfaction as reward for extra effort or temporary abstinence will worsen the problem. For addition to the material goods that can be expanded for all will, in itself, increase the scramble for those goods and facilities that cannot be so expanded. Taking part in the scramble is fully rational for any individual in his own actions, since in these actions he never confronts the distinction between what is available as a result of getting ahead of others and what is available from a general advance shared by all. The individual who wants to see better has to stand on tiptoe. In the game of beggar your neighbor, that is what each individual must try to do, even though not all can. The only way of avoiding the competition in frustration is for the people concerned to coordinate their objectives in some explicit way, departing from the principle of isolated individual striving in this sphere. That is to say, only a collective approach to the problem can offer individuals the guidance necessary to achieve a solution they themselves would prefer. The principle is acknowleged in the standard liberal analysis, but confined to the exceptional case.

How a satisfactory collective view is to be arrived at, and then implemented, remains a large and mostly unresolved problem of its own. Collective action can involve familiar distortions and inefficiencies. The means to a collective solution may be inadequate. To the extent that this is so, the analysis put forward here carries no clear-cut implications for immediate policy. The distortions and frustrations entailed in uncoordinated individual actions may still appear as the lesser evil. However, a change in the nature of a problem is not undone by deficiencies in the tools available for tackling it. Correct diagnosis is likely to yield some implications for policy, if only to stop banging into the wall.

By collapsing individual and total opportunities for economic advance into a single process grounded on individual valuations, the standard view has obscured a significant change in the nature of the economic problem. It has thereby overstated the promise of economic growth. It has understated the limitations of consumer demand as a guide to an efficient pattern of economic activity. It has obscured the extent of the modern conflict between individualistic actions and satisfaction of individualistic preferences. Getting what one wants is increasingly divorced from doing as one likes.

II

Together, these limitations imply a substantial modification in the menu offered by economic liberalism, including that embodied in programs of liberal socialism. The preponderant implication is that choices are more restricted and price tags are higher, in the form of costlier trade-offs, than the traditional menu has suggested. The traditional liberal opportunities, which are still held out as a prospect attainable by all who are prepared to adopt the requisite liberal values, appear instead to have the marks, in certain key respects, of minority status. Offered to the majority, they are available only to a minority. Tensions and frustrations have inevitably resulted.

That is one major undercurrent of the modern crisis in the liberal system. Positional goods, in the language introduced in the next chapter, become an increasing brake on the expansion and extension of economic welfare. Social scarcity tightens its grip. Economic liberalism is in this sense a victim of its own propaganda: offered to all, it has evoked demands and pressures that cannot be contained.

In a further sense, economic liberalism has been the victim of its own success. Its singular efficiency has resided in its capacity for decentralization of knowledge and of decision-making. This decentralization is achieved essentially by harnessing the ancient individual instinct of maximization of personal advantage (more strictly, of pursuit of individual interests, however self-oriented or otherwise they may be: "self-interest" should be understood as a shorthand way of expressing the wider concept of privately oriented behavior). Socially beneficial results have thereby been obtained without the necessity of socially oriented motivation. Good has been done by stealth. Adam Smith's invisible hand has linked individual self-interest with social need. But the conditions in which this link has been achieved over a wide area can now be seen not as stable conditions that can be relied on to persist or to be readily maintainable by deliberate action. Rather, they can be seen in important respects to have been special conditions associated with a transition phase from an earlier socioeconomic system. The generally benign invisible hand was a favorable inaugural condition of liberal capitalism.

There are two ways in which the novelty of the liberal capitalist order was associated with what can now be seen as transient inaugural conditions. First, full participation was confined to a minority—the minority that had reached material affluence before liberal capitalism had set the masses on the path of material growth. Second, the system operated on social foundations laid under a different order of society.

The successful operation of economic liberalism undermines both these supports. It spreads demand for participation to all. At the same time, it erodes the social foundations that underlie a benign and efficient implementation of the self-interest principle operating through market transactions.

Those who have understood the rationale of the free market as an organizing device have always recognized key areas of public life in which the maxim of laissez-faire—or nonintervention through public policy—was inappropriate. In these selective areas, public policies would be applied essentially as a supplement to market behavior directed to

maximization of individual advantage. The idea has been either to con-
strain such behavior by law, for example, through the income tax law, or
to influence behavior by deliberately adjusting market opportunities, for
example, through indirect taxes or subsidies or conditional grants. In
both instances, reliance is still placed on the self-interest principle for
compliance. A critical omission from this approach is the role played by
the supporting ethos of social obligation both in the formulation of the
relevant public policies and in their efficient transmission to market opportunities. Why expect the controllers, alone, to abstain from maximizing their individual advantage?

In brief, the principle of self-interest is incomplete as a social organizing device. It operates effectively only in tandem with some supporting social principle. This fundamental characteristic of economic liberalism, which was largely taken for granted by Adam Smith and by John
Stuart Mill in their different ways, has been lost sight of by its modern
protagonists. While the need for modifications in laissez-faire in public
policies has been increasingly accepted, the need for qualifications to self-
interested behavior by individuals has been increasingly neglected. Yet
correctives to laissez-faire increase rather than decrease reliance on some
degree of social orientation and social responsibility in individual behavior. The attempt has been made to erect an increasingly explicit social organization without a supporting social morality. The result has been a
structural strain on both the market mechanism and the political mechanism designed to regulate and supplement it.

In this way, the foundations of the market system have been weakened, while its general behavioral norm of acting on the criterion of self-
interest has won ever-widening acceptance. As the foundations weaken,
the structure rises ever higher. The deeper irony—which can also be seen
as a fortunate legacy—resides in the success of the market system in its
initial phase, on the shoulders of a premarket social ethos.

A system that depends for its success on a heritage that it undermines cannot be sustained on the record of its bountiful fruits. These
fruits themselves, real as they are, are yet a false promise. Offered in the
shop window, they outshine the competition. But delivery is limited to
select customers—the minority offering; worse, it is limited to early customers—the transient offering. It is possible that even an inferior selection of goods offered by the same store would still outshine any available
alternative. But that is another matter. What is seen to be on offer is the
selection in the window. If this offering is not what it looks, it is important to show how and why. Only in that way can expectations and performance be adapted to what can feasibly be provided.

part one
The Neglected Realm of Social Scarcity

2 A Duality in the Growth Potential

The central achievement of modern economic analysis has been to add up: to develop a theoretical basis and an associated accounting frame for the aggregation of economic activity within an integrated system. This system, represented conceptually and statistically in the national accounts, was critical to domestic stabilization policy, the prime objective of Keynesian fiscal management. Stabilization policy is concerned with minimizing the ups and downs of economic activity, particularly with avoiding mass unemployment and runaway inflation. Once established, this unsurpassed framework and body of data shed light on other major areas of economists' concern. Thus, a second focus of attention was distribution of income—in fact, concern with distribution had been the main impetus behind earlier, cruder, and less complete essays in measurement of national income, notably those associated with Arthur Bowley.[1]

A third major area to which the framework of national accounts could be applied was long-term economic growth. In a sense, the renewed interest in economic growth that took place following World War II was itself a product of the statistics. A run of numbers, showing a decided tendency to upward movement, demonstrated a pattern of growth of a regularity that might not otherwise have been discerned. Thus it could be said, after Molière, that the emerging time series of measured national product revealed the exponential growth rate as the prose that, in the absence of recorded measurement, economies had been talking unnoticed for nearly two centuries.

From the standpoint of all three areas of economic concern—stabilization, distribution, growth—the adding up of economic activity into the single output measure has yielded powerful insights. But at some points this focus on aggregation has obscured both the parts and the processes

[1] Arthur Bowley, *Three Studies on the National Income* (London School of Economics [1919-1927], 1938).

15

involved. In particular, it has obscured a duality in the potential for economic growth, a duality that also has important implications for distribution of the economic product and for the pattern and style of economic and social life.

I

Statistical measurement of national income and product, through its direct influence on economic and political expectations held by individuals and groups, has taken on a substantive importance of its own. These expectations, both individual and collective, have been based to some extent on misapplied aggregation of the economy's ultimate objective, or maximand. This objective is typically expressed as the satisfaction, to the greatest feasible extent, of demand for consumption of scarce goods and services by individuals, extending over time and thereby taking investment needs into account.

In a more comprehensive view, satisfactions from particular forms of work, as well as from particular social or physical environments, also need to be assessed because they influence the value attached to input and therefore to net output. The same output produced under more pleasant working conditions, whether these comprise more interesting work processes or longer coffee breaks, ought to be registered as larger net output. It represents the same gross output for less input. Leisure on the job is beginning to be recognized as a legitimate product of economic effort—on the important proviso that the work practices concerned are freely chosen in preference to more intensive work at higher rates of pay. But these wider desiderata have not been incorporated in either the professional or the popular concepts of economic output. If in Britain workers and managers show a persistent inclination to get up late and take leisure on the job, this is categorized, and generally condemned, as inefficiency and lost output. As a result, the concepts of economic efficiency, productivity, and growth, which all relate to the measure used for economic output, have been too crude; specifically they have been biased on the output as against the input side—to the individual as consumer rather than as producer. Yet broad questions concerning the measurement and interpretation of consumption have received little attention from economists.

Modern economic growth theory has been concerned with conditions that stimulate or impede the growth process from the supply side. The problem is one of harnessing and augmenting available resources of labor, capital, and technology to meet the competing demands upon them. Consumption represents the ultimate source of these demands. It represents the true subject and object of economic growth. Yet the composition of consumption—its content—is not brought into the analysis. In the standard view, growth provides the means of consumption; its form is then a matter of making the best choice fitted to prevailing consumer preferences. Thus a common riposte by economists to skepticism about the benefits of economic growth has been to turn the criticism to the use to which growth is put. The obvious corrective to dissatisfaction with the fruits of growth is then to redirect the additional resources to the preferred purpose.[2]

Underlying this approach is a view of consumption as a malleable aggregate. There is the product: its form can be fashioned to choice. Theoretical growth models can then be confined to a single consumption good. Practical consideration of growth prospects can be confined to the economy's supply capacity, possibly supplemented by some consideration of *aggregate* demand. Consumption comes into the picture only as a national income aggregate, and then as a determinant of the residual entity, savings.

To be sure, the market economy rests on valuations made by individual consumers. These valuations provide both the stimulus and the measure of economic activity in the market sector. The extent to which the preferences of consumers are transmitted to producers through the market process, and even the sequence of the transmission, has been questioned by a long line of critics, most recently and prominently by John Kenneth Galbraith. A further question arises from the failure of the market process to signal the demand for public or collective goods. These are goods such as police services, defense, or highways that in their nature become available to a group, rather than to a single purchaser, and that can therefore be provided more efficiently under some collective method of financing than in exclusive provision on market terms to individuals. A fairly wide range of views exists among economists on the relative significance of these market imperfections and market failures—on how far they make consumer valuations a misleading or inadequate indication of the preferences of consumers. But these qualifications are concerned essentially with perfecting the transmission from the preferences of the individual consumer to the delivery mechanism of the market and governmental suppliers. If both consumer preferences and full social costs could be correctly passed on to producers, fulfillment of these preferences of individual consumers would be the accepted goal of the system. The general view remains that consumption, whether in the form of private goods individually purchased or in the form of individual partici-

[2] This is a major theme of Wilfred Beckerman's book *In Defence of Economic Growth* (London: Cape, 1974); see also Walter W. Heller, "Economic Growth and Ecology—An Economist's View," *Monthly Labor Review* (November 1971). The argument occupies a prominent place in political hopes for benefits from future economic growth. See for example Anthony Crosland, "A Social Democratic Britain," in his *Socialism Now* (London: Cape, 1974).

pation in collective provision, provides the ultimate drive and purpose of the economic system.

Economic growth, then, is interpreted as growth in the capacity of the economy to meet these individual and collective consumption demands. How the demands can be met may be a serious technical problem —requiring the maintenance and stiffening of competition in the provision of private goods, and, more testingly, finding adequate means first of registering and then of financing individuals' demand for collective goods. The extent of interdependence in many forms of consumption in advanced, urbanized societies has brought increasing recognition that to give effect to public choice among the available economic alternatives represents a still unresolved intellectual and administrative problem, rather than requiring merely the sweeping away of impediments to the working of the market mechanism.

The core of the problem is that the market provides a full range of choice between alternative piecemeal, discrete, marginal adjustments, but no facility for selection between alternative states. Since the piecemeal choices between the opportunities that are available through market transactions at any given time involve unintended and at times undesired repercussions, choice in the small does not provide choice in the large. For example, as public transportation deteriorates, we are given an extra incentive to use our own private mode of transport which in turn results in further deterioration and a worsened position of public vis-à-vis private transportation. The choice is posed at each stage in a dynamic process; there is no chance of selection between the states at either end of that process. By contrast, the political mechanism, through which preferences between alternative states could in principle be posed, has not yet developed a satisfactory system for such decision. These issues are becoming better understood, though the extent of the ensuing dilemma is usually underestimated. Consequently, the capacity of both the market and the political system to meet expectations tend to be overestimated. They cannot deliver on what the public takes to be their promise.

But there is a prior and perhaps bigger question that has been widely neglected. This is how far—and more specifically, in what sectors— expansion of consumption is possible even in principle, that is, assuming away the technical problems just mentioned of transmitting individuals' preferences to market producers and to suppliers of collective goods.

The standard view of the economy does not focus on such limitations. Yet the extent to which consumption goods or facilities can be replicated or replaced by substitutes—their elasticity of supply and elasticity of substitution over the long term—is of central relevance for the growth process and its interaction with distribution. A fundamental distinction can be made in this connection, even on an a priori basis.

II

Certain goods and facilities from which individuals derive satisfaction are subject to absolute limitations in supply, deriving from one of a number of sources. The first though not the most significant such source of scarcity is physical availability.

Absolute physical scarcities have more usually been considered from the side of production. Thus, the limited availability of land was the centerpiece of classical economics as developed by David Ricardo and, from a different standpoint, by Thomas Malthus some 150 years ago.[3] Equally, concern about the implications of limited resources of agricultural land and of natural raw materials is at the center of the contemporary environmental-ecology movement, with its stress on physical limits to growth. To economists, the implications of these physical limits are not as clear-cut as they appear to natural scientists and laymen, because of the potential—and at any given time unknowable—scope for substitution. The enormous opportunities for substitution between the limited resources and reproducible materials as a result of technological advance is evident from the confounding of what now appears as the first round in ecological pessimism, in the Malthusian projections of the inevitable out-pacing of food supply by population growth. The four-fold increase in world population since Malthus wrote has gone along with a rise rather than a fall in food consumption per head, including a very sharp rise in what are now the industrial countries. This experience does not permit the comfortable conclusion that substitution will always continue to be adequate to counterbalance the constraints resulting from scarce physical factors of production. It does however give a verdict of non-proven on the analysis founded solely on physical limits to growth. That, in crude summary, is what has emerged from economists' criticism of the "ecological" antigrowth school.[4]

Though economists do not find it possible to make positive predictions on the implications of limited natural resources for the long run future and the possibilities of human survival, there is a less apocalyptic

---

[3] Thomas Malthus, *An Essay on Population* (1798) (London: Dent, 1914 and 1960). David Ricardo, *The Principles of Political Economy and Taxation* (1798), in P. Sraffa, ed., *Works of David Ricardo*, vol. I (Cambridge, Eng.: Cambridge University Press, 1962).

[4] See for example Robert M. Solow, "The Economics of Resources or the Resources of Economics," *American Economic Review*, Papers and Proceedings (May 1974); William D. Nordhaus, "World Dynamics: Measurement without Data," *Economic Journal* (December 1973); Mancur Olson and Hans H. Landsberg, eds., *The No-Growth Society* (London: Woburn Press, 1975); see also H. S. D. Cole and others, *Thinking About the Future* (London: Chatto and Windus for Sussex University Press, 1973); and Beckerman, *In Defence of Economic Growth*.

connection between absolute scarcities and economic growth. Insofar as the scarcities are themselves objects of consumption rather than factors of production, scope for substitution on the side of production disappears. In this sense, absolute limitations on final consumption possibilities are in economic terms "more" absolute than similar limitations on factors of production. An acre of land used for the satiation of hunger can, in principle, be expanded two-, ten-, or a thousand-fold by technological advances. These advances may occur in one or all of the processes that come between the productive agricultural use of that acre and the end product in the form of nutrient. From the same productive acre, more and more food can be and has been produced. By contrast, an acre of land used as a pleasure garden for the enjoyment of a single family can never rise above its initial productivity in that use. The family may be induced or forced to take its pleasures in another way—substitution in consumption—but to get an acre of private seclusion, an acre will always be needed. The significance of this distinction is that it marks the existence of absolute scarcity in one economic dimension, namely consumption. It is with this type of insufficiency, stemming primarily from social rather than physical limitations, that this book is essentially concerned.

Figure 1 gives a summary of various broad kinds of absolute consumption scarcities and presents them in a simple categorization. The first category comprises physical (though not exclusively natural) scarcities. Examples would be a Rembrandt painting or exclusive access to a particular natural landscape which is physically unique. Consumers derive at least part of their satisfaction just from the inherent characteristics —that is, from the paintings or acres as paintings or acres, rather than as objects that are scarce.

A second classification of consumer scarcity is social: consumer demand is concentrated on particular goods and facilities that are limited in absolute supply not by physical but by social factors, including the satisfaction engendered by scarcity as such. Such social limits exist in the sense that an increase in physical availability of these goods or facilities, either in absolute terms or in relation to dimensions such as population or physical space, changes their characteristics in such a way that a given amount of use yields less satisfaction. This is equivalent to a limitation on absolute supply of a product or facility of given "quality," and it is in this sense that it is regarded here as a social limitation.

This social limitation may be derived, most directly and most familiarly, from psychological motives of various kinds, notably envy, emulation, or pride. Satisfaction is derived from relative position alone, of being in front, or from others being behind. Command over particular goods and facilities in particular times and conditions becomes an indicator of such precedence in its emergence as a status symbol. Where the sole or main source of satisfaction derives from the symbol rather than

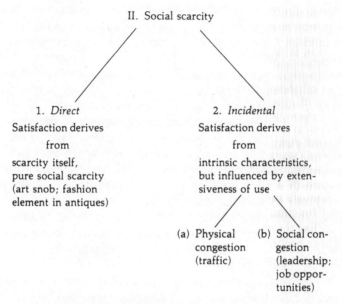

I. Physical scarcity (natural landscape; Old Masters)

II. Social scarcity

1. *Direct*
Satisfaction derives
from
scarcity itself,
pure social scarcity
(art snob; fashion
element in antiques)

2. *Incidental*
Satisfaction derives
from
intrinsic characteristics,
but influenced by exten-
siveness of use

(a) Physical
congestion
(traffic)

(b) Social con-
gestion
(leadership;
job oppor-
tunities)

Figure 1. A Categorization of Consumption Scarcity

the substance, this can be regarded as pure social scarcity (figure 1, II [1]).

Such satisfaction may also be associated with absolute physical scar-cities. Thus to at least some people, part of the attraction of a Rem-brandt, or of a particular natural landscape, is derived from its being the only one of its kind; as a result, physically scarce items such as these be-come the repository of pure social scarcity also. (If the owner of an origi-nal painting finds his own utility from such ownership diminished by the existence of good copies, that can be taken as a sign that pure social scar-city is present.) But the scarcity itself need not be associated with abso-lute physical limitations. It can be socially rather than physically de-rived, through the influence of fashion. Thus, a cachet of this kind can be attached, at a given time, to particular antiques which cannot be repli-cated, but derive their scarcity *value* only from the (changeable) fashion that designates them as a sought after emblem. Antiques in the sense of uncommon junk, and addresses of wavering fashion, are the main exam-ples. Scarcity is, so to say, deliberately created and in a sense manipu-lated.

These are examples of "pure" social scarcity in the sense that satisfac-tion is derived from the scarcity itself. But social scarcity may also be a by-product, or incidental (figure 1, II [2]). A social limitation may be derived from influences on individual satisfaction that are independent of the satisfaction or position enjoyed by others and that are yet influenced by consumption or activity of others. Essentially the phenomenon of congestion or crowding is in that category. Congestion is not limited to mutual impediment in physical form, as in traffic congestion and excessive urbanization, important as these are. The same phenomenon, of individual satisfaction in a specific activity being obstructed by the similar activity of others, can arise in purely social relationships. The most prominent examples are leadership positions, both in work relationships and in political or civic roles. Shared leadership neither fulfills the same function nor yields the same satisfaction as individual leadership. The first thing one wants to know about the vice-president of a bank or business corporation is how many others there are. When an extension in participation in a controlling group is conceded under pressure from those previously excluded, a typical response is for the broadened group to lose in function and for effective decision-making to remain with something like the original group operating as an informal caucus.[5] Since jobs or other positions at the top of a hierarchy almost always have high status, which is generally valued in itself, they also have some attributes of pure social scarcity. Even if you don't like performing as the boss, you may still want to show that you can, that you can have and do what others cannot have and do. But top positions are regarded here, as shown in the categorization of figure 1, as valued primarily for their intrinsic attractions. Social scarcity in this case is primarily incidental, the outcome of social congestion.

The distinguishing characteristic of these goods and facilities is not, of course, scarcity as such. All economic goods and facilities are scarce in the sense of being attainable only through the sacrifice or displacement of other satisfactions. It is scarcity that gives goods their economic dimension. More of this means less of that. But this regular economic scarcity merely reflects the limits on contemporary availabilities: by tomorrow, more of both this and that may be available, though still subject to new, wider limits. Such are the characteristics of what can be regarded for the moment as standard economic goods, scarce at any moment of time but increasing in availability through growth in production over time. Contrasted with these standard economic goods are the absolute scarcities,

[5] Examples abound in organizations of every type. Staff meetings in business and government develop their own ecology, their effective life being inversely proportional to the rate of expansion in attendance. Students have succeeded in gaining entry to governing bodies of Oxford colleges—but the faculty remains free to arrange a regular working lunch immediately beforehand. In international financial negotiations, the working dinner has long provided a sanctuary for inner groups when broadened participation in the formal group has made it unwieldy or unrepresentative of the relative strengths of the interests involved.

physical and social, of the kind that have just been discussed. Their wider economic significance will be treated in Chapter 3. A brief word, though, should first be said about the origin of this way of looking at things.

III

Absolute scarcities in consumption opportunities, in the sense of satisfactions that in their nature are possible only for a minority, are the subject of scattered references rather than systematic treatment in economic literature. The concept was clearly recognized, but discussed only very briefly, by Philip H. Wicksteed in *The Common Sense of Political Economy*, published in 1910. Wicksteed insisted that whereas Napoleon might wish to encourage the belief that every soldier carried in his knapsack a marshal's baton, it was obviously impossible that *every*—as distinct from *any*—soldier could rise to the position of marshal. "For the existence of one marshal implies the existence of a number of soldiers who are not marshals." In the same way, certain forms of wealth could never be universalized: "if we cannot all be marshals, neither could we all belong to the servant-keeping class."[6]

The distinction that Wicksteed pointed up was carried a little further by Sir Roy Harrod in a short essay in 1958,[7] and then neglected by almost all economic writers, including Harrod himself.[8] Harrod had referred to "an unbridgeable gulf" between what he called "oligarchic wealth and democratic wealth." Democratic wealth (Harrod used the term wealth broadly, in the sense of long-term income) comprises such command over resources as is available at a particular moment of time to everyone. It is limited by, and can rise only with, the average level of productivity. Oligarchic wealth (or income) is what is possible for the few but never— whatever the level of average productivity—for all.

Oligarchic wealth is defined in two aspects. The first is simply com-

---

[6] Philip H. Wicksteed, *The Common Sense of Political Economy* (1910) (London: Routledge and Kegan Paul, 1933), II, 657. Wicksteed also foresaw that economic growth by itself, with no redistribution, could remove the servants from the homes of the middle class, because a less hard pressed populace would no longer choose to send its daughters to clean other families' houses.

[7] Roy Harrod, "The Possibility of Economic Satiety—Use of Economic Growth for Improving the Quality of Education and Leisure," in *Problems of United States Economic Development* (New York: Committee for Economic Development, 1958), I, 207-213. Harrod does not refer to any previous body of thought, and there is nothing in his exposition to indicate that Harrod was aware that he was making an original contribution himself.

[8] An important exception is Staffan B. Linden who, in *The Harried Leisure Class* (New York: Columbia University Press, 1970), resurrected Harrod's theme and developed it in a number of directions. Important ingredients of the analysis were introduced by Tibor Scitovsky in a 1959 essay, "What Price Economic Progress?" in his *Papers on Welfare and Growth* (London: Allen and Unwin, 1964).

mand over the services and products of more than one man's labor, whether one's own or the labor of others (strictly, of the man of average productivity). "The average person can afford no more personal services than he could in the Stone Age."[9] One man's servant is another man's service. Consumption of particular kinds can only be oligarchic in this dimension. This reckoning includes not only the purchase of services on an appreciable scale (since someone who purchased the equivalent of one full-time servant could consume no goods at all if he was to remain within the limit of one man's labor). Service-intensive consumption also includes, as Harrod points out, use of material goods such as large houses, country estates, yachts, and so forth, which meet their full purpose only when considerable amounts of personal service are devoted to their upkeep.

The second aspect of oligarchic wealth is access to more than a proportionate share of goods and facilities that are scarce in some absolute sense. "If an unequal distribution prevails, the richer people will price these rare things beyond the pocket of the average man. Or if really equal shares prevailed, one would have to arrange a rationing system."[10]

Harrod's concern in this discussion was "the possibility of economic satiety." The distinction between democratic and oligarchic wealth was introduced in order to refute the common argument that because some individuals enjoyed incomes far in excess of the contemporary average, this indicated that similar scope for enjoyment of higher incomes by all could be expected in the future as a result of economic growth.[11] Harrod's distinction, between the kinds of consumption available only to a privileged minority and the consumption available to all even at a much higher average level of productivity, suggested that the threshold of economic satiety must always be lower for society as a whole than for the rich minority. Paradoxically and rather nobly, though perhaps intellectually assisted by his affinity with the British tradition of enlightened elitism, Harrod, a founder of modern growth economics, led the field in pinpointing what growth could not achieve. In his brief essay, he identified the economic wants and not just the cultural or spiritual values that would go unmet by economic growth, however long sustained. This approach suggests that economic growth is either a less clear-cut or a more limited concept than implied in the standard view which compounds growth rates in average living standards over future decades and generations.[12] Harrod himself questioned whether the living standard of the

[9] Linder, *The Harried Leisure Class*, p. 123.

[10] Harrod, "The Possibility of Economic Satiety," I, 209.

[11] Ibid., p. 207.

[12] The game seems to have been started by Keynes, in his 1930 extrapolation in "Economic Possibilities for our Grandchildren," *Collected Writings* (London: St. Martin, 1971-1973), IX, 325-326, that the standard of life in "progressive countries" in a

average American could be doubled or quadrupled without an artificial inflation of material consumption of a kind that might even detract from the consumer's true welfare—and would thereby presumably cast doubt on the meaningfulness of the concept of the standard of living and of its growth. In a vein that recalls a famous essay by Keynes,[13] Harrod looked with apprehension to the prospective "passing away of the economic phase" in human history, arguing that it would invite boredom for those he presumed to be outside the small minority capable of cultural appreciation, which would resuscitate man's preoccupation with war.

But having raised this distant prospect of gloom, Harrod—again in the manner of Keynes a generation earlier—pressed the analysis no further. In particular, he paid no attention to the process by which satiety of the attainable wants (democratic wealth) was expected to come about. This omission is crucial. For the resolution of the forces involved will depend on their interaction, in the day-to-day influence of both the market and political pressures. Uncoordinated action by individuals on the basis of the situation which they confront on their worm's eye view cannot be expected to lead to the outcome that appears rational from observation of the influences pointed to by Harrod, and by Keynes before him, on their aggregate view. The existence of absolute limitations on certain sectors of consumption is not reflected at the relevant decision point, which is at the individual level. Individual transactions involve social costs additional to those borne by the people who undertake them.

---

hundred years would be four to eight times existing levels. William J. Baumol and William G. Bowen, in their pioneering study of *Performing Arts: The Economic Dilemma* (New York: Twentieth Century Fund, 1966; Cambridge, Mass.: MIT Press, 1968), p. 406, extrapolated for illustrative purposes an optimistic growth rate of 4 percent to produce an increase in "total output" by fifty times in the century from 1965 to 2065—with only a rather mild qualification of the significance of the comparison ten lines further down. No such qualifications were incorporated into the much cited projections of Herman Kahn (in Herman Kahn and Anthony Wiener, *The Year 2000*, New York: Macmillan, 1967); or in the significance attached by Norman Macrae in *The Economist* of January 22, 1972 to a projection that median family income in the United States would reach $250,000 early in the second half of the twenty-first century.

[13] "Economic Possibilities for Our Grandchildren," p. 326. Keynes here made his own distinction between "those needs which are absolute in the sense that we feel them whatever the situation of our fellow human beings may be, and those which are relative in the sense that we feel them only if their satisfaction lifts us above, makes us feel superior to, our fellows." Needs of the latter class—defined in a more narrow frame than by Harrod in that they were confined to pure social scarcity in the terminology introduced in the present chapter—might indeed be insatiable; they would rise with the general living standard. But this was not "so true" of the absolute needs, for which satiety was in prospect, in Keynes's remarkable insight from the depths of the depression, within a hundred years.

So the social constraints imposed by absolute scarcities are imperfectly transmitted to the individual—no single individual is confronted with the limitations that confine society as a whole. However small the favored minority, no individual knows that he will be excluded from it; all can therefore set their sights on participating in it. Any soldier may have the marshal's baton in his knapsack. The distinction between democratic and oligarchic wealth does not emerge at the individual or micro level. As average productivity grows, and democratic wealth grows with it, the appetite for oligarchic wealth will also grow, and in practice at a faster rate. In the aggregate, it is an appetite that cannot be satisfied. Attempts to satisfy it may remain rational for the individual, at least while others are making the same attempt. The combination of a rising potential for democratic wealth and a static potential for oligarchic wealth must be expected to produce a rise in effective demand for the latter in terms of the former. More wealth of the kind attainable by all paradoxically means an increased scramble for the kind of wealth attainable only by some.

An interaction of this kind was hidden by the aggregate view of Harrod and of Keynes before him. The next chapter attempts to delve into some aspects of the process involved by introducing the concept of the material economy and the positional economy—the basis of which is Harrod's democratic and oligarchic wealth. It suggests that the interacting process between the material economy in a state of growth and the positional economy in a stationary state has important implications for the pattern of economic growth, for the connection between growth and the distribution of economic resources, and for the relationship between what individuals expect and what they get.

The more carefree society has been regarded by many thoughtful economists as the ultimate goal of economic striving. This goal has been an especially strong theme in the tradition of English liberal humanism—and also in the Marxism of Karl Marx. But it is now questionable whether the road to the carefree society can run through the market economy, dominated as it is by piecemeal choices exercised by individuals in response to their immediate situation. The choices offered by market opportunities are justly celebrated as liberating for the individual. Unfortunately, individual liberation does not make them liberating for all individuals together.

3 The Material Economy and the Positional Economy

The material economy is defined as output amenable to continued increase in productivity per unit of labor input: it is Harrod's democratic wealth. The material economy embraces production of physical goods as well as such services as are receptive to mechanization or technological innovation without deterioration in quality as it appears to the consumer. It is assumed that a continued increase in the "materials productivity" of output—that is, in final output obtained per unit of raw material input—will be sufficient to contain emerging shortages of raw materials as a result of technological progress, which is broadly what has happened up to now.[1] The positional economy, which is the basis of Harrod's oligarchic wealth, relates to all aspects of goods, services, work positions, and other social relationships that are either (1) scarce in some absolute or socially imposed sense or (2) subject to congestion or crowding through more extensive use. The focus of the present analysis is on the interplay between these two divisions of the economy. What happens when the material pie grows while the positional economy remains confined to a fixed size?

In the first instance, the pieces of the positional pie will tend to be bid up as they become scarcer in relation to the rising effective demand in terms of material goods.[2] Suppose that the relative preferences of individuals as between material and positional goods are unchanged as their incomes rise—that, if able to buy more of both at the same price, their demand for both increases proportionately.[3] If, therefore, positional goods remain in fixed supply while material goods become more plenti-

---

[1] Robert M. Solow, "Is the End of the World at Hand?" *Challenge* (March/April 1973), and Solow, "The Economics of Resources or the Resources of Economics."

[2] The process could be illustrated in textbook terms in a conventional Edgeworth box diagram, with indifference curves of conventional shape, and the effect of expansion of material output being represented by a horizontal elongation of the box.

[3] Represented in successive indifference curves of unchanged shape.

ful, the price of positional goods will rise, as consumers' relative intensity of demand for them increases in terms of material goods. The tendency for positional goods to increase in relative price will be reinforced if rising incomes increase the demand for them faster than for material goods. This tendency may be expected on a number of grounds.

Demand for positional goods in the form of personal services tends to increase in association with the use of material goods, because the use of many of these goods involves the consumer in the expenditure of both effort and time. Consequently, as more are acquired, the relative value placed on economizing effort and time through access to the necessary personal services wil increase; and the relative price of these services will rise accordingly, in the absence of sufficient technological innovation. Thus, at least beyond some threshold below which consumption involves little absorption of time, demand for positional goods increases merely to "service" additional availabilities of material goods. Also, the demand for a number of positional goods may be rising on its own, as primary biological needs for sufficient food, shelter, warmth, and so forth are met. Accordingly, the relative price of positional goods can be expected to increase on two grounds, from the side of demand as well as from the side of supply.[4] The tendency for the relative price of services to increase with the level of average productivity is widely documented.[5]

The combined effect of these influences, clearly apparent in budget studies of consumption, is that goods and services sharing some or all of the characteristics of positional goods attract an increasing proportion of family expenditure as family income rises. Prominent examples are expenditures on education, vacation housing, and a variety of personal services.

I

The rise in the price of positional goods will choke off any excess demand for such goods. To the extent that there is "pure" social scarcity, in that satisfaction is derived from scarcity itself, the price mechanism is the basic regulator containing demand within the limits of inherently restricted supply. Allocation proceeds, in effect, through the auction of a

[4] In technical terms, the outward shift in the supply curve of material goods and the purchasing power that it creates generates an increase in demand, probably of magnified proportions, for positional goods; the combination of high income elasticity of demand and zero elasticity of supply produces an increase in relative price.

[5] See for example Tibor Scitovsky, "What Price Economic Progress?" (1959), *Papers on Welfare and Growth* (London: Allen and Unwin, 1964); Baumol and Bowen, *Performing Arts*; and in the international context, Bela Balassa, "The Purchasing Power Parity Doctrine: A Reappraisal," *Journal of Political Economy* (December 1964).

Income elasticity of demand, United States, 1960

	Percent increase in consumption with 1 percent increase in income
All goods	0.9
All services	1.1
Leisure	1.3
Education	1.6
Travel	1.4
Food away from home	1.2
(Owned vacation home)	(3.3)
(Lodging out of town)	(3.1)

Source: Robert T. Michael, *The Effect of Education on Efficiency in Consumption* (New York: National Bureau of Economic Research, 1972), pp. 35, 39, 59.

restricted set of objects to the highest bidder. This is process A in figure 2 (see p. 30), which relates various mechanisms of allocation to the categories of figure 1. Where social scarcity is not pure but a by-product of positional goods, in the sense that satisfaction is influenced by the extensiveness of use by others, the resultant congestion or crowding reduces the "quality" as perceived by the consumers. This process of crowding can then have a number of different results. It may induce a deliberate attempt to preserve the initial quality by restrictions of various kinds to access to the goods or activity. If these take the form of congestion taxes set so as to limit traffic to the precrowding level, this regulator would be precisely equivalent to auction of the scarce resource of noncrowded traffic space (figure 2, IIIB [i] [a]).

Crowding may be avoided in a second and quite different way in cases where the scarce facility is itself of fixed quality for some reason, for example, a particular leadership position or favored job. Excess demand for access to such a position may then be absorbed by increasing the severity of the selection process through closer screening. There is, in principle, no reason why these scarcities too should not be allocated by auction. The purchase of public offices in eighteenth-century England, and in some countries to this day, is a direct example of this process. The pressure of demand for such positions (which may also be seen as an excess supply of applicants) can also be dealt with by the auction process in an indirect way. It can involve what is in effect a Dutch auction—that is, the seller starts by calling the prices high and steadily reduces them to the

I. Physical scarcity (natural landscape; Old Masters)

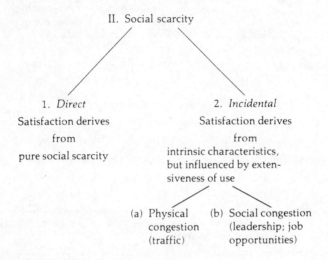

II. Social scarcity

1. *Direct*
Satisfaction derives
from
pure social scarcity

2. *Incidental*
Satisfaction derives
from
intrinsic characteristics,
but influenced by exten-
siveness of use

(a) Physical
congestion
(traffic)

(b) Social congestion
(leadership; job
opportunities)

III. Allocation processes

Excess demand contained by:

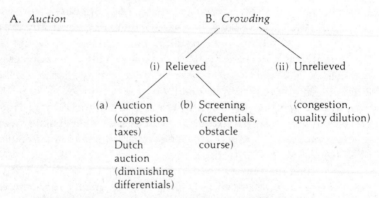

A. *Auction*

B. *Crowding*

(i) Relieved

(ii) Unrelieved

(a) Auction
(congestion
taxes)
Dutch
auction
(diminishing
differentials)

(b) Screening
(credentials,
obstacle
course)

(congestion,
quality dilution)

Figure 2. A Categorization of Consumption Scarcity

point at which the market clears. This procedure may in practice take place over time, through a lowering of salary differentials to the point at which demand for the positions involved is pared down to their supply. The modern prevalence of career ladders and established pay scales in large organizations makes any such adjustment in response to direct market pressures intensely unpopular. For this and other reasons, discussed in section II below, the more common method of allocating applicants to attractive jobs has been to make the requirements for entry to them more difficult—lengthening the obstacle course. This process involves the escalation of education credentials rather than of money payments needed for entry. The job formerly open to high school graduates now demands a college degree.

Finally, the process of crowding may be left unchecked (figure 2, IIIB [ii]). The increased supply then entails a reduction in quality, in the sense that a congested road is of lower quality than a clear one, which is a restraining influence on demand. The classical example of this process in economic literature is the crowding of a new highway that proceeds to the point at which travel along it is no faster than on the old road.[6] Beyond some point, the overburdening of limited capacity is self-regulating, at the level set by the next best available alternative.

There are, then, a variety of mechanisms for the filtering process by which excess effective demand is adjusted to the limited supply of positional goods. The first mechanism is through the classical process of price rationing: the deterrent of the auction room. This mechanism absorbs no economic resources and represents merely a transfer of claims to resources. The auction process can also be used to anticipate (in the sense of forestall) deterioration in quality through crowding. The remaining types of filtering devices function through the spontaneous development of "real" obstacles which absorb resources and thereby involve potential social waste. Unrelieved crowding or congestion which creates its own difficulties is one form. Another is screening, which operates not by diluting the quality of the output, as in the case of unrelieved crowding, but by adding to the necessary input. It does this by increasing the resources that the individual seeking access to the scarce facility has to "invest" in order to gain selection. For the economy as a whole, both these adjustments absorb real resources and involve a lengthening in the production chain, an increase in intermediate output. The process can therefore be regarded as adding to "needs" in the sense of what, in prevailing circumstances, appear to be regrettable necessities (discussed in Chapter 4). Requirements of this kind are an additional means to satisfaction. The competition for positional goods that gives rise to them can therefore be thought of as representing a potential misallocation of resources and activities. It is not possible to speak of actual misallocation since we do not have as yet a precise criterion of what alternative allocation would be best. That is, we cannot say definitively how else to deal with the problem under constraints of this kind.

II

Of the three basic mechanisms through which the limited supply of positional goods is adjusted to the demand, potential social waste is therefore associated with two—crowding and screening to avoid crowding. In addition, both these processes, as well as the third, the auction,

---

[6] Frank H. Knight, "Some Fallacies in the Interpretation of Social Cost," *Quarterly Journal of Economics* (1924).

disturb the harmony of expectation and outcome on which the smooth and efficient working of a decentralized market economy depends. The processes by which positional goods are allocated thereby have a number of general effects which help to explain some of the frustration and disappointment that has become evident in the recent development of advanced economies. They embody a false hope of what economic growth means for the individual. By promising to satisfy individuals' demand for what only some among them can have, the processes distort the pattern of output within the market economy. They also distort the extent of market activity in social life as a whole, by bringing a larger portion of such life into the commercial sector than would occur if individuals could foresee the full results of their actions. (This "commercialization effect" is discussed in Chapter 6.) Finally, the means by which positional goods are allocated make it impossible to separate relative apportionment of resources—distribution—from additions to the available supply of resources—growth—in the way that underlies the traditional approach of economics or of political economy, including that of liberal socialism.

These implications are developed in ensuing chapters. It will be convenient first to illustrate the working of the three processes in the cases of three different positional goods: scenic or leisure land, suburban living, and access to leadership positions. These are discussed as major examples, although they are clearly not the only ones.[7]

(1) *Auction: the case of leisure land.*

Exclusive access to beautiful countryside is a luxury good across a wide variety of tastes and cultures. "Luxury good" is used here in the sense of a commodity or service for which, as income rises, effective demand rises more than proportionately—that is, one that has a high income elasticity of demand. A poor man may appreciate natural beauty as much as a rich man, in the sense that he derives as much satisfaction from it (supposing for the purpose that there is some way by which their respective satisfactions can be compared). But in the subjective hierarchy of wants common to both men, exclusive access to landscape ranks behind wants for food, shelter, and a variety of appurtenances which are in part necessary to make best use of such exclusive access.

---

[7] Thus the auction process applies also to allocation of antiques; the crowding process to tourism; and the screening process to a variety of activities in which relevant information is costly to acquire. A. Michael Spence, *Market Signaling: The Informational Structure of Hiring and Related Processes* (Cambridge, Mass.: Harvard University Press, 1974). Activities of the latter kind include the setting of managerial objectives to test managers rather than to optimize their performance. Costs of this type, however, are borne by the firm, unlike the costs of educational screening which are borne by others and will on that account tend to be excessive.

This relationship can be observed both historically over time and among people in different positions at a moment of time, that is, both in time series and in cross section. Thus, until the present century, only rich aristocrats had an income sufficient to have satiated other effective demands to an extent that left something over for the purchase of land for "consumption" purposes—land to walk in, shoot in, play in, keep others out of. And today, even at the average income level of the United States, ownership of significant amounts of land for leisure is believed to remain disproportionately large for upper income groups and, among these, ranks high in incremental demand and in prestige.[8] Distribution of leisure land, that is, has been more unequal than distribution of income and wealth, which is to say that leisure land has consistently high income elasticity of demand in cross section.

Correspondingly, in the historical time trend, demand for leisure land has extended farther down from the very top of the income and wealth pyramid. The country house of Victorian times was confined to a tiny portion of the population, those in the aristocracy and upper middle class. The country cottage or vacation home today is a symbol of the successful modern middle-class professional.[9] Although only a small pro-

---

[8]An indirect indication of this is provided by the fact that the proportionate role of land in personal wealth rises with the size of the estate. It is safe to presume that large estates are held at least in part for the satisfaction they give as well as for the financial return. Official estimates for Britain in 1973 show that holders of net wealth in the two largest classes (£ 100,000 and above) held 58 percent of all land, compared with 18 percent of total net wealth. (*Royal Commission on the Distribution of Income and Wealth*, 1975, Cmnd 6171.) In the United States, some spread of ownership of leisure land is available through the purchase of condominiums.

[9] The proportion of households in the United States owning a second home was estimated at 4.6 percent in 1970, compared with 2.9 percent in 1967; the average annual rate of construction of second homes increased from 20,000 in the 1940s to 55,000 in the 1960s. The percentage of households owning a second home in 1970 rose steadily from 3 percent for families and individuals with less than $2,000 reported income to 19 percent in the highest income group, above $50,000. U.S. Department of Commerce, Bureau of the Census, *Characteristics of Second Home Owners for the United States, 1970*, Census of Housing, HC 51 (13) and *Current Housing Reports*, Series H-121, no. 16). A survey of chief executives of the Fortune 500 leading corporations, in which over half gave data, showed that 60 percent had "getaway" places, though some of these were rented. Robert S. Diamond, "A Self Portrait of the Chief Executive," *Fortune* (May 1970).

In England and Wales, the number of second homes is estimated to have quadrupled between 1955 and 1970; by the latter year, 2 percent of families owned a second home. Three-quarters of the users of second homes (who include a small number of renters) are in professional or managerial occupations; in a middle-class area of Kensington, a quarter of households had second homes, compared with none in a working-class area of Hackney. C. L. Bielckus and others, *Second Homes in England and Wales* (Ashford, Eng.: Wye College School of Rural Economics and Related Studies, 1972), pp. xi, 43, 46. A survey of 190 managing directors with head offices in the London region found the proportion with second homes rising from 19 percent for the

portion of these present-day properties include significant acreage of land, the demand for the houses themselves is linked to the leisure value of the land, and additional building in the areas involved is restricted by administrative controls. Planning controls or restrictive zoning may serve a variety of purposes, of which protection of natural scenery is one.

Since the supply of natural scenery is fixed, an increase in effective demand for its exclusive possession will, in the first instance, drive up the price of such possession. At any given time, the effective demand for exclusive access to scenery is represented by the differential in the price of land concerned, compared with its value for agricultural production or some other nonscenic use. The premium on scenic land will of course vary with ease of connections with the major cities in which the demand originates. Improved transport can greatly enlarge the supply of scenic land for which an effective demand exists. This transportation advance will hold down the price of leisure land for the period in which new land is still available to be drawn into leisure use. But this will be only a transient influence; once such land is absorbed, the characteristics of a fixed supply will again come into play.

In the early stages of industrialization, and even of affluence, the leisure premium on land was in some places close to zero; it is only in the past decade or so that hill lands in Wales and West Virginia have acquired a value above their relatively low worth in agriculture. The value of scenic land, and of houses situated on it and protected in their accesses and views, has risen relative to other prices on average.[10]

---

group with salaries below £ 10,000 to 25 percent for those between £ 10,000 and 15,000 and 35 percent for those with incomes above £ 15,000. Michael Young and Peter Willmott, *The Symmetrical Family* (London: Routledge and Kegan Paul, 1973), pp. 239-246.

In France, the high proportion of urban dwellers living in apartments and the relatively recent reduction in the agricultural labor force and consequent abandonment of rural dwellings have combined to raise second home ownership to an estimated 18 percent in 1967. Slightly more than two-fifths of the second homes were owned by top professional people and industrialists; 12 percent were inherited farms or country cottages. H. D. Clout, "Second Homes in France," *Journal of the Town Planners Institute* (December 1969), pp. 440-443. In Sweden, more than one-fifth of householders are estimated to have second homes; 30 percent of the owners are described as "manual workers," who account for 45 percent of national employment (Bielckus and others, *Second Homes*, p. 45). Thus home ownership seems to be consistently biased to upper income and occupational groups, but the bias is smaller in the countries where second home ownership is more widespread. See also Peter Downing and Michael Dower, *Second Homes in England and Wales* (London: Countryside Commission, 1973), p. 20.

[10] No indices are available for scenic land as such, but local evidence of this tendency is legion. As one example, a study of land values around sixty artificial lakes in Wisconsin showed increases from an average of $100 an acre in 1952 to $250 in 1962, a

Such increases in land prices will have a number of effects. Suppose first that the land is owned privately and there are no differential taxes on appreciation of land value. The existing owners of the land will enjoy windfall gains on its capitalized value. At the early stages at which scenic or leisure land first becomes economically scarce, that is, at which a premium in its price emerges above the agricultural value, the capital gain will accrue to the owners of the land in its agricultural use. But once the land is acquired for its leisure value, it will tend to come into the hands of upper middle income and wealth groups, because only they will be prepared to pay the leisure premium on it. That is to say, because the price of scenic acres in the south of England or in Maryland has been bid up by gentlemen farmers, only they, or others who share both their tastes and the financial capacity to indulge them, will find their purchase an economic proposition (quite apart from the tax advantages involved). These groups will then benefit from the further appreciation in values that takes place in the next round, as expansion in the sector of material output pushes effective demand for leisure land a little farther down the income and wealth ladder.

This sequence will involve a cumulative process of capital appreciation which will accrue to the benefit of the early rich and their heirs. The concentration of such capital gains in their hands will be checked to the extent that others are able to purchase land of this kind for investment purposes rather than for their own "consumption." But this tendency is unlikely to be very marked in practice. Those who are in a position to devote resources to exclusive rights over natural scenery will often also attach special value to possession as such. For this reason, and because of the difficulty of ensuring adequate maintenance, the rental market in "home estates" is poor, and that in large gardens is nonexistent.

Thus the result of the auction process of matching growing demand with static supply, as applied to scenic land, is an increase in *relative price* and an associated capitalization of the underlying asset, which can be expected to accrue to old wealth and thereby, in itself, to increase the concentration of wealth holding.

This process provides a particularly clear illustration of the fallacy of aggregation in the assessment of opportunities for economic advance. An individual can improve his capacity to acquire scenic property by improving his position in the income and wealth distribution, that is, by getting richer vis-à-vis his fellows. The same result will not be achieved if

---

period in which the all-items consumer price index rose by 14 percent and the index of all wholesale prices by 7 percent. E. J. David, "The Exploding Demand for Recreational Property," *Land Economics* (May 1969), pp. 206-217.

he gets richer along with his fellows, that is, if his income and wealth rise in line with a general increase in average income and wealth in the community. Indeed, as the general level of income rises, acquisition of scenic or other property for leisure use, at the rising relative price, entails progressively increasing sacrifice of other goods. Thus for the early rich, who acquired an effective demand for such property when it was economically a free good, the sacrifice was zero.[11]

Positional goods come first into the hands of the early rich, at a time when the income of others remains absorbed by their still unsatiated demand for material goods. Where, as in the case of scenic land, the positional goods are in durable form and thereby become capitalized, this priority in historical sequence of access provides a cumulative advantage.[12] The old rich make capital gains on positional assets they acquired early, and these gains make it harder for the new rich to rise on the relative wealth scale.

In other words, what matters in the acquisition of scenic property is less one's own present income than the present and past incomes of other people. To secure the objects in the auction catalog, it is *relative* rather than *absolute* income and wealth that count. A head start in this competition for relative ascendancy accrues to those who acquired such assets in earlier, less expensive auctions. At the limit, the only people who can now afford to buy at the auction will be those who have similar assets to sell.

(2) *Crowding: the case of suburbanization.*

A suburb—the perimeter of country around a major city (*American Heritage Dictionary*)—derives its distinctive characteristic from its relationship to other sociogeographical forms, the city and the country. It derives nourishment from both. Proximity to the city allows suburbanites to enjoy certain benefits of urban living—access to jobs, entertainment, and cultural ambiance that depend on large and concentrated populations—while escaping other aspects of city life. (These benefits will be available even if suburbanites pay the full costs of city services they use; to the extent that they do not, the balance of advantage in suburban living will be compounded.) Proximity to the country provides benefits of cleaner air, cheaper land, and easy access to open space. As one economist has put it, individuals throughout the industrial world have pat-

---

[11]It should be recalled that this entails not free land but merely an absence of a "leisure" or scenic premium above the value of the land in agricultural use.

[12]Leadership positions, which are major examples of positional goods, also embody a capitalized element to the extent that access to these positions is facilitated by an educational and cultural background that is transmitted by incumbents in such positions to their children.

terned their demands for living space according to the rule: "I will try to live as close to the city as possible, provided that, in order to gratify instincts evolved in an earlier, and more rural, period of my society's history, I must have at least a quarter of an acre of actual or potential garden."[13]

These attractions of suburban living provide incentives to both city dwellers and country dwellers to move to the suburbs. This process of movement will in turn change the characteristics of suburban life, at first to its net benefit but after some point to its detriment. With a declining city on its inner side and another suburb rather than open country on its outer side, the essential character of a suburb will be altered and in part destroyed. In practice, the changed external relationship will itself set in motion internal changes, notably increased land prices and consequential increases in housing density and expansion of commercial and industrial development. Individual choices, each made separately and thereby necessarily without taking account of the interaction between them, combine to have destructive social consequences. These consequences are destructive in the sense that they produce a worse result for the individuals concerned than could have been obtained by coordination of individual choices by some method that took account of the mutual interaction. This general class of problems of social interaction has been brilliantly analyzed by Thomas Schelling under the rubric "On the Ecology of Micromotives."[14] The separate actions induced by the opportunities that present themselves to each individual do not add up to a consistent whole.

The suburb, created as a refuge from the city, becomes transformed by the refugees it attracts.[15] It may be noted in passing that essentially the same process, in which participation in an activity changes its form, occurs in tourism. "The tourist, in his search for something different, inevitably erodes and destroys that difference by his very enjoyment of it."[16] This economic anomaly embedded in tourism was first brought into prominence by E. J. Mishan in his challenging assertion of *The Costs of Economic Growth*.[17] The fact that some tourists are not in search of

[13] Robin Marris, "First Commentary," in Robin Marris, ed., *The Corporate Society* (London: Macmillan, 1974), p. 110.

[14] "On the Ecology of Micromotives," in Marris, ed., *Corporate Society*, pp. 19-64.

[15] "A lot of people thought they were moving out to the quiet and beauty of the countryside—but the city followed them, with all its problems of traffic, housing, and congestion." U.S. Department of Housing and Urban Development, *Third Annual Report* (1967).

[16] Isobel Cosgrove and Richard Jackson, *The Geography of Recreation and Leisure* (London: Hutchinson, 1972), as quoted in George Young, *Tourism, Blessing or Blight?* (Harmondsworth, Eng.: Penguin, 1973), p. 178.

[17] E. J. Mishan, *The Costs of Economic Growth* (London: Staples Press, 1967).

something different does not remove the anomaly, as was implied in a counterpolemic by Wilfred Beckerman.[18] For if the increased activity of tourists at large deprives only one of their number of a satisfaction previously available, orthodox economic analysis provides no basis for judging the increase in tourism to be of net benefit. The victim has no way of indicating his valuation of the opportunity he has lost—no travel agency can provide him with a charter flight to the past. The ambiguity does not itself justify the sweeping restrictions on tourism proposed by Mishan, which, as Beckerman points out, would involve a large distributional gain for the rich and the fastidious. The key point is that more than a distributional issue is involved. Wider participation affects not just how much different participants get out of the game, but changes the game itself. It changes the set of choices available to all.

So the choice made by each individual in a piecemeal way ceases to be a valid guide to what individuals would choose if they could see the results of their choices along with other peoples' choices. Suppose everyone spoils it a bit for everyone else. Without mutual coordination, the best tactic for every isolated individual will be to rush in before others have spoiled it even more. Each individual might nonetheless prefer a regime in which all agreed to hold back, and in which no one had the "freedom" to renege on such agreement.

Returning to the process of suburbanization, inhabitants who wish to recapture the original attractions which newcomers have degraded (in the literal sense) now transplant themselves in a new outward move. This in turn will set off a new cycle of attraction and repulsion. (Similar waves occur in tourism: after the Cote d'Azur, the Costa Brava, and then Tunisia.) In practice, these processes are usually qualified or checked by planning restrictions of various sorts (referred to later in this chapter).

The distinctive feature of the suburb is that its attractiveness as a residential location is strongly and perhaps predominantly influenced by its position relative to neighboring locations—city and country—rather than by its absolute size or other characteristics. Its own relevant features are to a substantial extent derivative. In this sense, suburban living of given quality characteristics is a positional good, limited in absolute availability by the context of surrounding conditions and influences.

Suburban living provides a means of sharing certain advantages of the city and the country while avoiding certain disadvantages. It offers a means of picking and choosing from what was earlier—before improved communications made suburban living practicable—an indivisible package. Among the now disposable elements of the package are the mix of taxation and municipal services prevailing in local government districts that contain a range of income groups. The mixed income locality will

---

[18] Beckerman, *In Defence of Economic Growth*, pp. 51-52.

normally offer public services of lower quality and perhaps also smaller quantity than the higher income groups would choose on their own, because people with higher incomes tend to demand more of all goods, including public goods. Alternatively, if public services are offered to the tastes of the better off, they will tend to pay more than their share of the costs, since they will normally contribute more than their poorer neighbors to local taxes.[19] A better fiscal buy for the wealthy can therefore be attained in a district with few low income residents. A fiscal stimulus of this kind has been an important element in the growth of homogeneous suburbs. The process becomes self-reinforcing, as the departure of high income residents from the cities puts further fiscal burdens on those who remain. Together with a reduction in the quality of city services, this provokes further departures, building up to cumulative flight.[20] To the extent that the prosperity of the homogeneous suburb is dependent on economic contact with the city, including the supply of lower paid labor nearby, the fiscal attractions of the suburb themselves have the characteristic of a positional good, available to a minority but not to all.

If the process of suburbanization is unimpeded by planning or other restrictions, excess demand for this positional good involves, in the first instance, a process of *crowding* that changes—and beyond some point, worsens—the quality of suburban characteristics. This development in turn induces creation of new suburbs with undefiled characteristics, but since these also in time tend to attract demand that is excessive for the maintenance of maximum quality, the leapfrogging process will tend to continue. Congestion is stabilized at the point at which deterioration reduces the attractiveness of the facility to that of the next best alternative; metaphorically, the superhighway is reduced to the carrying capacity of the old road. Visually, we have Long Island.[21]

This leapfrogging process involves potential social waste, in so far as the combined result of the series of individual moves leaves all concerned

[19] William J. Baumol, "Environmental Protection and Income Distribution," in Harold M. Hochman and George E. Peterson, eds., *Redistribution Through Public Choice* (New York: Columbia University Press, 1974).

[20] This process is concisely described by William J. Baumol, "The Dynamics of Urban Problems and Its Policy Implications," in Maurice Peston and Bernard Corry, eds., *Essays in Honour of Lord Robbins* (London: Weidenfeld and Nicolson, 1972), pp. 380-393. For results of an econometric study providing supporting evidence for the hypothesis of self-perpetuating flight from the city, partly through the fiscal influence described above, see D. F. Bradford and H. H. Kelejian, "An Econometric Model of the Flight to the Suburbs," *Journal of Political Economy* (May/June 1973). See also J. Richard Aronson, "Voting with Your Feet," *New Society* (August 29, 1974).

[21] "In town after town, suburbanites find that exclusive zoning strategies no longer work, and may even promote the very sprawl, scrambled land use and urban chaos that these strategies were intended to prevent . . . And the centerless growth continues. On Long Island, New York, the urbanization line is instantly visible from the air. It moves, the planners say, two miles a year. In Middlesex County, New Jersey, it is

worse off than they would be if they concerted their actions in the knowledge of the likely responses by others. Those involved in the process are
victims of "the tyranny of small decisions." That is to say, they are
obliged to make choices covering a range or a time span too small to take
all relevant factors into account.

Choices are often made on this piecemeal basis. For example, purchase of books at discount stores eventually removes the local bookshop.
Yet bookbuyers can never exercise a choice as between cheaper books
with no bookshop and dearer books with one. The choice they are offered is between books at cut price and books at full price; naturally,
they take the former. The effective choice of continuance of a bookshop
at the expense of dearer books is never posed.[22] Everyone has a choice of
living in the city as it is or in the suburb as it is, but not between living in
the city and suburb as they *will be* when the consequences of such choices
have been worked through. The house in the suburbs appears desirable
in itself (just like the lower price tag on the book). Whether its attractions
outweigh the subsequent deterioration of the suburban amenities and
perhaps the effective destruction of the city, which this choice in company with other people's carries in its train, is never put to the test. Since
the only choice available to individuals acting in isolation is the attractive half of the sequence, the issue is preempted.

In practice, however, destructive effects within the suburb itself can
be checked in a variety of ways, notably through planning and zoning
restrictions, both on outward expansion of suburbs and on development
within them. To the extent that such restrictions preserve the quality of
suburban living by limiting the number of newcomers, existing suburban
locations will then reap capitalization gains; and excess demand will be
contained by price.[23] This is the auction process of matching positional
goods to increasing demand that was discussed previously in the context
of limited availability of scenic property.

---

not so easily visible; says one planner, 'There is no front. It's like Vietnam. It's hap-
pening all over.' " Kathleen Vilander, "Outer-City: Suburbia Seeks New Solutions,"
Real Estate Review (Summer 1973).

[22]For a discussion of externalities of this type (but not specifically the case of the
suburb) see Alfred E. Kahn, "The Tyranny of Small Decisions: Market Failures, Imperfections, and the Limits of Economics," *Kyklos* (1966), pp. 23-46; and Burton A.
Weisbrod, "Collective-Consumption Services of Individual-Consumption Goods,"
Quarterly Journal of Economics (August 1964), which emphasizes the inability of the
market to cater to option demand—the amount individuals would be willing to pay to
have some facility available for their contingent use.

[23]Restrictions on new developments depress the price of any individual property
or unit of land, but convey favorable external effects on surrounding units. The sum
of internal (that is, direct) effects and external effects can be presumed to be positive as
long as they have support of the locality as a whole.

As growth in material productivity adds to effective demand for living in environments that are socially or physically scarce, the excess pressures of demand on these facilities lead either to a deterioration in their quality, or to protection through exclusion, including exclusion by price. The first course—quality deterioration through the tyranny of small decisions—involves social waste. The second course—protection through exclusion—involves a hidden redistribution of economic welfare in favor of those established in the areas at the expense of those attempting to move in (including existing residents seeking more house room). People living in the protected areas gain and people excluded from them lose. These transfers will often be regressive, accruing to the rich at the expense of the poor. Explicit measures of redistribution in the reverse direction would be needed to counter this latter influence.

The uneven incidence of implicit benefits from zoning or planning controls on different individuals and groups, related in part to their past income, has become an important and largely hidden element in economic inequality in modern societies. The focus in the present chapter is the effect on allocation of resources and on related social patterns. The principal result is a tendency to draw excess resources into opportunities that are attractive in themselves but that deteriorate in quality as more people crowd into them.

(3) *Screening: the case of leadership jobs.*

Electricians have helpers, managers have secretaries, head teachers have assistant teachers, supervisors supervise. Between many if not most jobs there is a hierarchical relationship: while the nature and extent of that relationship depend partly on particular institutional forms, it is in some degree inherent in the tasks to be performed and in the requirements of communication and control. A job at the upper end of a particular hierarchy is normally preferred; in terms of job satisfaction, it almost invariably carries greater status. Since, for reasons of efficient administration, organizational hierarchies are pyramid shaped, with supervisors at each level having a number of underlings, and themselves being responsible to a single higher supervisor, the number of positions available at higher levels is limited in some fractional ratio by the number of inferior positions. The height of the pyramid, or any section of it, depends on the width of the base.[24]

In this sense, jobs anywhere above the base level of the hierarchy can be regarded as positional facilities, limited in absolute availability by structural influences. The two key such influences are the size of the la-

[24] H. Simon, ''The Compensation of Executives,'' *Sociometry* (1957), in A. B. Atkinson, ed., *Wealth, Income and Inequality* (Harmondsworth, Eng.: Penguin Education, 1973), pp. 199-202; Robin Marris, *The Economic Theory of Managerial Capitalism* (London: Macmillan, 1964).

bor force and the average span of control, that is, the number of employees who report to the same supervisor immediately above them, which sets the angle of the pyramid. Positions more than halfway up the pyramid, and those offering professional independence, can be regarded as superior jobs and as more likely to carry positive job satisfaction. An expansion in the capacity of the economy to supply goods, whether it results from improved technology, an increased capital stock, or an increased supply of labor, has no necessary tendency to expand the proportion of superior jobs. Nor does such expansion result from the structural shift common to all advanced economies toward employment in the service sector at the expense of manufacturing as well as agriculture. The growth in service employment has been accompanied by spreading bureaucratization, and increasing concern has been voiced about the routine nature of jobs in the lower echelons and the lack of opportunities for promotion. [25]

Since economic expansion increases the resources that can be made available for education and training, and in practice also increases their share of resources, the labor force as a whole becomes better equipped to occupy superior jobs. How then will the increased demand to perform higher level jobs be matched to the limited availability of such positions?

One indirect form of adjustment is a change in the character of superior jobs; they may become less superior. In a world where more people feel themselves to be the intellectual and/or technical equal of those higher up, bosses become less bossy. The pains of subordinate status, and the pleasures of superior status, may thereby be reduced a little, with a corresponding diminution in excess demand for superior positions. Assertion by trade unions, clerical and manual, of minor managerial functions should be seen in this light. Although such practices are usually regarded as inefficient, they may represent a rational exchange of some material output and income for a degree of control over the work situation. A similar trade off may be chosen in a different way when professional people and craftsmen prefer to work, as consultants or contractors, for themselves. Such outlets may be seen as partial substitutes for the limited supply of superior jobs of the more traditional type.

More generally, the classic method of adjustment to an excess supply of labor capable of performing superior jobs is given in the market model through a reduction in the pay and fringe benefits attached to those jobs. Demand for superior jobs is based partly on the work satisfaction and status they provide. To this extent, applicants might continue to prefer such jobs even if financial remuneration fell below the level necessary to meet costs of training incurred by the individual. Superior jobs might then be allocated by Dutch auction, with salary levels being bid

[25] This point is discussed further in Chapter 12.

down to the point at which available positions would just be filled by applicants of suitable quality. In this simple market model, remuneration could therefore be reduced by the competition of competent applicants to levels below those of jobs lower down in the hierarchy of employment. Such competition would be expected to intensify as the satiation of more primary wants increased the appetite for these upper echelon jobs and as more extensive education made more people competent to perform them. In the market model, top jobs could eventually pay least, if sufficient numbers became competent and eager to perform them.

Some responsiveness in relative salary levels to shifts in potential supply and demand undoubtedly exists. The great expansion in supply of college graduates in the United States in the 1950s and 1960s eventually led to a surplus, and between 1969 and 1973 the excess in average mean income of male college graduates over high school graduates was reduced from 50 to 41 percent.[26]

Yet flexibility in relative pay in different occupations is inhibited by a number of factors. These include (1) conventional pay differentials or norms; (2) high "transactions" costs in filling senior posts from outside the firm or organization or department, resulting both from necessary on-the-job training and from the cost of acquiring information about the capability of potential candidates; and (3) the ability of existing incumbents in superior jobs to influence their own pay scales either through the exercise of economic power over their contribution to "team" productivity, or more simply through their access to relevant scarce information.[27]

The structural changes in the workforce of advanced economies, referred to above, have increased the importance of influences of the kind just mentioned. Fewer people grow things or make things: more people service, entertain, consult, supervise. The effect is to reduce the area of the economy in which personal productivity can be identified and to increase the influence of accepted or imposed norms in the determination of relative pay. That may be the most significant feature of the modern transformation in the structure of the labor force as between manufacturing and service industries. In the service economy, personal productivity is subjectively assessed rather than objectively measured.[28]

[26] Richard B. Freeman, "Overinvestment in College Training?" *Journal of Human Resources*, 10 (Summer 1975), 290.

[27] Lester C. Thurow, *Investment in Human Capital* (Belmont, Calif.: Wadsworth Publishing Co., 1970), and the same author's *Generating Inequality* (New York: Basic Books, 1975).

[28] Trends in service employment, and an optimistic interpretation of shifts toward it, are discussed in Daniel Bell, *The Coming of Post-Industrial Society* (London: Heinemann, 1974). For a more critical assessment see Anthony Giddens, *The Class Structure of the Advanced Societies* (London: Hutchinson University Library, 1973). On the theme of proletarianization of the lower clerical grades in the United States see

Modern economic growth has been marked by successive shifts in employment from primary industries (agriculture and mining) to secondary industries (manufacturing) and from these to the tertiary sector (services); this latter sector has been subdivided and extended by Daniel Bell to the quaternary sector (exchange and information) and quinary sector (research and government). The recent shifts from production of things to the doing of things can be interpreted in a wide variety of ways. For Bell, Herman Kahn, and other enthusiasts of the postindustrial cornucopia, they are the source of the enlarged surplus over what would be available from primary and secondary production alone. For neo-Marxists, the prime significance of the expansion of the tertiary sector lies in the absorption of the surplus.[29] Another interpretation, suggested by the present analysis and drawing some inspiration from Simon Kuznets,[30] is that the great expansion of employment in service sectors, such as transportation, government, education, recreation, and finance, has reflected new needs directly associated with the changes in economic structure that are involved in growth. A part of what is conventionally recorded as consumption and governmental services should therefore be reclassified as intermediate output.[31] Finally, a facetious interpretation offered by Bertrand Russell ahead of his time in 1935 deserves pondering:

> Work is of two kinds: first, altering the position of matter at or near the earth's surface relatively to other such matter; second, telling other people to do so. The first is unpleasant and ill paid; the second is pleasant and highly paid. The second kind is capable of indefinite extension: there are not only those who give orders, but those who give advice as to what order should be given.[32]

There are, therefore, a variety of powerful reasons why coveted jobs are not allocated predominantly by price. In this arena, there are strict

---

also Gavin Mackenzie, *The Aristocracy of Labor* (Cambridge, Eng.: Cambridge University Press, 1973). See also Chapter 12 below.

[29] Bell, *The Coming of Post-Industrial Society*; Paul A. Baran and Paul M. Sweezy, *Monopoly Capital* (New York: Montly Review Press, 1966; Penguin, 1968).

[30] Simon Kuznets, *Modern Economic Growth* (New Haven: Yale University Press, 1966), p. 225, and "The Share and Structure of Consumption," *Economic Development and Cultural Change*, 10 (January 1962), 41-42.

[31] The concept of needs as intermediate output is developed in Chapter 4 below.

[32] Bertrand Russell, "In Praise of Idleness," in Eric Larrabee and Rolf Meyersohn, eds., *Mass Leisure* (New York: Free Press, 1958). Empire building and covering up by bureaucrats in private corporations, with a view to maximizing not the profits of the firm but their own personnel record and security, can lead to artificial extensions of the Russell type. Protective cover is provided by imperfect information within the firms and by economies of scale which limit competition by nonbureaucratic rivals.

limits to the auction market process, which would here take the Dutch auction form of bidding salary levels down. The alternative process of regulation is to relieve the crowding of these scarce jobs by means of screening.

Performance of superior jobs will vary according to the personal qualities of those who do them. This is true of all jobs; but since responsibility for supervising the work of others, or of enjoying freedom from supervision in one's own tasks, makes it difficult for remuneration to be adjusted closely to the level of performance (if only because poor performance can involve large negative contributions to output),[33] screening of personal attributes is always likely to be more important for superior jobs.

Such screening involves a double judgment: on the attributes of the candidates and on the attributes required for the job. So long as job performance is improved by superior attributes, an improvement in the quality of candidates will open the way to increased productivity. This result may be achieved by raising the threshold required for entry: screening will be in a finer mesh. The higher the qualifications of the staff, the better their performance. In less bureaucratized occupations, the increased productivity imparted by education will show up automatically in increased output and earnings. The educational process itself makes those who have passed through it more productive, both individually and socially, that is, for the economy as a whole.

This view of the economic impact of education formed the basic hypothesis of the development of the concept of human capital, which blossomed in the late 1950s and rose to what seems to have been its apogee in the 1960s. The hypothesis helped to explain a major finding of neoclassical economic analysis, namely, that the growth in output in the United States and other industrial countries in the twentieth century far exceeded the growth that could be traced to input in the form of labor and capital. The quality of both was enhanced by education, together with research, through improvement in human skills and the quality of technology. The product of education was not limited to culture and humanism. Education, in this approach, produced investment in human beings with direct economic returns equivalent to those from investment in physical assets.

The analysis was important in a number of ways. In practical policy, it provided an economic rationale for the major expansion of edu-

---

[33] As witnessed by the large sums in severance pay (golden handshakes) that firms find it worth their while to incur to be rid of top executives whose performance is judged to have lapsed. The virtual impossibility of adjusting remuneration to the true value of performance of complex tasks is also illustrated by the general recognition that some form of licensing of professional practitioners is to the public benefit, though not necessarily under the exclusive control of the profession involved.

cation, especially higher education, that occurred in the 1960s in all countries big and small, advanced and underdeveloped.[34] In economic ideology, the analysis extended the concept of capital accumulation to a form enjoyed by the majority of the population in greater or lesser degree; with every man a (human) capitalist, the old socialist distinction between the earnings of labor and the earnings of capital dissolved. In academic development, the human capital analysis represented an important step in the bold attempt, centered at the University of Chicago but spreading far outward from there, to unify the social sciences on the foundation of the individual optimizing his or her behavior, in areas extending beyond the traditional sphere of market consumption, to include education and health, and more recently crime, fertility, marriage, religion, and suicide.[35] In each of these spheres, individual action is analyzed by reference to a rationalistic pursuit of private objectives.

The limitations of individual optimization in wide areas of economic as well as social life are a recurrent theme of this book. (The unintended results of personal competition for facilities subject to physical or social limits are discussed in this chapter, and the dependence of market organization on moral values that are ultimately inconsistent with individual optimization is discussed in Part III.) The immediate concern here is with the connection, which is central to the human capital approach and partly implicit in it, between the private and the social return from education.

The starting point of the approach is the differential added by education to an individual's lifetime earnings, a differential that is observed essentially from the differences in present earnings of otherwise like individuals with dissimilar education. The addition to lifetime earnings, appropriately discounted by a selected interest rate (a selection that has to be made from a fairly broad relevant range and that makes a crucial difference to the result) is then adjusted for the real cost of acquiring such education, of which the main component is earnings foregone during the period of learning.

[34] The step between economic theory and governmental action has probably never been so short as from the formulation of human capital theory to the explosion of educational spending, which helps explain why the disillusion that ensued with the practical results brought a rapid boomerang reaction on the theory too.

[35] On the key concepts and methods in calculation of returns to education in the human capital approach see the contributions by T. W. Schultz, W. G. Bowen, and M. Blaug, in M. Blaug, ed. *Economics of Education*, vol. I (Harmondsworth, Eng.: Penguin, 1968), summarizing a large literature. A succinct development of the broader implications of the Chicago approach was given by Harry G. Johnson in his inaugural lecture at the London School of Economics, "The Economic Approach to Social Questions," *Economica* (February 1968); for a more formal treatment see the same author's *The Theory of Income Distribution* (London: Gray-Mills, 1973). The pioneering extensions into the fields of crime, marriage, religion, and suicide have been led by Gary

This procedure raises a number of questions. There is the problem of separating the effect of education from the effect of native ability and family background. Education also makes it easier for employers to detect existing abilities and accompanying characteristics such as motivation and discipline. The fact that employers pay for evidence of educational success—for the educational certificate or credential—does not indicate what they are buying. They may be paying for education's contribution to high potential productivity or merely for education's signaling of where high potential productivity lies.

In this latter function, education serves as a pure screening device or filter, through which employers identify individuals with certain qualities that the educational process tests and certifies but does not itself produce. Such qualities typically comprise a combination of intelligence, motivation, and discipline necessary to absorb on-the-job training.[36] Since direct information about these attributes would be extremely expensive for employers to acquire, a proxy for the information is obtained —notably in credentials of some form as evidence of the candidates' passage through the educational system.

Economic calculations of the return to education now usually attempt to isolate the effect of ability as well as of family background. Thus in two widely used estimates, E. F. Denison and Gary S. Becker found that after allowing for such influences, about two-thirds of the "gross" effect calculated for education still remained.[37] But the significance of such estimates is limited by the lack of any real measure of ability. I.Q., the proxy that has to be used, has been shown—for example, by studies in the U.S. navy—to be only weakly related to ability to perform productive tasks. Kenneth Arrow, in the course of a weighty critique of the human capital approach, asked the devastating question: If employers cannot measure ability directly, why should we expect economists to be able to do so?[38] In an empirical test of the screening hypothesis, Paul Taubman and Terence Wales have estimated that in the absence of

---

S. Becker. See in particular his "A Theory of Marriage," *Journal of Political Economy* (July/August 1973 and March/April 1974). The latter issue contains proceedings of a special conference on Marriage, Family, Human Capital, and Fertility, including perceptive critiques of Becker's economizing approach by William J. Goode and Marc Nerlove.

[36]Lester C. Thurow and Robert E. B. Lucas, "The American Distribution of Income: A Structural Problem," U.S. Congress, Joint Economic Committee, March 17, 1972. See also Samuel Bowles, "Understanding Unequal Economic Opportunity," *American Economic Review* (May 1973).

[37]Quoted in Blaug, ed., *Economics of Education*, I, 225.

[38]Kenneth J. Arrow, "Higher Education as a Filter," *Journal of Public Economics* (July 1973).

screening, returns to investment in college education might be reduced by 50 percent, without allowing for greater foregone earnings at lower educational levels.[39]

Education in its economic function therefore is a filter as well as a factory. This dual role has a number of important implications for the effects of expansion of education. An expansion in the "output" of educational credentials will, by itself, reduce the information conveyed by the particular credentials involved.[40] In the United States in the early 1970s, when 70 percent of those leaving school were high school graduates, the graduation certificates were a less distinctive identifying mark than a generation earlier, when barely 40 percent graduated. By the 1970s the credential indicating the position of the holder as within the top 25 percent of survivors in the educational obstacle course had become the college degree; and for the top 8 percent of survivors, which had been indicated by college degree holders in the 1930s, employers would now have had to require a master's degree.

The expansion of educational credentials also has probably increased the attention paid to presumed differences in their quality. Expansion of new universities in England has not weakened the hold Oxford and Cambridge graduates have on particular professions and instead may have increased the value set by employers on the Oxbridge degree.[41] Not only does it convey information the employers can trust but, in addition, it enables them to buy the elite contacts of the employee. The importance of such contacts is systematically understated in the simple model of the economy in which firms respond to information and opportunities equally known and available to all.

As mentioned earlier, an increase in effective demand for superior jobs can be expected to accompany the growth of the material sector, because with material wants better satisfied, people are readier to devote more resources to improving their work situation. The result, through the processes just described, is likely to be to increase the resources devoted to formal education, but also to reduce the efficacy of a given unit

[39]Paul Taubman and Terence Wales, *Higher Education and Earnings* (New York: McGraw-Hill, 1974), pp. 23 and 171.

[40]This tendency has a long pedigree: "The indiscriminate collation of degrees has justly taken away that respect which they originally claimed as stamps, by which the literary value of men so distinguished was authoritatively denoted." Samuel Johnson, *A Journey to the Western Islands of Scotland* (New Haven: Yale University Press, 1971), p. 17.

[41]"Expansion of university education brings more men with degrees on the job market. As a result, mechanisms of differentiation are established; the more numerous the graduates, the more selective the mechanism." David Boyd, *Elites and Their Education* (Windsor, Eng.: NFER Publishing, 1973), p. 143. Boyd drew this conclusion from empirical studies of recruitment in the British Civil Service, judiciary, armed forces, Church of England, and clearing banks.

of education in securing access to higher level jobs. When education expands faster than the number of jobs requiring educational credentials, employers intensify the screening process.[42] In this respect, an individual's education carries some external costs for the rest of society.

Education has more usually been associated with external benefits, based on the assumptions that educated people make better citizens, they are more productive, and the resulting benefits are not all captured in their own higher earnings—for example, they pay more taxes and enhance the productivity of those with whom they work.[43] The influences discussed above—focusing on the role of education as a signaling device —qualify and may negate these external benefits. Their presence means that the increase in personal productivity as measured by market earnings is not matched by an increase in social productivity. Education adds to personal earnings, but not commensurately to social product.

To the extent that education conveys information about the innate or accultured *relative* capacity of the individual who has undergone it, more education for all leaves everyone in the same place. The test of relative capacity could in principle have been carried out as well at a lower general level: addings layers to the level to which the competition for credentials is pushed merely absorbs educational resources without adding to the productivity of the winners in the competition. On this model, one man's higher qualification devalues the information content of another's. Once again, it is a case of everyone in the crowd standing on tiptoe and no one getting a better view. Yet at the start of the process some individuals gain a better view by standing on tiptoe, and others are forced to follow if they are to keep their position. If all do follow, whether in the sightseeing crowd or among the job-seeking students, everyone expends more resources and ends up with the same position.

In practice, however, not everyone will follow; only those who assess that the individual benefit received from keeping up is worth the additional cost or effort will do so. Individual benefit derives from three elements: the additional pay attached to the superior job to which education gives access; the educational experience in itself (the "consumption" benefits of education which no one has found a way of measuring); and the relative satisfaction derived from performance and tenure of the job

----

[42] In his careful survey of the literature of the economics of education in 1962, William G. Bowen acknowledged the influence, but confined it to a footnote. "It may well be that as a higher proportion of the people in a country receive a college education, employers, in order to recruit people possessing a certain level of ability, will find themselves forced to recruit college graduates—even though college training may be unnecessary for the job." "Assessing the Economic Contribution of Education" (1963), in Blaug, ed., *Economics of Education*, I, 81.

[43] For a succinct discussion of the range of influences involved see Thurow, *Investment in Human Capital*.

itself. The valuation placed on the latter two benefits can be expected to rise at least with income levels, that is, to be normal rather than inferior goods, and probably to rise faster, that is, to be "superior" or luxury goods with an income elasticity of demand above unity.

A general expansion of educational levels, when it adds to the amount or quality of education and training that individuals need to acquire for access to superior jobs, does not have a clear-cut effect in allocating individuals among these scarce and coveted jobs. The expansion in educational resources, provided it accrues to those selected by cognitive ability, will in itself help those who can make the best use of their education. These, in a loaded phrase, are the meritorious.[44] But the resulting excess of apparently qualified candidates induces an intensification of job screening that has the effect of lengthening the obstacle course of education and favoring those best able to sustain a longer or more costly race. These are the well off and the well connected.

But this is the situation ex post, reached at the end of the process involved. Expectations which form the basis for demand for education and training are more likely to be shaped by the educational qualifications of current incumbents of different jobs.[45] This is the evidence available to new entrants, who are unlikely to allow for the effect of their own decisions in raising the ultimate hurdle to selection. If theorists of human capital fell into this trap, why expect acquirers of human capital to avoid it? Job expectations will then frequently be frustrated, as the expansion in supply of qualified applicants raises the threshold of necessary credentials. Where the frustration of expectations is particularly sharp, the effect may be to deter new entrants to comparable education courses, which will eventually lead to a shortage of qualified personnel, to competitive bidding for applicants, and reattraction of entrants for training. A cycle of this kind of shortage and surplus is clearly visible among physicists in the United States.[46] However, where educational expansion overcrowds superior positions as a whole, rather than one specific field, the effect will be to push competition by hitherto qualified applicants down the hierarchy of jobs: screening will be intensified at each level.

[44] "Merit is a bit of an accident not only in its origin, but also in its being treated as merit." Amartya Sen, *On Economic Inequality* (Oxford: Clarendon Press, 1973), p. 105.

[45] An empirical study of how students in Canada made their decisions found that estimates of their lifetime returns were "determined by students largely on the basis of casual and impressionistic observation of the living standard of people of different ages and educational attainments." John F. Crean, "Foregone Earnings and the Demand for Education: Some Empirical Evidence," *Canadian Journal of Economics* (February 1973).

[46] Richard B. Freeman, "Supply and Salary Adjustments to the Science Manpower Market: Physics, 1948-1973," Harvard Institute of Economic Research Discussion Paper 318, September 1973.

Jobs for which a high school diploma was previously sufficient will then require some college education. Individuals who decline to join the educational upgrading, or who have simply assumed that the education they acquire will admit them to the kind of jobs that are open to those having this level of education at the time it is acquired, will suffer a devaluation of their credentials in terms of job access. Thus in the early 1970s, more than 20 percent of male graduates from the class of 1970-71 were employed in nonprofessional and nonmanagerial jobs, compared with less than 14 percent of the class of 1958 at a similar period in their working lives.[47] There may still be disillusionment with benefits of university education, as was apparent in the reduced pressure of applications for university admissions which became marked in Britain and the United States in the mid-1970s. But as the average level of educational qualifications in the labor force rises, a kind of tax is imposed on those lacking such qualifications, while the bounty derived from possessing a given qualification is diminished. The general educational upgrading depreciates the credentials currency so that those who do not lay in more of it will lose out in job purchasing power. This process, which is checked by adjustments in relative pay, operates insofar as competition for more attractive jobs lengthens the line waiting to acquire such jobs and thereby raises the barriers that have to be surmounted for entry.

Education may then "become a defensive necessity to private individuals even if there are no net social returns to education . . . Education becomes a good investment, not because it would raise an individual's income above what it would have been if no one had increased their education, but because it raises their income above what it will be if others acquire an education and they do not."[48]

An "inflation" of educational credentials of this kind involves social waste in two dimensions. First, it absorbs excess real resources into the screening process: the lengthened obstacle course is unlikely to be the most profitable way of testing for the qualities desired, because its costs are not borne by the employers whose demands give the credentials their cash value. Second, social waste will result from disappointed expectations of individuals and from the frustration they experience in having to settle for employment in jobs in which they cannot make full use of their acquired skills. Professor Jan Tinbergen, the first co-winner of the Nobel Prize for economics, has gone so far as to incorporate into a formal model any shortfall between the educational requirements of a job and the education possessed by its incumbent as a negative element in individual welfare.[49]

[47] Freeman, "Overinvestment in College Training?" p. 294.
[48] Thurow and Lucas, "The American Distribution of Income," p. 38.
[49] Jan Tinbergen, *An Interdisciplinary Approach to the Measurement of Utility or Welfare* (Dublin: Economic and Social Research Institute, 5th Geary Lecture, 1972).

III

We may now pause to assess the common general effects to be expected from the impact of growth in the expanding material sector of the economy on the static positional sector in the three main facets examined —leisure land, suburban location, and job hierarchy, representing respectively the processes of auction, crowding, and screening.

In each of the three cases, material growth intensifies what may be termed positional competition. By positional competition is meant competition that is fundamentally for a higher place within some explicit or implicit hierarchy and that thereby yields gains for some only by dint of losses for others. Positional competition, in the language of game theory, is a zero-sum game: what winners win, losers lose. The contrast is with competition that improves performance or enjoyment all round, so that winners gain more than losers lose, and all may come out winners— the positive-sum game.

In the material sector, competition yields net benefits in the positive-sum sense by stimulating efficient performance of tasks and by directing individual effort into more productive uses. In the positional sector— comprising goods, services, jobs, and other social positions that are either scarce in some absolute or socially imposed sense or subject to congestion or crowding through extensive use—competition will also improve both individual performance and allocation of individual effort. This result is the positive aspect of competitive selection for positional facilities. But in addition, competition in the positional sector serves as a general filtering device through which excessive demand has to be matched to available supply. This aspect—which I seek to isolate by the term "positional competition"—at best yields no net benefit and usually involves additional resource costs, so that positional competition itself is liable to be a negative-sum game. Competition in the positional sector, however, may still yield net benefits if its contributions to individual efficiency and allocation of resources outweigh additions to resource costs and misallocation. But this cannot be judged from the conventional measures of economic output, since these measures gloss over the negative or deadweight elements of positional competition.

The outcome is a systematic bias in the signals of available choices and opportunities as conveyed at the individual level. *The choice facing the individual in a market or market-type transaction in the positional sector, in a context of material growth, always appears more attractive than it turns out to be after others have exercised their choice.* A disjunction between the terms of individual and social choice offered by market opportunities represents, in the standard analysis, a case of market failure. This failure calls for correction by internalizing, that is, incorporating in the market situation confronting the individual, the external cost that is imposed on others. The existence of the positional sector in the context of growth in the material sector can thus be seen as a kind of "system externality." That is to say, the unregistered external cost is attached to the whole run of transactions in this sector. The distortions involved in positional competition are so broad ranging that they are not easily amenable to the conventional correctives, notably indirect taxes and subsidies.[50]

The consistent bias is to present the individual who looks forward to an income rising in line with national income with too favorable a view of the opportunities with which he or she—and the community as a whole—will be faced. The juxtaposition of growth in the material sector and fixity (stagnation without its pejorative connotation) in the positional sector induces a rising trend in the relative price of positional goods. It also may absorb real resources into the process of allocating the scarce positional goods. The price rise may not be reflected in specific goods and services—prices of houses in particular suburbs may fall, specified educational credentials may be attainable at lower costs. The effective price increase may then rather be reflected in depreciation in the quality or worth of these instrumentalities as means to the objective that the individual seeks. Thus a particular suburb becomes less effective in delivering the objective of quiet living combined with easy access to city and countryside; a particular educational credential becomes less effective in providing entree to particular jobs and, more generally, as an implicit designation of the holder as among the cleverest or most diligent of the contemporary age group.

There is a shortfall in performance not because performance gets worse but because the demands on performance become greater. It is as if a coal fire burned with continued efficiency, but the outside temperature dropped or the insulation deteriorated. More coal would then be needed to produce the same degree of warmth and to offset a deterioration in the physical environment. For the individual, increased positional competition involves a deterioration in the social environment. More individual effort and resources have to be expended to achieve the same result.

This condition does not yet signify, however, that resources are misallocated for the community as a whole. Misallocation can be meaningfully adduced only if alternative means that are less wasteful socially can be specified for dealing with the demands held by individuals. The point to be stressed at this stage is the bias in the signals. Individual demand in

[50] Mishan points out that these standard correctives were themselves designed to deal with exceptions to the general benevolence of the working of the price system. "When external effects are seen, as is increasingly the case today, as being widespread and pervasive, Pigou's remedy implies an unmanageable maze of taxes and subsidies." E. J. Mishan, "On the Economics of Disamenity," in Marris, ed., *The Corporate Society*, p. 340.

the positional sector is a misleading guide to what individuals would demand if they could see and act on the results of their combined choices. Whether expressed in market transactions or translated into a political demand of what government should do to meet the individual wants considered in isolation, individual demand for positional goods seeks the undeliverable. The economic product it evokes then comes out flawed.

4 The Ambiguity of Economic Output

The flaws in the economic product that result from positional competition are not revealed in the national accounts. There is no obviously practicable way by which they could be. But the limitations of statistical measures of gross national product and its components have been increasingly discussed in recent years. Many economists have acknowledged these limits and have undertaken pioneering work to extend them through refinement of the existing yardsticks. Much work has also gone into the exploration of new measures, specifically into construction of social indicators that attempt to gauge a restricted number of key outputs of the system in the form of proxies for happiness or well-being. Meanwhile, public commentators and politicians have become somewhat more wary of equating GNP with economic performance as a whole, without any clear notion of what to put in its place—which is hardly surprising in view of the unresolved debate within the economics fraternity.

The debate turns on a fundamental question which has been around for a long time—the precise nature of economic output. There has always been a deep ambiguity in the concept of economic output; the ambiguity has grown as economies become richer and more complex.

The heart of the problem can be summarized as follows: The "economic" element in human activity comprises the satisfaction of wants (ends) with means that are, in some sense, scarce. Consequently, rational action necessitates selection and choice: if more of this for this, then less of this for that. But what precisely is the distinction between means and ends? At some points the distinction is apparent enough. Thus land, labor, and capital equipment used for the production of wheat and its transformation into flour and bread are the means to the production of bread. Bread, therefore, represents the end output and wheat, flour, tractors, flour mills, and so forth represent intermediate output, a stage toward the completed product of bread. The consumer's primary want is for bread; so bread is the final output of the system. But is it? The consumer's primary want can also be seen not as bread itself but as nourishment with bread-like flavor; and bread can be viewed as merely intermediate to the true final economic output, the stilling of hunger in a particular way.

In this example, the distinction is essentially metaphysical: whatever the view, it is the bread actually produced that constitutes the economic output. In satisfaction of more complex wants, however, the distinction is more substantial. Much travel, and particularly the journey to and from work, is undertaken not in its own right but as a means of satisfying wants for other goods and services. The same is true of many items bought by final consumers: garden equipment is acquired to produce more pleasant gardens, a banking account and credit card to ease the administrative task of acquiring other goods and services, a pocket calculator to help complete one's income tax returns. (In each case, there may also be some satisfaction from use of the service or good itself.)

Such "intermediate" consumer goods and services are not in any sense less productive or pressing than "final" goods. Since they are a means to satisfaction of wants for final goods, such a comparison is meaningless —a category error, confusing alternative ends with means to a single end.[1] No one suggests that the firm producing sheet steel is less productive than the firm that turns sheet steel into cars. In the enterprise sector, intermediate goods have an accepted place. In practice, consumers also perform a processing role. Some of their purchases are in effect inputs, which only after treatment and processing will emerge as the final output they seek. It is merely the conventions and practical exigencies of national accounting that create the convenient fiction that once goods or services are acquired by consumers they have reached the stage of final consumption.

What is missed by the neglect of this processing function, when it relates to consumers, is the effect of changes in the efficiency of converting the input, that is, the intermediate good the consumer buys, into the desired final output. Suppose that the process becomes less efficient in the technical sense of requiring a larger input to produce a given output —because, for example, additional heating is required to maintain a given temperature in a cold winter, or because additional years of full-time education are required to attain the credential necessary for entry to a given job. In such cases, increased expenditures on the intermediate good

---

[1] The Soviet concept of national income is confined to material production and excludes most services. The statistical outcome (as distinct from the rationale) of this exclusion has certain affinities with exclusion of intermediate consumer goods; an important and irrational practical result seems to be to encourage a general neglect of services as against material output. Visiting economists waiting for their lunch in Moscow restaurants have plenty of time to reflect on this distortion and perhaps to draw excessive conclusions from it.

that serves as an input appear in the conventional measure of national accounting as adding to consumption, but actually will leave the consumer no better off in terms of the object of his or her consumption. An increase in positional competition, as will be discussed below, can be regarded as lengthening the chain of necessary intermediate consumption in this way.

I

Another way of looking at consumer intermediate goods is to see them as "defensive" goods (sometimes termed "regrettable necessities"). This phenomenon is then seen as a kind of counter to a "bad," in the sense of a negative good, deriving its value only from the existence of the negative factor that is being countered. Viewed from this perspective, more is not necessarily better than less: fire stations in regions free of fire risk are without economic value and may simply spoil the view. The point is that the value of these intermediate goods derives entirely from the final output to which they contribute. If the risk of fire rises, additional fire stations will make economic output higher than it would be without them, but production, in the sense of net or final product, will be no higher than in the period when the danger of fire was less.[2] This example serves as the parallel to an elongation in the chain of necessary intermediate product.

This general categorization has been developed as part of the recent critique of national accounting practices. It is usually applied to certain public expenditures, for example, defense, police, fire protection, and so on, that cannot be seen in themselves as adding to individual welfare but that leave individuals better off than if the expenditures had not been incurred. The concept applies equally to private expenditures that are induced as an offset to some deterioration in the individual's position, for example, expenditure on extra laundry services made necessary by a smokier atmosphere.[3] Additional education acquired so as to safeguard one's access to a particular job at a time that general educational expansion is raising the level of required credentials can be considered in the same category, except to the extent that it is enjoyable in itself and/or adds to social as well as private productivity.

Since the borderline between intermediate and final output is not clear-cut, a qualitative hierarchy of output suggests itself, with regrettable necessities at the bottom and ultimate goals at the top. This approach

[2] For a comprehensive discussion of this and related issues see Thomas Juster, "A Framework for the Measurement of Economic and Social Performance," in Milton Moss, ed., *The Measurement of Economic and Social Performance* (New York: National Bureau of Economic Research, 1973).

[3] See Wilfred Beckerman, " 'Environment,' 'Needs' and Real Income Comparisons," *Review of Income and Wealth* (December 1972).

represents a major break in economic analysis; in the absence of adequate statistical or even conceptual formulation, it remains essentially a critique of existing concepts and measurements. But the critique itself has important implications for interpretation and policy. It is a key tool in understanding and explaining positional competition.

The present-day national accounts focus predominantly on gross output. Gross output is a blown up version of input, measuring the scarce resources that are used in the process of production; it represents the economic contribution to welfare, whatever that may be. "Economic activity" precisely describes this broad concept, nicely begging the question of what the activity is for. Net or final output is a more ambitious concept, attempting a measure of welfare itself, or at least of economic welfare (welfare resulting from the use of scarce resources as distinct from economically free resources such as sunshine and inner contemplation). The national accounts measure economic activity, broadly though not exclusively delineated by market transactions, regardless of its purpose. Consumers and government are regarded as final consumers, with the enterprise sector, in its current expenditures, as intermediate. The net concept of production is represented at one point in the treatment of capital formation by an allowance imputed for capital consumption (depreciation of equipment). The allowance, when deducted from gross investment, yields net investment and net national income.

It has been observed that the orientation of national accounting to the gross concept reflects the preoccupation of the 1930s with cyclical unemployment and of the 1940s with war potential. It leaves the framework less satisfactory in dealing with contemporary problems of growth and welfare than the more "net" orientation found in the work of Kuznets, a founding father of national income measurement in its modern phase.[4] The fact that no account is taken of the disutility of work—or for that matter of its occasional positive utility—is a striking indication of the "gross" nature of the measure of economic output. Kuznets has recognized that the major changes in structure that accompany the process of economic growth, such as urbanization, necessitate additional consumption expenditures, for example, for commuter travel; and he has acknowledged that these ought perhaps to be classified as additional costs of production, that is, intermediate product rather than additional real net product.[5]

Defensive goods, it has been argued, are a facet of some wants being a means to the satisfaction of other wants. The concept therefore admits of a hierarchy of wants. Although the concern is with the bottom end of the hierarchy, by implication there must also be a top end: ultimate

[4] Juster, "A Framework for the Measurement of Economic and Social Performance"; Kuznets, "The Share and Structure of Consumption."

[5] Kuznets, Modern Economic Growth, p. 225.

wants in some sense. The admission is a crucial one and serves to reopen an old philosophical problem of the purpose of economic activity. (This problem is discussed below.) But there is also a more practical implication, central to our immediate concern, which involves the distinction between what consumers really want and what they do to get it. This distinction rests on an implicit two-fold division in consumer preferences. The implied division is between goods and services that yield direct primary satisfaction in themselves and those that yield zero or negative satisfaction (defensive consumption). But conceptually there is nothing unique about the zero line in this context. Consumer spending that is undertaken primarily as a means to satisfaction from other forms of consumption, but that nonetheless yields slight satisfaction in itself—holiday travel, say, or, for many people, expenditure on education—has more in common with consumption wholly directed to intermediate ends than with an activity that itself rests on prior intermediate expenditures—activities on the holiday beach, or enjoying the pleasant job to which intensive education leads. That is to say, distinctions in demand that separate consumer satisfaction on either side of the zero line also separate satisfactions at different distances from that line.

II

Once admitted, the hierarchy of wants is a continuum. If this is so, questions long banished from economic discussion return. The relevant problem is not only how much is the individual willing to spend on this or that activity or purchase, but what for? The latter question cannot be answered in the precise and objective form of a sum of money and has thus far proved impervious to any alternative quantification. For the purpose of economic measurement, then, the question remains nonoperational. But it can be used as a tool in assessing the significance of economic magnitudes estimated conventionally. The wide range of activities and expenditures related to positional competition are a prime example of the relevance of asking "what for." Education enjoyed in its own right is capable of indefinite extension; as an instrument for entree into top jobs, it is not. In the first case, the private benefit is equally a social benefit. In the second case, the only social benefit is the contribution to improved sorting of people as a whole for jobs that suit them best, a benefit that will normally be well below the private benefit from improving one's own selection chances. Individual demand for purely private goods can be satisfied by additional supply through the market process. But individual demand for positional goods cannot be satisfied in the same way. Instead, it will tend to evoke additional defensive needs—needs in the sense of regrettable necessities or defensive consumption.

The relevance of this condition for public policy is that attempts to satisfy an expansion in individual demand in the positional sector will be frustrated by a *pari passu* increase in individual needs. In the area of the economy represented by positional goods, growth in aggregate availabilities is unattainable since it is subject to the limits of social scarcity. The growth shown here in conventional measures of economic output reflects no more than the inability to distinguish defensive or intermediate expenditures by individuals from expenditures and activities that add to primary satisfactions. The bigger the proportionate role that positional competition attains in individual activity, the more serious the distortion. The consumer dollar then turns out to be a less sure guide to the allocation of economic activity in response to the preferences of consumers themselves. To see this in perspective, it is useful to consider the problem in its historical philosophical setting.

The philosophical problem of the nature of the economic objective, or maximand, has been covered over in the formalization of economics in its modern neoclassical development as a science of choice in the use of limited means for given ends. The problem arises from the expanding frontier of wants themselves, a frontier that is pushed out by the very means of satisfying existing wants. It follows that the satisfaction of wants in a proportionate sense, that is, the extent to which existing demands are satisfied, may never increase. If the objective of economic activity is narrowly defined as the maximum satisfaction of individual wants within the constraint of limited resources, this seems to invite the conclusion that increases in resources (and thereby in the availability of goods) does nothing to increase welfare, since wants increase correspondingly. The extent to which existing demands are satisfied may never increase because wants rise commensurately with resources. So economic advance appears as one of those hoax races that leave the participants in the same place.

The weak point in this line of thought, a line that recurs in various critiques of material growth over the centuries, is that it applies a criterion fashioned for use in static situations to dynamic ones in which the previously fixed parameters—in this case wants—themselves change. And wants, at least in western culture, are sought-after objects susceptible to development and "improvement." What else, after all, are cultivated tastes than additional, especially refined wants?

III

This wider objective was undoubtedly obscured in early classical economics, based on the simple Benthamite calculus, in which wants are entirely subjective and therefore of equal status, one with the other. (Pushpin is as good as poetry.) So it was not only Marx but Alfred Marshall, the heir of the classical tradition in English economics, who parted company from Ricardo and his followers in emphasizing that man was not to be regarded as a constant quantity. Wants and tastes must be expected to evolve along with the development of the means of production, distribution, and consumption, and Marshall's Victorian confidence left no doubt that the evolution was upward into increasingly elevated planes.[6]

But the notion that welfare is about the quality of wants, rather than merely the algebraic difference between subjective wants and their satisfaction, is not dependent on any law of historical progress. It was a central theme of Frank Knight, who in the generation after Marshall combined antipathy to deliberate measures of social reform with a deep philosophical pessimism about the capacity of liberalism to satisfy man's ethical and moral needs. Knight stated flatly:

> The chief thing which the common sense individual actually wants is not satisfaction for the wants he has, but more, and better wants . . . Life is not fundamentally a striving for ends, for satisfaction, but rather for bases for further striving . . . true achievement is the refinement and elevation of the plane of desire, the cultivation of taste.[7]

Knight concluded by faulting "the economic assumption" that men produce in order to consume; the opposite was nearer the truth.

Marshall and Knight formed part of the mainstream of economic liberalism. Yet their philosophical reflections were essentially asides, cut off from their systematic economic exposition and often regarded by contemporaries and followers as personal indulgences.[8] The barrier and stumbling block was market valuation, the bedrock of classical and neoclassical economics to this day. Market valuation is grounded on existing wants; it reflects the subjective priorities of present-day consumers, weighted by the purchasing power at their disposal. It retains the Benthamite subjectivity which was blind to any gradation of wants or recognition of needs. For, in short, it assumes "consumer sovereignty," or more correctly, the sovereignty of consumer dollars. In this mercantile populism, the cultivation of tastes is an elitist intrusion. More: any change in tastes, even if entirely spontaneous, removes the established basis for judging whether economic progress has taken place. The established test is whether a given set of tastes is better satisfied.

The dynamic concept, in which fulfillment of given wants generates new and higher order wants, was more easily captured in Marxist analysis. A passage from the *Grundrisse* touches the heart of the contemporary dispute about the objective of economic growth:

[6] Alfred Marshall, *Principles of Economics* (1920), 8th ed. (London: Macmillan, 1969), pp. 73-74 and Appendix B, p. 630.

[7] Frank H. Knight, "Ethics and the Economic Interpretation," in *The Ethics of Competition* (1935) (London: Allen and Unwin, 1951), pp. 22-23.

[8] Thus Marshall is nowadays chided from time to time for his sentimental lapse into biological environmentalism.

As soon as consumption emerges from its initial state of natural crudity and immediacy—and, if it remained at that stage, this would be because production itself had been arrested there—it becomes itself mediated as a drive by the object. The need which consumption feels for the object is created by the perception of it. The object of art—like every other product—creates a public which is sensitive to art and enjoys beauty. Production thus not only creates an object for the subject, but also a subject for the object. [9]

Higher class wants have increased welfare. This much is now widely accepted as a matter of practical and philosophical judgment, even if no systematic basis has yet been found for accommodating it into economic analysis. An increase in unfulfilled wants or needs can therefore not be taken, in itself, as detracting from welfare. [10] This point has come to be a standard counterblast against Galbraith's teasing assertion of the "revised sequence," in which output induces wants rather than wants inducing output [11]—a line of thought that had earlier been encapsuled in the elegant formulation of de Jouvenel: *la civilisation de toujours plus*. [12]

That welfare is increased by additional wants, as well as by their fulfillment, is a convincing riposte, in terms of economic philosophy, to the Galbraith-de Jouvenel position. There is elasticity in the economic maximand. But the philosophical reflection bursts the narrow bounds of the neoclassical economic frame. For admission of elasticity into the economic maximand breaks the link between welfare and satisfaction of a given set of wants on the basis of market choice. If the set of wants changes because of a change in tastes (as distinct from a change in demand on the basis of given tastes), the economist's standard measure goes out of commission. No comparison of welfare can be made where tastes vary; instinct that the change must be for the better is simply instinct, no more.

A greater practical difficulty is that once defensive consumption is admitted into the arena, shifts in output that appear to be in response to a change in consumers' tastes may then alternatively be a response to a change in the physical or social environment. If the environment deteriorates, for example, through dirtier air or more crowded roads, then a shift in resources to counter these "bads" does not represent a change in consumer tastes but a response, on the basis of existing tastes, to a reduction in net welfare which the conventional national accounts hide. [13] In

[9] Karl Marx, *Grundrisse* (London: Pelican Marx Library, 1973), p. 92.

[10] For a good discussion of the point see Beckerman, *In Defence of Economic Growth*, pp. 87-93.

[11] John Kenneth Galbraith, *The New Industrial State* (Boston: Houghton Mifflin, 1967).

[12] Bertrand de Jouvenel, "Organisation du travail et l'amenagement de l'existence," *Free University Quarterly*, VII (August 1959).

[13] This point is brought out sharply by Beckerman in " 'Environment,' 'Needs' and Real Income Comparisons," but essentially ignored in his book *In Defence of Eco-*

the same way, more intensive competition for positional jobs will also disguise a reduction in net welfare, which in this case occurs through absorption of additional resources in credentials-producing educational activities. Accordingly, once defensive consumption is acknowledged, the signals of market demand lose reliability as guides to economic welfare.

Arrival at a true assessment of national product as a measure of economic welfare that is distinct from economic activity is therefore bedeviled in practice by both statistical and conceptual difficulties. The one serious quantitative attempt so far made at a gauge of economic welfare is essentially a modification of the national accounts.[14] More ambitious attempts to indicate net or final output, or the welfare produced by the economic system, have had to resort to the avowedly unsystematic measures yielded by "social indicators." These comprise a hybrid collection of indicators of various facets of economic and social well-being—for example, health as indicated by mortality rates (rather than money spent on doctors and hospitals); contentment and safety as indicated by the inverse of suicide and accident rates (as distinct from spending on prevention services and safety devices); air quality as indicated by pollution content (as distinct from spending on antipollution devices).[15] The signif-

---

nomic Growth. For a pioneering discussion of the conceptual problems of comparing national income between countries or periods where conditions and/or tastes (including habits) differ see Dan Usher, *The Price Mechanism and the Meaning of National Income Statistics* (Oxford: Clarendon Press, 1968). An interesting early essay on aspects of this theme is S. Herbert Frankel, " 'Psychic' and 'Accounting' Concepts of Income and Welfare" (1953), in R. H. Parker and G. C. Harcourt, eds., *Readings in the Concept and Measurement of Income* (Cambridge, Eng.: Cambridge University Press, 1969), pp. 83-104.

[14] William D. Nordhaus and James Tobin, "Is Growth Obsolete?" in *Economic Growth* (New York: National Bureau of Economic Research, 1972). By far the most important adjustment was allowance for the value of leisure and nonmarket activities. On the other side, deductions were made of instrumental expenditures by private households on commuting and by government on defense, police, sanitation services, road maintenance, and so on; further deductions were made for "disamenities of urbanization," measured from estimates of the income differentials needed to hold people in localities with greater population densities (a basis that omits any deterioration common to all areas). The net outcome, dominated by the adjustment for nonmarket time, was a measure of economic welfare (MEW) for 1965 of rather more than double the equivalent net national product, but with a probably slower rate of growth. Thus in 1947-1965, net national product per capita rose by a compound 2.0 percent; the growth rate of MEW, on three alternative measures which made different assumptions on the change in real value of nonmarket time, was -0.1, 0.4, or 1.6; in 1929-1965, growth on the NNP basis of 1.7 percent compares with 0.5, 1.0, or 2.3 on the MEW basis (Nordhaus and Tobin, *Economic Growth*, p. 56). The desirability in principle of much more far-reaching adjustments was discussed by Robin Matthews in his "Comment" in Nordhaus and Tobin, *Economic Growth*, pp. 87-92. See also Juster, "A Framework for the Measurement of Economic and Social Performance."

[15] The parentheses indicate in each case the comparable gross concept in the national accounts.

icance of these social indicators is limited first by the statistical difficulty of finding measurable proxies for the "output" that is to be assigned; and second, by the absence of any common unit of measurement to link and aggregate the separate measures, comparable to that of money in GNP. This lack of a weighting system for social indicators is a conceptual limitation for which no solution is yet in sight.

Yet public and professional interest in social indicators has not been diminished by their evident limitations. An alternative and more welfare-oriented measure of output than GNP evidently remains in strong demand from the users of these statistics. This demand may be taken as a prima facie indication of the inadequacy of the GNP accounts. The dissatisfaction does not, by itself, indicate that the figures are becoming worse over time, that is, that the gap between GNP and a true measure of economic welfare is growing, but it is clearly consistent with such a divergence. It is not difficult to find deductive reasons why this may have taken place. One set of such reasons relates to ecology and the physical environment; these have been widely discussed. Whether actual pollution increases faster than material output is not the main consideration. There is little doubt that such a tendency exists in potential, that is, in what pollution would be if nothing was done to check it. Since the preventive or defensive measures that industry, government, and consumers take to counteract pollution are mostly reflected in GNP, there is an upward bias to recorded national output when compared to other countries or past times in which the level of pollution is or was lower.[16]

The concern in our analysis is with a different family of defensive expenditures, those motivated to protect the position of the individual in the social environment. Statistical measures of consumption and economic product are exaggerated by the failure to allow for the increase in intermediate consumption which individuals face in their attempt to secure the satisfactions they seek in the positional sector.

Positional competition, as has been pointed out, enlarges the negative or deadweight element in market competition and voluntary exchange. It is a process that can be seen as a continuation of a broad historical tendency. Its cumulative effect is a profound qualitative change in the impact of the market system, and more generally of pursuit of individualistic economic goals.

---

[16] This will be the case where the pollution is uncorrected and where correctives are applied by consumers or government, and counted as final product. No distortion will exist where correctives take the form of current expenditures by business enterprises, which are counted as adding to costs, provided that associated increases in output prices are assessed as such. This condition is not always met: safety and "environmental" features that raised prices of new automobiles in the United States in the early 1970s were classified, after much soul-searching by the national account statisticians, as improvements in quality.

IV

In the early stage of Britain's economic growth, when only a small minority of rich people had claim to surplus beyond the needs of subsistence, Adam Smith saw the rich man as being obliged by the inadequate capacity of his stomach to sell his surplus to buy "those baubles and trinkets which are employed in the economy of greatness" and as a result of this exchange, to provide the means of support to others who supplied his needs. This is the process by which Smith, in *The Theory of Moral Sentiments*,[17] sees the working of an invisible hand as guiding self-seeking individuals to socially beneficial results. The rich are in this way "led by an invisible hand . . . and, thus without intending it, without knowing it . . . advance the interest of society."[18] It was only because the individual could be deceived to believe in "place" and "riches" that "the individual effort necessary for the progress of society and moral standards" could be sustained. Therefore the rich man could be encouraged to chase "trinkets" so long as this contributed to the wider end. For the poor man and for society, the exchange was plainly a good deal—the poor reaped large consumer surplus. This was a key element in Smith's rejoinder to Hobbes; it showed why pursuit of individual interests need not result in the destructive Hobbesian conflict.

The modern problem is that it is no longer trinkets that are the prime object of the chase but scarcities desired in their own right. Stomachs have not expanded but other human needs—notably those of the mind and the psyche—have expanded in a way Smith did not envisage. More precisely, fulfillment of primary biological needs has provided greater scope for the development and satisfaction of these other needs.

In the eighteenth century, the goods and services supplied to the rich —the domestic services, the rarities, the favored positions—appeared to Adam Smith as trinkets and baubles precisely because effective demand for them was so small on the part of others whose far more urgent needs went unsatisfied. For those whose stomachs are empty, the exchange of diamonds—or personal respect—for water and bread involves minimal cost in terms of available alternatives. The price of luxuries that are bid for and consumed predominantly by the rich, at this stage in history, far exceeds their opportunity cost to the rest of society. If such demands

---

[17] Adam Smith, *The Theory of Moral Sentiments* (1759) (London: Bell, 1907).

[18] Cited in A. L. Macfie, "The Invisible Hand in the 'Theory of Moral Sentiments,' " in *The Individual in Society* (London: Allen and Unwin, 1967), p. 124. This is a more limited view of the invisible hand than in the famous reference in *The Wealth of Nations*, though Macfie, following Keynes and Sidgwick, regards the theistic and optimistic assumptions of the *Moral Sentiments* as providing the psychological and theological basis for the more general equilibrating device extolled in the later volume. See also Samuel Hollander, *The Economics of Adam Smith* (London: Heinemann, 1973), pp. 246-256, and Chapter 10 below.

were removed, luxury values—and measured national income—would collapse. To the extent that the services yielded by the luxury good are essentially symbolic, demonstrating the superior ability of the purchaser to afford it (the trinket function deriving from pure social scarcity in the terminology of Chapter 2), the decline in absolute values would not indicate an equivalent loss of satisfaction.

In a poor society, the consumption of the mass of the population is concentrated on basic material goods. The positional sector is correspondingly uncrowded: in many of its aspects, the frontier of wants is still open. Positional competition is therefore largely confined to the purely representational, to indications of relative superiority. These may be socially resented but they are economically benign, promoting the harmony of interests in the way Smith described.

By contrast, as general standards of living rise, demand for luxuries becomes more extensively diffused throughout the population. Where the demand falls on positional goods whose availability is limited in some absolute sense, their relative price will increase; and to the extent that particular positional goods are actively sought for the performance of a specific function beyond "representation," this price increase will induce attempts by individuals to find substitutes in the ways that have been described. Such attempts absorb real resources. They yield a benefit to the individuals concerned, but for society, they are at best a stand-off. Rather than trinkets, the distinctive appurtenances of the rich then become squirrels' wheels for those below: objects of desire that the most intensive effort cannot reach. Competition moves increasingly from the material sector to the positional sector where what one wins another loses in a zero-sum game. As the frontier closes, positional competition intensifies.

The values embodied in trinket-luxuries, as indicated, would collapse with a redistribution of income, and opponents of such redistribution have long put great emphasis on the fact and drawn incorrect inferences from it.[19] Correspondingly, a growth in the general level of income is incapable of adding to the sum of services yielded by positional goods.

The following contrast then appears. Insofar as the main brunt of

[19] Wicksteed was among the first economists to warn that average national income gave a misleading indication of the resources that would be available to all if incomes were divided equally, since the values created by rich men bidding up prices of resources in scarce or inelastic supply (the services of the best surgeons, as well as land) could not be converted, at prevailing relative prices, into the goods that would be in demand with equal distribution. (*The Common Sense of Political Economy*, II, 649-656.) Trinkets cannot be turned into bread. This limitation has often been seen and presented as implying that redistribution destroys wealth. But this interpretation misses the ambiguity embodied in the issue. What constitutes "wealth" is itself governed by how claims on it are distributed. A hundred dollars' worth of diamonds cannot be turned into a hundred dollars' worth of bread, but, say, the ten dollars' worth

unsatisfied demand is for material goods which require additional inputs of labor, capital, or technology, redistribution of income that the rich currently spend in order to impress each other is little substitute for general economic growth in its effects on the poor. But insofar as latent demand is for goods, services, or facilities with a positional element, generalized growth will be no substitute for redistribution. Demands of the latter kind tend to grow as general standards rise. Just as there was a tendency in times of material poverty to exaggerate what redistribution of income could do to diffuse what was then the most sought-after prerogative of the contemporary rich, their material comfort, so there is a tendency in times of material affluence to exaggerate what growth can do for diffusion of the new distinctive preserve of the rich, their positional prerogatives.

What the wealthy have today can no longer be delivered to the rest of us tomorrow;[20] yet as we individually grow richer, that is what we expect. The dynamic interaction between material and positional sectors becomes malign. Instead of alleviating the unmet demands on the economic system, material growth at this point exacerbates them. The locus of instability is the divergence between what is possible for the individual and what is possible for all individuals. Increased material resources enlarge the demand for positional goods, a demand that can be satisfied for some only by frustrating demand by others. The intensified positional competition involves an increase in needs for the individual, in the sense that additional resources are required to achieve a given level of welfare. In the positional sector, individuals chase each others' tails. The race gets longer for the same prize.

---

of bread that can be substituted may be valued more highly, after the redistribution of income, than the quantity of diamonds valued at a hundred dollars before redistribution.

[20] This theme is discussed in more detail in Chapter 12.

part two
The Commercialization
Bias

5 The Economics of Bad Neighbors

The scramble to acquire larger shares of fixed availabilities involves a distortion frequently alluded to in casual conversation. It makes people too money-minded. This judgment is usually associated with criteria beyond economic calculation or directly opposed to it. However, a rationale can be provided in straight economic terms on the basis of choice conventionally grounded in individual wants. Excessive preoccupation with monetary gain can reflect the qualitative change in the impact of market activity that occurs when the cumulation of individual demands produces unintended and wasteful side effects over a widespread area.

Earlier, positional competition was analyzed as a major example and expression of potential distortion arising from autonomous market transactions. Such competition not only draws resources away from the output of final consumption goods and services in the commercial sector; it also draws resources away from the noncommercial sector, from activities that remain partly or wholly outside the market and the cash nexus. These activities include subsistence production (production for one's own use rather than for sale), formal or informal grants in goods or kind, and leisure. Performance of work for lower remuneration than would be commanded elsewhere also contains an element of subsistence production since it produces for oneself the nonmarketable satisfaction of doing a job one prefers. People who enjoy their jobs, in effect, sell part of their work activity to themselves in return for direct satisfaction. The product is not available for marketing for cash; if cash is needed, different work carrying higher pay and less or negative enjoyment must be undertaken. Less obviously, extramarket activities include a wide variety of actions prompted consciously or unconsciously by social habit or a feeling of social obligation.

All these practices have some cost in terms of time, and positional competition increases that cost. This has helped to upset a long-held expectation about the potential fruits of economic growth—namely, that

71

they will be taken increasingly in the form of relief from material pursuits.

I

The subjective cost of time to the individual depends on the value he or she attaches to alternative uses of it. The time devoted to leisure and other non-income-earning activities will rise or fall with (1) the rate of pay on the work activity that is given up in order to make room for the additional leisure time, and (2) the subjective value that is attached to the pay that is given up. The effect of a general increase in productivity and the rate of pay will be to raise the "felt" cost of leisure on the first count (more pay and therefore more goods being sacrificed for each hour not worked) and to lower it on the second count (the marginal utility of income falls and of leisure rises as income becomes more plentiful in relation to leisure). The second effect can be expected to predominate as individuals increase their consumption in all forms including leisure, with the exception of "inferior" goods whose consumption declines as living standards rise. This supposes no complications from expanded needs in the sense defined earlier and no change in the nonmonetary valuation (positive or negative enjoyment) attached to work. This simple world has been the implicit model behind traditional expectations that rising productivity would gradually lead to the decline of economic cares and to a more leisured and cultivated society.[1]

The real world is demonstrably not like that.[2] Why? One reason has been hammered home with wit and insight by Staffan Linder in his lament for *The Harried Leisure Class*.[3] Linder's central explanation of this

[1] This expectation was perhaps the longest surviving legacy of Victorian optimism. It was an important theme of Keynes's famous 1930 essay "Economic Possibilities for our Grandchildren," p. 328, and of C. A. R. Crosland's *The Future of Socialism* (London: Cape, 1956, rev. ed., 1964). In more guarded form it reappeared in economists' "anti-antigrowth" ripostes in the early 1970s. Beckerman, *In Defence of Economic Growth*; Samuel Brittan, "The Economics of the Alternative Society" in his *Capitalism and the Permissive Society* (London: Macmillan, 1973).

[2] Various statistical measures of leisure have shown a substantial increase, notably the coverage and length of paid holidays; there has also been some continuing, but decelerating, reduction in the length of the working week in manufacturing and clerical jobs, but not in professional and high-salaried jobs, probably reflecting the consistently higher degree of work satisfaction in the latter. It has been estimated that in the U.S. labor force as a whole, workers took only about 8 percent of the increased productivity in the 1960s in the form of leisure; this was somewhat *less* than during preceding decades. Geoffrey H. Moore and Janice Neipert Hedges, "Trends in Labor and Leisure," *Monthly Labor Review* (February 1971), p. 11. See also George Katona, Burkhard Strumpel, and Ernest Zahn, *Aspirations and Affluence* (New York: McGraw-Hill, 1971), chap. 9; John D. Owen, *The Price of Leisure* (Rotterdam: Rotterdam University Press, 1969); Scitovsky, "What Price Economic Progress?" Young and Willmott, *The Symmetrical Family*, chaps. 4, 5, 6, 9.

[3] Linder, *The Harried Leisure Class*.

phenomenon—the tendency for greater affluence to make modern man more harried rather than less—is the increasing time absorbed by the process of consumption itself. As output of material goods increases, while the time in which to use them remains constant, time becomes scarcer in relation to goods (the goods intensity of time rises). To the individual, this is reflected in two ways. He is under increased pressure to economize on his own use of time so that he can spread it over his extended range of consumption, which is itself time absorbing in greater or lesser degree. He also faces a parallel increase in the cost of buying time through the hire of personal services. This cost tends to rise as productivity rises elsewhere in the economy. The result is that these gains make it more expensive in terms of production foregone to devote labor to pure service for which no increase in productivity is possible. Since rising living standards also induce and permit the suppliers of services to follow their preferences for more pleasant or less demeaning work, remuneration for such services must be increased further to offset the disamenities for which a price can now be asked. The steep increase in the cost of domestic service in rich countries is the most prominent example.

Hence the pressure to do more things in—and at—the same time: Linder's image of modern man finding himself "drinking Brazilian coffee, smoking a Dutch cigar, sipping a French cognac, reading *The New York Times*, listening to a Brandenburg Concerto and entertaining his Swedish wife—all at the same time, with varying degrees of success."[4]

Increased time pressure induces the substitution of time-saving for time-intensive consumption goods. Gary Becker, who pioneered modern application of economic analysis to the consumer's use of time, points to the time saved by shaving oneself rather than visiting a barber shop. Becker cites this example as a neglected source of increase in productivity —time productivity—in services.[5] But while the neglect of the consumer's own time costs in the conventional national accounts may in this way understate the relative increase in productivity of services vis-à-vis goods, full allowance for these time costs would tend to overstate, through a kind of double counting, the aggregate increase in productivity. For when the consumer feels his time to be sufficiently scarce to adjust his consumption in order to economize time, it can no longer be assumed that the new and time-saving forms of consumption add satisfaction in themselves. Instead, they may serve as, in effect, intermediate goods, providing additional resources in the form of time through which some other, and separately measured, form of consumption may be enjoyed. Thus Becker's consumer may lose satisfaction from his switch to self-shaving as such, but may do so in order to use the extra time for tennis.

[4] Ibid., p. 79.
[5] Gary S. Becker, "A Theory of the Allocation of Time," *Economic Journal* (September 1965), p. 508.

The benefit from his spending time on tennis ought then to be assessed net of his loss of satisfaction from barber's gossip.

This example illustrates an important and neglected facet of adjustment in modern life patterns under the impetus of increasing productivity in the material sector. It is worth emphasizing with an arithmetical illustration. Suppose the consumer's satisfaction from time spent playing tennis and at the barber's is as indicated in the table below; for simplicity, assume that the cost of both activities per hour is the same, and that self-shaving absorbs negligible time and negligible cost.

	Units of satisfaction from extra hour of		Total hours available	Disposition of time (hours) giving maximum satisfaction
	Tennis	Barber		
1st hour	3	1	1	Tennis 1 (3 units)
2nd hour	2	0	2	Tennis 2 (5 units)
3rd hour	0	0	3	Tennis 2 Barber 1 (6 units)

With three hours available, the consumer does best to play tennis for two hours and have his session at the barber's in the third. If now his available time is squeezed to two hours, he will do best to abandon the barber, shave himself, and preserve his second hour of tennis.

Thus, while the "product" from self-shaving is hidden in the time released for the preferred and therefore more productive activity of tennis, it would be incorrect to treat this time as pure gain: against the satisfaction from tennis must be set the loss of satisfaction from visits to the barber's shop. In terms of the example, the net gain, compared with an enforced hour at the barber's shop, is the 2 units from the second hour of tennis *less* the 1 unit from the abandoned hour at the barber's.

Alternatively, suppose that the consumer gets no positive satisfaction from time spent at the barber's and switches from shaving himself in a time-intensive way to shaving himself faster with more costly equipment. The extra equipment is bought to open the way to consumption activities otherwise excluded by the shortage of time—say, early morning tennis. The national accounts will record a double addition to consumption—the car-fitted electric razor and the additional payments for tennis services—although the addition to consumption satisfaction is limited to the latter.

When the consumer's time is scarce, therefore, any one time-consuming activity is undertaken at the expense of another, and it becomes economic for the consumer to engage in certain transactions as a means of purchasing time. In effect, shortage of time pushes more consumer activities into the category of instrumental or intermediate activities, and since there is no way of allowing for this in the national accounts, the effect is to introduce an extra element of double counting into consumer expenditures.

In this sense, expenditure not only on a variety of services such as taxis or credit cards but also on time-saving goods and services themselves can be considered as defensive, undertaken in order to permit other forms of consumption. The fact that the expenditure is undertaken indicates that the new package still constitutes a gain on the old, in the eye of the purchaser: the extra tennis is worth the additional cost of the electric razor. But the gain is exaggerated in the national accounts by adding both the expenditures that eat into available time and other consequential expenditures made to economize it. If an increase in income permits an extra shopping trip and this in turn necessitates a taxi home to make up for the time spent buying, then it is reasonable to regard the increase in welfare as confined to the extra goods acquired. The taxi fare is an indication of increased welfare, and not a part of it. Heightened time pressure induces a new layer of consumption to be undertaken, in the twentieth-century habit, not for its own sake but for the sake of something else. The more intensive the consumption pattern, the greater the number of layers, and the more that these are likely to represent time savers rather than the final objective of consumption activity. Pressure on time, like pressure on geographical or social space, adds to the consumption activities that have to be undertaken as means to other forms of consumption.

An additional reason why the pressure of time rises with affluence is suggested by the earlier analysis of the uneven structure of growth in the advanced economy. This influence matches Linder's inroads into available consumption time with a parallel increase in pressure for more time to be spent in production (or more strictly, in market activity). Concentration of productivity growth in the material sector leads, in the ways described, to increases in effective demand for positional goods. The processes of crowding and screening absorb additional real resources in allocating the limited availability of such goods and facilities. To this extent, part of the addition to national product is absorbed in increased input and yields no net gain in welfare. Crowding may add directly to the time cost of the positional good, for example, in spreading suburbanization outward, which increases the time spent in commuting.[6] More generally, the increase in individuals' "needs" created by positional competition has

---

[6] I am indebted to Tibor Scitovsky for this example.

a cost in time represented by the extra money that has to be earned to pay for the additional needs.

This is the rat race at the societal level. It must be expected to increase the value that individuals attach to additional income obtained by sacrifice of leisure or otherwise by substitution of a preferred activity for a less preferred one, for example, a shift from work at home to work in the market, or from work that yields positive satisfaction to less pleasant but more financially remunerative work. The increased "need" for market earnings intensifies the scarcity of time by increasing pressure for its use in maximizing earnings from work.

This distortion directly counters the effect that the income tax may have in discouraging market activity vis-à-vis leisure and nontaxable job perquisites. Because income taxes reduce total incomes as well as reducing the income reward from working as against the leisure reward from not working, their net effect on work effort cannot be established a priori. (There is of course a clear-cut effect in diverting effort into tax-avoiding activities.) The need to work more if spending power is to be maintained (the "income effect" of the tax) will wrestle with the cheapening of leisure in terms of consumption foregone (the substitution effect). Various limited empirical investigations have not produced any clear and general tendency in this respect. By contrast, the opposite tendency stemming from positional competition, that for market activities to be overstimulated, will often involve no such conflict of forces. The addition to needs, or deterioration in the social environment with which the individual is faced, will in many cases represent not a worsening in the terms on which effort exerted in market activities can be exchanged for goods, but the equivalent of a "lump sum" deterioration—common to all—irrespective of the supply of effort. It is the counterpart of a drop in the winter temperature hitting both workers and idlers alike. For the individual there is then no cheapening in the terms on which additional leisure can be obtained for a given reduction in earned income—that is, no substitution effect—to counter the negative income effect. So the consumer will seek to restore the balance by sacrificing some leisure as well as some final consumption goods; the reduction in welfare increases the incentive to work, and to work for money rather than satisfaction. Admittedly, not all positional competition will be of this type. Increased competition for top jobs will leave opportunities for leisure unaffected, at least to the extent that leisure can be enjoyed without the income that these jobs provide; intensified job competition may thereby increase the temptation to "drop out." But many forms of positional competition have a direct impact on welfare from nonworking time—notably, the effects of crowding and suburban spread.

The same influences also cast light on the pervasive modern tendency for workers to move from agriculture, often from farming on their own account, to industry. This tendency has been identified as an important source of increased productivity and growth in advanced economies as well as in developing economies;[7] it rests on the higher earnings in industry, which workers who have left agriculture have evidently seen as a recompense for any loss of work satisfaction and independence. The analysis above suggests that the inducement to individuals to make the switch will not necessarily reflect a comparable social advantage in the form of increased productivity in the economy. In part, it may reflect excess stimulation to money earnings as against work satisfaction, which results from positional competition through the processes that have been discussed.[8] More cash income is needed to retain access to certain desired facilities; for example, as rural communities decline, journeys to the city become necessary for certain conveniences and accommodations that were previously available locally. At the limit, only investment bankers or corporate lawyers can afford to own farms in areas within convenient traveling distance of large cities and rich suburbs.

II

Both sources of increased time pressure identified in the last section —the additional time needed for consumption and the additional income needed to maintain position in its broad sense—help to explain another phenomenon which some have observed in modern economies, and for which an economic solution is not usually offered: a decline in sociability and, specifically, friendliness. Friendliness is time consuming and thereby liable to be economized because of its extravagant absorption of this increasingly scarce input—the straight Linder effect. It has been widely observed, both in casual impression and in some survey data,[9] that concern for the wider family is greater among the lower income groups than among the higher. Decreased dependence by the well off on mutual aid is one explanation;[10] another is the higher valuation set on their own time, consuming time as well as working time. Both elements may be tending

[7] For example, in the major study by E. F. Denison, *Why Growth Rates Differ* (Washington, D.C.: The Brookings Institution, 1967).

[8] I am indebted to Mr. J. C. R. Lecomber for this point.

[9] Potomac Associates, *Survey of National Concerns* (1970).

[10] See P. Kropotkin, *Mutual Aid* (London: Heinemann, 1904), p. 286, where Kropotkin quotes "a lady-friend who has worked several years in Whitechapel" as follows: "I know families which continually help each other—with money, with food, with fuel, for bringing up the little children, in cases of illness, in cases of death. The 'mine' and 'thine' is much less sharply observed than among the rich." See also Michael Young and Peter Willmott, *Family and Kinship in East London* (London: Routledge and Kegan Paul, 1957). Simon Kuznets, from the perspective of a growth economist analyzing the process of economic development, emphasizes the burdens of mutual aid in the extended family: "from the standpoint of the economically successful individuals or of the growth potential of the economy as a whole they entail a large cost." "The Share and Structure of Consumption," p. 40.

to reduce friendliness and mutual concern in society as a whole as it becomes richer in material goods and ever more pressed for time.

The impact of time pressures on sociability—in the sense of friendliness, social contact, and mutual concern—is made particularly severe by the fact that these social relationships do not, by their nature, have the character of private economic goods: which is to say that the costs and benefits of specific actions do not fall primarily on those undertaking them. There also are externalities, or external costs and benefits, which individuals who seek to maximize their own advantage from each transaction will not take into account.

Friendship contains an element of direct mutual exchange and to this extent is akin to a private economic good. But it is often much more than that. Over time, the friendship "transaction" can be presumed, by its persistence, to be a net benefit on both sides. At any moment of time, though, the exchange is very unlikely to be reciprocally balanced. One partner puts himself out. In a deep friendship or love between two people, the mutual benefit in taking the long view rather than the short can be assumed to be sufficiently ingrained for this basis of exchange to emerge implicitly. There will be sufficient trust for the implied contract of give and take to be honored and faithfully interpreted over time. But deep friendship and love are of course more than implied contracts of long-term exchange. They involve a greater or lesser degree of altruism. To put it another way, the well-being of the other partner adds directly (though not necessarily equally) to one's own, or more radically, m₁y be integrally merged with one's own well-being.[11] However, even here, behavior is likely to be influenced by the norm or standard of such reciprocity prevailing in the society at the time.

This behavioral norm—how other people expect me to behave and how I can expect others to behave—has the character of the economist's public good in the sense that it affects everyone and can be shut out or appropriated by none. In more casual friendship and everyday social relations, the public good of the norm of sociability will be crucial, dominating the direct benefit or private good aspect of the particular relations. The casual nature of such contacts means that they rarely "pay" as piecemeal individual transactions. Perhaps the most obvious example is the mutual hello exchanged between passers-by. Since its essence is reciprocal exchange and any specific biliteral contract to enunciate it would be virtually impossible to arrange, social convention is its only basis: as is evident in its present-day decline, even in rural areas.

This is a peripheral example of an important social phenomenon: the existence of felt obligations to act in certain mutually supportive ways in

[11] For a concise formal discussion see Robert H. Scott, "Avarice, Altruism, and Second Party Preferences," *Quarterly Journal of Economics* (February 1972), pp. 1-18. See also Kenneth E. Boulding, "Notes on a Theory of Philanthropy," and William

given circumstances, formally undefined but grounded in the prevailing conventions of good social behavior. Such obligations are usually considered to be the province of sociologists and are regarded by economists as fixtures; which, in practice, means they are ignored. But social norms of this kind have a definite economic content, as public goods. For economists to exclude them from the set of interactions they are concerned with is to impart a bias in economic calculation comparable to the bias resulting from earlier exclusion of the economic effects of pollution or congestion.

III

The economic aspect of these behavioral norms can be illustrated in a simple way in the context of mutual support. Suppose that action under this head always has a discernible giving end and receiving end. People rotate in these positions. If the rotations are frequent, *and* occur between the same individuals, the exchange will be close to a private good even without altruism. My gesture to you today is likely to be repaid by you tomorrow, and that is enough to encourage it. Now suppose the rotations are both less frequent and linked by long chains rather than recurring pairs. Suppose some social action costs me a small amount very frequently and that its reciprocation will occur rarely, at unknown intervals, and from unknown individuals, but will be of great benefit. Friendliness to a stranger is one example; mutual readiness to aid someone attacked in the street is another. Since the great majority of specific transactions of this kind undertaken by everyone will involve a net (though small) cost, no such transactions will occur on the basis of immediate advantage alone.

Yet since all individuals gain more from the minority of transactions in which they benefit than from the majority in which they lose on a piecemeal basis, there is clearly a failure in organization. The piecemeal basis of motivation is inefficient: there is a tyranny of small decisions.[12] The gap has traditionally been bridged by social convention. The social norm that it is right to be friendly to strangers, or to come to the aid of victims of attack, is necessary to induce the provision of friendliness or mutual protection in the amount that is worth everyone's while. The Good Samaritan remedies a market failure.

The extent of this failure is likely to rise with the increasing scarcity of time, which makes it more pressing to pass by on the other side. As the market becomes more extensive, covering a wider sector of life, more

---

S. Vickrey, "One Economist's View of Philanthropy," in Frank G. Dickinson, ed., *Philanthropy and Public Policy* (New York: National Bureau of Economic Research, 1962).

[12] See Chapter 3, note 22.

Good Samaritans are needed. Yet as the subjective cost of time rises, pressure for specific balancing of personal advantage in social relationships will increase.[13] As long as the time cost is relatively low, whether because of fewer alternatives for use of leisure or because of fewer opportunities or pressures for additional work effort, the net cost of each specific time-absorbing activity connected with friendship or other social relationships will also be relatively low. In fact, it may not even be seen as a cost. Perception of the time spent in social relationships as a cost is itself a product of privatized affluence. The effect is to whittle down the amount of friendship and social contact to a level that leaves everyone wishing they had more at the expense of fewer material goods. This effect is doubly perverse since the relative value attached to friendship and other human relationships must be expected to increase as pressing material needs are increasingly met.

The huge increase in personal mobility in modern economies adds to the problem by making sociability more of a public and less of a private good. The more people move, the lower are the chances of social contacts being reciprocated directly on a bilateral basis. A casual favor or gesture is less likely to be returned. There also is then less scope for a long run view to be taken in a bilateral friendship exchange: before my gesture to you today has been reciprocated by you tomorrow, you may have moved away. In the language of the market, it pays less to invest in friendship when you or the other person may soon negate the specific prospective return by disappearing. This influence is strongest with geographical mobility, but increased social mobility—moving out of one's class—has the same general effect.

The inadequacy of individualistic calculation in this sphere is brought out by Tibor Scitovsky in the following way.[14] It takes two to be sociable. Therefore, since sociability is not bought and sold, an external economy is involved, and individual decisions will lead to suboptimal, that is, too little, sociability. The optimum requires what Scitovsky calls socially rational behavior, where individual rationality is modified by adherence to moral rules, conventions, gentlemanly manners, or the like.

[13] I have been able to find only two allusions to this issue in the economic literature, both of them brief: Trygve Haavelmo, "Some Observations on Welfare and Economic Growth," in W. A. Eltis and others, eds., Induction, Growth and Trade (Oxford: Clarendon, 1970); and Roland N. McKean, "Growth vs. No Growth: An Evaluation," in Olson and Landsberg, eds., The No-Growth Society (1975). McKean's position is close to that taken here. "Increasing material wealth, specialization, and population make it more costly and less rewarding to each individual to be considerate of others and to adhere to customs or ethical rules." See also the symposium on 'Time in Economic Life," Quarterly Journal of Economics (November 1973).

[14] In his book The Joyless Economy (New York: Oxford University Press, 1976), pp. 173-174. Professor Scitovsky kindly summarized this approach in commenting on an earlier draft of this section.

To be more specific, when the externalities are negative, there is need for restriction or prohibition enforced by laws and regulations. What is less widely recognized is that when there are external economies, as with friendship, the optimum requires *more* individual initiative. Law cannot bring this about; it must rely on moral or social conventions. In the example of friendship, this would mean being hospitable partly because one does not want to go against the long-standing tradition of hospitality; and such traditional behavior should get one closer to the social optimum than behavior dictated solely by the individual rationality of strict time budgeting.

The increased pressures on time from the tendencies discussed in this chapter—briefly, time-absorbing consumption and positional competition—help explain why these social conventions have come under increased strain. Additional influence in the same direction is exerted by other characteristics of advanced economies, notably, by the great increase in mobility. Nor can these adverse influences be expected to be offset by a strengthening of demand for friendship and other aspects of sociability, such as will occur if sociability is a luxury good for which demand rises more than proportionately to income. For if sociability develops progressively more of the characteristics of a public good whose benefits are diffused—and increasing productivity together with increasing mobility tend to make it so—then sociability will become less responsive to individualistic demand. We may want sociability more than ever; yet we cannot, individually and separately, express that want in a way that secures it. This analysis helps explain a frequent casual observation, which otherwise appears economically puzzling: that human contact in advanced economies is increasingly sought but decreasingly attained.

It is important to be clear that the distortion with which we are here concerned arises from the essence of the market process itself. The market framework, as has been well established in response to a widespread popular misunderstanding, permits in principle altruistic or communally directed objectives to be pursued so long as they are held by individuals and can be effected by their own actions. It is individual action to optimize individual objectives that is the crux. But there is one objective that the market mechanism cannot optimize. That objective is altruistic concern for the partner in the market transaction—what Wicksteed called "tu-ism." Efficient allocation of resources through the market demands that individuals always try to get the best deal, and then use the resources for whatever objective they happen to have, provided only that this is not the objective of *not* getting the best deal in the specific transaction. Individualistic maximization is crucial to the market process. Yet as has been seen, it is precisely this maximization that makes individuals underproduce the amount of sociability they want. Social convention may of course make them overproduce it, in cloying chumminess and repressive punishment or disfavor for deviations from the social norm. The choice between the two should depend on whether and where a deficiency of social consideration, rather than an excess, is likely to have greater drawbacks.

What is primarily at issue in the present discussion is not how sociable or altruistic individuals, taken together, are in their objectives, or whether they should become more so; but rather how the prevailing objectives of sociability or altruism can best be applied.

IV

As a secondary matter, a market economy probably encourages the strengthening of self-regarding individual objectives and makes socially oriented objectives more difficult to apply. The reason is that interests of self-concern and self-regard can be enlisted much more effectively in support of commercial sales efforts. Admittedly, corporations have no direct stake in their customers' motives. So why should they not urge potential purchasers of their product to buy also for others, or for common use, rather than for themselves?

The problem is, which others? Who deserves, and needs, Brand X? This is information usually not known precisely by the consuming altruist himself, who delegates the decision to a particular charity which he provides with a check. Power of purchase and choice of purchase are then divided and the force of a sales message becomes diffused. For a sales effort with impact, therefore, the identity of the person who deserves and needs Brand X selects itself. The corporation, to make its sale, is driven to urge those who have spending power to spend it on themselves.

Consumer advertising comprises a persistent series of invitations and imperatives to the individual to look after himself and his immediate family; self-interest becomes the social norm, even duty. The same ethos, albeit propagated for different motives, pervades what is in some respects the antimarket—the consumer movement of Ralph Nader and his followers in the United States and other countries. The individual is urged to secure maximum value for money for himself or herself. The approach is to the individual as maximizing consumer, rather than as cooperating citizen.

This is not to question the particular benefits that accrue from the consumer approach. Advertising may, and consumer services normally will, convey pertinent information that enhances satisfaction from consumption and thereby improves the efficiency of production. What is emphasized here is that this increase in "local" efficiency will have countervailing adverse effects for the economy as a whole to the extent that a sharpening of individualistic calculation erodes conventions of social responsibility and obligation. Such conventions, as indicated above, are necessary to counter the tendency of individualistic calculation to leave the community with less sociability than individuals themselves would choose if they felt the full consequences of their actions.

Whereas individualistic calculation is inherently antipathetic to sociability, the connection with objectives of self-regard and self-concern is in principle weaker. Consumers might simply become more skilled in their calculations without becoming more egotistical. But it seems doubtful that this separation could be achieved without a conscious effort.[15] The double barrage of consumer information from salesmen and their monitors has shown little sign of any such effort, and some indications to the contrary. Thus consumer periodicals, and the press at large, pay increasing attention to management of personal finances, including advice on tax avoidance: fully rational on the individualistic calculus, but also likely to discourage and to erode feelings of social obligation. The same inference may be derived from the increasingly explicit appeal to outright selfishness that can be observed in some commercial advertising.[16] Such direct counters to conventional morality are the exception, and may be intended tongue in cheek—a kind of dare. Yet they reflect, in extreme form, the conflict between traditional morality, with its stress on duty and social obligation, and individual maximization of consumption as a goal in itself.

[15] The experience of the consumer cooperative movement in Britain and other European countries suggests that social and consumerist objectives are difficult to run in harness.

[16] Two examples from the *New Yorker* in the spring of 1974: "Does your mother-in-law deserve Peter Dawson Scotch?" (implied answer: yes, if she comes carrying gifts for you rather than laden with luggage for her own stay) . . . "think before you share it." And from Johnnie Walker Black Label: "Honor Thy Self." Thus does the substitute religion reverse the message of the original variety. The reversal can be explained in terms of individual maximization as readily as in terms of changed morality. The purveyors of whiskey will find their services in greater demand if their customers wallow in self-indulgence. The purveyors of spiritual values of the other kind will find their own services most in demand if their customers feel the need to surpass natural instincts.

6 The New Commodity Fetishism

The way in which productivity growth in the material sector pulls the pattern of individual activities toward vain but costly attempts to achieve parallel growth in the positional sector has been discussed (Part I). The previous chapter suggested that this tendency has contributed to the perceived shortage of time, which in turn has exacerbated the pressure of positional competition, so that these two tendencies have become self-reinforcing. The increasing premium that people have put on their time has intensified a number of problems in economic and social organization. Most important, it has eroded sociability. This erosion has been deepened by the influence of advertising and the self-interest ethos of the market, including the antimarket ethos of consumerism. The present chapter suggests that the upshot of these several connected influences have together created a bias to material commodities.

This bias is a commodity fetishism in the fundamental sense of excessive creation and absorption of commodities and not merely an undue conceptual preoccupation with them in the original sense of Marx—a masking of social relationships under capitalism by their mediation through commodity exchange.[1] By "commodity" I mean here goods, and also services, sold on a commercial basis through the market or its equivalent. The concept of a commodity bias, therefore, implies that an excessive proportion of individual activity is channeled through the market so that the commercialized sector of our lives is unduly large. A related concept which is suggested by this approach is a "commercialization effect" —meaning the effect on satisfaction from any activity or transaction being undertaken on a commercial basis through market exchange or its equivalent, as compared with its being undertaken in some other way.

The increasing commercialization of life in advanced countries is a complex phenomenon. Its discussion in the present context implies no

[1] Karl Marx, *Capital*, vol. I, chap. 1, "The Mystery of the Fetishistic Character of Commodities" (London: Dent, 1951).

more than that positional competition, and the increase in material productivity that underlies it, have strengthened this tendency. Other factors such as the decay of traditional social ties and the great increase in
geographical mobility have obviously also played an important contribu-
tory part. The phenomenon could be analyzed fully only in terms of the
interaction of these and other influences in the general process of what
social scientists during the headier days of the 1950s and early 1960s liked
to refer to as "modernization." The focus here is on the specific, contribu-
tory influence of positional competition and what goes along with it.

The commodity bias affects not only the development of the nonmaterial sector, through its influence on sociability and on instrumental
means to positional goods which create new needs, but also the satisfaction derived from the material goods themselves.

I

Consumers derive satisfaction not from goods as such, but from the
various assortments of properties or characteristics that they embody.
This common sense concept has been formalized in a development of
consumer theory by Kelvin Lancaster under the revealing rubric, "Goods
Aren't Goods."[2] In this conception, "consumption is an activity in which
goods, singly or in combination, are inputs and in which the output is a
collection of characteristics." Particular goods may derive additional or
changed characteristics when used in combination with other goods.[3]

By a simple extension of this concept, the utility derived from goods
can be seen as emanating not only from their embodied characteristics
but also from the environmental conditions in which they are used. The
most obvious of such conditions are associated with direct interaction
between use of goods or services by different individuals—conventionally analyzed by economists as external costs or benefits. As has been
seen, the spreading of car ownership, through congestion, affects the
transportation service of a particular car; and the spreading of university
education, through the impact on the information content of given credentials, affects the service of a degree as a career entry ticket. Other
environmental conditions that may affect commodity characteristics are
social friendship and mutual aid. Such conventions respond over time to
changes in individual actions, but at any given time have an equal impact
on all, irrespective of specific individual behavior.

Social norms deriving from conventions and general standards of
human relationship over time may also be associated with specific ser-

[2] In A. S. C. Ehrenberg and F. G. Pyatt, eds., *Consumer Behavior* (Harmondsworth, Eng.: Penguin, 1971), pp. 340-360. The original article, "A New Approach to
Consumer Theory," is in *Journal of Political Economy*, 74 (1966), 132-157.

[3] This gives the formal basis for complementarity between goods, in which more
of one good enhances the utility derived from the other.

vices. The services of a doctor may yield, besides a direct improvement
in health, additional characteristics stemming from the patient's trust in
the doctor's judgment, his assessment of the doctor's motivation, and his
assurance or anxiety about his prospects of securing similar services in
the future. These latter characteristics are likely to be influenced by the
social basis under which medical services are supplied—whether in piecemeal market transactions, private insurance, or comprehensive public
insurance—and perhaps also by the underlying social ethos as it affects
obligations and entitlements to mutual aid in the society. The effect of
commercialization of medicine in the United States in weakening the
doctor-patient relationship is a matter of common experience and widespread comment. One striking example of the accompanying diminution
in trust is contained in a survey of the American Medical Association in
1969 showing that one in five of all physicians in the United States had
been or was being sued for malpractice.[4] This, in turn, has stimulated the
pursuit of "legally defensive" professional practice, marking a further
twist in the diminution of trust between doctor and patient.

The characteristics yielded by the provision of other services, such
as educational instruction, political or administrative leadership, or com-
panionship, also may be affected by the basis on which such services are
provided. The product or service that is supplied solely under the motive
of satisfying private wants—whether these wants are for money, power,
or a quiet life—can be seen as different from the product or service supplied at least partly under the motive of satisfying the wants or needs of
others, including society as a whole.[5]

This neglect of the social context in which individual acquisition
of goods and services takes place comprises a central aspect of modern

[4] Cited in Richard M. Titmuss, *The Gift Relationship* (London: Allen and Unwin,
1970), p. 166. The number and cost of malpractice suits has since risen sharply, and is
now recognized as a major problem in U.S. medical practice. The perverse effect of
market incentives on transactions that depend on mutual trust has been recognized in
orthodox economic analysis as resulting from a difference in relevant information
available to the two parties to the transaction.

[5] By broadening the view of economic welfare from consumption in its narrow,
direct sense to consumption in its social context, this approach responds to the modern Marxist criticism that neoclassical welfare theory "considers objects as ends in
themselves" (Herbert Gintis, "A Radical Analysis of Welfare Economics and Individual Development," *Quarterly Journal of Economics*, November 1972). The criticism
applies particularly to the burgeoning application of orthodox economic analysis to a
range of social questions (see Chapter 3 above). While the relevant environmental
conditions also can be treated more conventionally as externalities or public goods
yielding utilities or disutilities additional to the utilities derived from individual consumption, such treatment obscures the association that may exist between these externalities and certain structural forms of consumption; specifically it obscures certain
distinctive characteristics of market provision as such, or the "commercialization effect."

commodity fetishism. It involves an excess preoccupation with commodities—including for this purpose specific professional services—as instruments of satisfaction. Orthodox economic analysis is concerned with the commodities people have, not with the way they get them. Yet the relevance of this dimension is uncontroversial when applied to at least one activity—sex. "Bought sex is not the same." And this has a wider significance.

The effect on the characteristics of a product or activity of supplying it exclusively or predominantly on commercial terms rather than on some other basis—such as informal exchange, mutual obligation, altruism or love, or feelings of service or obligation—has been termed here the commercialization effect. Economists have recognized, however reluctantly, that something like this commercialization effect applies to sexual activity. Some would explain this influence by irrational social taboos or conventions that bar this activity from the market sector; others by a rational, but unique, assessment by the "consumer" that the nature or quality of the product or relationship here depends on the basis on which it is provided: a commercialization effect specifically acknowledged in the concept of prostitution.

Yet sexual prostitution can be seen as merely the polar extreme of a continuum in the more general commercialization effect. Thus, in the sexual relationship itself, a more explicit basis of exchange involves a diminution of unspecified mutual obligation, which in turn lowers the quality of the product. The move toward an exchange basis may take a variety of forms short of open commercialization—from the one-off barter transaction of a dinner for a sexual favor to the lengthy marriage contract recommended by the magazine *Ms.*, in which mutual obligations of both parties on household duties, sexual tolerance, and a host of other matters are drawn up and specified in the explicit detail of a business contract. Such barter exchanges or contractual commitments focus, in effect, on the narrow commodity aspect of the relationship—the sexual and other favors to be exchanged—to the neglect of the associated external conditions such as the spirit in which the exchange is undertaken.[6]

Whether or not the more commercial arrangements diminish the totality of mutual obligation and trust in the particular relationship involved, they will almost inevitably erode social expectations that mutual

---

[6] An alternative explanation of the inferior "quality" of sex when it is for pay has been suggested to me, I believe seriously. For some men, their sexual partners may be, in my terms, "positional goods." Accordingly, the female suppliers of such goods must be careful to maintain their status value, which precludes general marketing: only inferior women, therefore, will be available on the market. This skillful combination of the new Chicago economic approach to social questions with the traditional male approach to sexual questions fails to explain why many men consider (for any given sexual partner) bought sex inferior in itself.

obligation and trust will be available without similar specification in other, future relationships of the same kind. The more that is in the contracts, the less can be expected without them; the more you write it down, the less is taken—or expected—on trust.[7]

II

By influencing social norms and expectations in this way, commercialization or its equivalent embodies its own dynamic. More specifically, the dynamic is that of privatization,[8] or internalization, of benefits that were earlier assumed to be available through the influence of conventional norms of give and take. A key social function of such simple yet pivotal norms is to restrain people from maximizing their individual satisfaction in every specific transaction where this would conflict with their long-term self-interest.

Social norms are not always necessary to induce people to take a long-term rather than a short-term view of their self-interest. Good-will accumulated by an established firm; an individual's reputation for truth and honesty among continuing acquaintances; an expected lifelong friendship—these are all cases where the inducement to take a long-term view of self-interest, as a result of being internalized, is built-in. These are cases in which qualities such as trust, mutual support, reciprocity have the characteristics of private goods so that the benefits and costs of a particular pattern of behavior fall on the individual concerned. The problem arises, as pointed out in the previous chapter, when the effects of individual behavior are diffused and uncertain in their incidence.[9] It is then that social norms, or alternative inducements or coercion, are required to evoke socially directed action. And self-interest alone, even long-term self-interest, is then not sufficient to ensure compliance since the individual can take a free ride on compliance by others, while others can take a free ride on compliance by him. This "public goods" problem is discussed further in Chapter 9.

It follows also that a weakening of social norms, where they serve to

[7] The commercialization effect in its sexual illustration is discussed in greater detail in the appendix to this chapter.

[8] See footnote 16 below.

[9] The problem has therefore been heightened by increased geographical mobility, which has general effects similar to those noted in the context of sociability. The fact that modern property developers do not live in the neighborhoods they remold, and often nowhere near them, has been widely cited as an explanation of the reduced weight they have given to esthetic and social considerations compared with their predecessors, at least in European cities. Similarly, the mobility of corporation executives has tended to make corporate decisions less sensitive to their impact on local communities, at least until checked by a political reaction. Professor Kenneth Boulding has suggested Pittsburgh as an example of the good effects of having people live in the nests they foul.

uphold public goods, is likely to become self-aggravating. Once such conventions can no longer be counted on as the typical basis of behavior —that is to say, once the typical behavior to be expected of partners is an attempt to capture maximum private benefit from specific transactions— then the change in behavioral norms will feed on itself.

There will then be a "tipping" effect of the kind analyzed by Schelling in the context of neighborhood tipping in the housing market. In this process, individual behavior on the basis of given preferences produces a chain of reactions that works itself out only after culminating in a pattern that no single individual would himself choose.[10] In Schelling's example, a moderate urge among residents to avoid being in a small minority of their race may cause a nearly integrated housing pattern to unravel and highly segregated neighborhoods to form, although the only racial preference existing was to avoid being in a minority of one-third or less. In the present example, erosion of conventions about mutual obligations could extend a certain distance within society without setting off dynamic effects—people being prepared to take some risk that the reciprocity they expect for their own socialized behavior may go by default. But beyond the point at which the risk looks too high, behavior "tips" to securing fair exchange within the individual transaction. Commercialization, in the sense of securing fair exchange in each specific transaction, then becomes general. It is the essence of such situations, grounded in their public goods aspects, that individuals are never faced with the effect of their own behavior in influencing the social norm. The impact on themselves is usually infinitesimal and, in any case, dominated by the direct or private result of their actions.

Generally, market institutions are inefficient at any collective provision and may fail completely at collective provision of social norms. Correspondingly, they have a tendency to overproduce specific commodities or services at which they are efficient. The outcome is a commodity bias. Bars are for beer rather than for gossip; note the telling construction of the American bar, where customers sit facing the bottles and the barman rather than each other, and the natural pickup technique is to say *to the barman*, "buy the lady a drink." In the modernized English pub, the infrared grill replaces the dartboard.

More precisely, the market is inefficient at providing those collective goods for which limitation or exclusion is impractical or costly.[11] Where the turnstile or its equivalent can be used to limit access to those who are willing to pay, collective goods can be, and are, provided privately on a

[10] Thomas Schelling, "On the Ecology of Micromotives," in Marris, ed., *The Corporate Society*, pp. 43-55.

[11] For a full discussion, but one confined to the "narrow" commodity view, see James M. Buchanan, *The Demand and Supply of Public Goods* (Chicago: Rand McNally, 1968).

commercial basis. But in the approach taken in this chapter, the exclusion itself may change the characteristics of the collective goods provided. The market may supply the same narrow commodity or service, but with different characteristics in its environmental use. The most graphic illustration would perhaps be the pub dartboard screened by a turnstile—a facility differing so radically from the traditional open area that it has to my knowledge never been tried. If, then, the game of darts is inextricably bound up with open socializing, the market incentive and the market pressure will be to offer other things instead.

So there are tennis clubs for tennis; commercial dating services; country clubs and total living environments tied to rental or ownership of particular residences. In each case, the individual's demand is catered to in a package suitable for marketing, which may or may not be the package that the individual would himself choose if he were presented with the full potential choice. A full choice would include a municipal park and a town plaza, financed by local or national taxes; and perhaps tax-financed subsidies for private individuals, firms, or groups that provided comfortable or attractive facilities for socializing without direct charge: a subsidy for the open-access club.

In practice, the individual is confronted with choices only on a piecemeal basis and has to take as a fixture the relevant conditions of use. Thus the choice is not between private motor transport and public transport, but between buying an auto and putting up with the existing bus service; not between relying on private or public recreational facilities, but between supplementing existing public facilities or making do. Moreover, each initial choice tips the balance toward itself. With a double lock on your door, private guards at the apartment gates, and the private bills all this involves, your enthusiasm for bearing additional taxes to pay for more public policemen is likely to wane. Personal security and access to country lakes are increasingly being bought in the United States on an exclusive basis; in their traditional form as open to all citizens, they have ceased to be available in many areas as a direct result of those facilities becoming market commodities, that is, privatized.[12]

---

[12] A typical "total security environment" being developed in the San Francisco Bay Area offered the following: "Only residents with special keys can drive through the four entry gates. Once inside, private underground parking is available. Visitors park outside and enter through lobby doors which are controlled by intercoms to each apartment. The front door of each apartment is equipped with two locks, including a high security deadbolt. Inside the complex, residents and their guests can enjoy nearly four acres of privacy. Islanded in the centre of the lake is a spacious recreation center containing saunas, gym, steam room, tanning rooms, billiards, fireplace lounge, lockers, color T.V., stereo system and a kitchen." *Sunday Tribune*, Oakland, Calif., August 5, 1973.

A less blatant version of this phenomenon can be observed in new towns and suburbs in Britain. A clerk living in Bracknell remarks: "a funny thing is that you're sup-

Those interested primarily in the narrow commodity or activity will be well served; those who place a positive value on exclusion or exclusiveness will find their social environmental preference satisfied. On the other side, those who prefer social contact focused on casual meetings and activities or relationships less specifically geared to particular forms of consumption will be neglected; so also will those who place a positive value on open access, on nonexclusion. Their bad luck is that they derive utility from environmental characteristics that are outside the capacity of the market to provide. Since people with the first two sets of preferences have the engine of internalization on their side—which is to say that they have tastes that commercial enterprises find it profitable to cater to—the balance of forces in the market will tend to swing increasingly in favor of commodities, exclusion, and commercialization.

This phenomenon is the generalized bias of the market: to cater to those particular consumer demands that are amenable to commercialization.[13] It is a bias that operates through the wider extension of property rights and excluding devices, that is, gates and locks that to many tastes are unpleasant in themselves. The intense unpopularity of the introduction of museum charges in Britain by the Heath government in 1973 may have been directed at the symbol of the turnstile as much as at the modest charge. This charge removed not only 10 pence from the pocket but also the pleasure derived by some visitors from the existence of a part of the cultural heritage as common property available freely to all.

It is a paradox in the extension of choice through the market mechanism that the spread of restrictive laws and barriers takes place in the name of freedom. This paradox is lost sight of in the conventional focus on the narrow concept of a commodity or service. To advocates of greater internalization of benefits from collective goods, the more flexible property arrangements and additional excluding devices that are needed merely add to the efficiency of the market exchange. "If the owner of a hunting preserve is allowed to prosecute poachers, then prospective poachers are much more likely to be willing to pay for the hunting permits in advance."[14] A specific commodity or service can always be pro-

---

posed to be in the country but there are hardly any parks around that you can go to. In London we had Hyde Park and Hampstead Heath of a Sunday. This is supposed to be the country but it's all private." Quoted in Young and Willmott, *The Symmetrical Family*, p. 49.

[13] The same influence explains why externalities are biased to costs rather than benefits and cannot be expected to balance. In the production of goods and services, external economies are an oddity (the standard example is bee pollenate, and that has been disputed) because normal market forces provide an incentive for these economies to be internalized, and for external diseconomies not to be.

[14] James M. Buchanan, "An Economic Theory of Clubs," *Economica* (February 1965), p. 14.

duced more efficiently when property rights are strictly delineated. Public rights in use, without effective obligations on individuals to maintain and protect the facility, lead to the familiar tragedy of the commons. (Everyone benefits from the upkeep of the common, but no one has the motivation to tend it himself, so there develops the opposite and fatal incentive to graze and overgraze it before others complete its ruin.[15]) Yet a common facility can give satisfaction in itself. Its loss through commercialization involving exclusion both removes one item in the circle of economic choice and curtails personal liberty in various dimensions, for example, of movement. This restriction needs to be put in the scale against the increase in narrow efficiency, that is, in output in relation to input of commodities on their market valuation, and in choice *within* the commercial sphere that privatization will usually involve.[16] Privatization will also affect the distribution of income. Unless the system of tax or other form of finance supporting the public good is extremely regressive, privatization will be detrimental to the poor, by removing what to them (though not of course to society) was a free good.

In the ways described above, major changes in social patterns or social norms can take place without being willed by any individual and without being consistent with any summation of individual wishes. A "tip-over" of activities from social to market provision is a neglected example of the social irrationality that can result from rational individual economic behavior.

Irrationality in this sense, and indeed the economic significance of the commercialization effect itself, is denied, usually implicitly, in much of the extension of economic analysis into the realms of neighboring social sciences.[17] This extension, characterized by exponents and critics

[15] See in particular G. Hardin, "The Tragedy of the Commons," *Science* (1968).

[16] I have discussed various other aspects of what I regard as the weak link between personal liberty and economic choice in my "Empty Shelves on the Market Counter," *The Banker* (June 1973). Privatization is used here to denote a move away from provision of goods or services on a communal or subsidized basis to provision on a commercial basis, in which revenue is raised by specific charges paid by the user rather than through a system of tax finance or other collective means (of which the most famous example was communal labor to maintain the medieval commons before their privatization through enclosure). Privatization is a prominent example of commercialization, though the latter term is used more widely to cover the substitution of commercial exchange for implicit barter arrangements and conventions about mutual support.

[17] In the conventional treatment, a switch in an economic activity from outside to inside the market sector, or from partial to more complete exchange on market terms, normally represents an unqualified improvement in economic welfare, at least if it leaves the distribution of income unchanged. The improvement stems from the gain from trade voluntarily conducted. It makes at least one person better off without making anyone worse off, thereby yielding a "Pareto improvement." This Pareto im-

alike as "economics imperialism," was begun by Joseph Schumpeter in his classic work *Capitalism, Socialism and Democracy* in 1942[18] and developed by followers such as Anthony Downs, Gary S. Becker, Harry G. Johnson, and many others. The common assumption, almost always hidden, is that the commercialization process does not affect the product, so that the product, independent of the process by which it is acquired, sufficiently defines the objective. This again rests on the economist's traditional view, now beginning to be questioned, that consumption is the sole economic maximand, with consumption seen as a collection of outputs represented in specific commodities or services.

The validity of the so-called economic view of democracy has been questioned by some political scientists, particularly those who stress the functional role of participation.[19] In the Schumpeter-Downs model, democracy is essentially a choice exercised periodically by the mass of the people among alternative and open ruling elites, who in turn are induced by the force of competition (from rival elites) to offer policies tailored to attract electoral support. The political arena in this approach is akin to the market mode for fulfillment of personal wants. It is an extension of the department store—and the problem is to find the managers who can

---

provement forms the basis of traditional support among neoclassical economists— and some who would reject that label—for a wide range of policy issues and, in particular, for redistributive measures to be in cash rather than in kind. The present focus on the environmental use-cum-provision characteristics of consumption is a reminder that commercialization has additional effects which also need to be brought into the reckoning. The crucial limitation in the conventional analysis is that it does not allow for a change in the nature of the product according to the method of provision.

[18] Joseph A. Schumpeter, *Capitalism, Socialism and Democracy* (New York: Harper, 1942). The characterization "economics imperialism" was introduced by Kenneth Boulding. See, for example, his "Economics as a Moral Science," *American Economic Review* (March 1969).

[19] It is notable that one of the first textbooks to apply the economic method to political science, the widely used Robert A. Dahl and Charles E. Lindblom, *Politics, Economics, and Welfare* (New York: Harper and Row, 1953), still recognized a functional difference between the political and the market mode. "On the whole, the process of making market choices tends to narrow one's identifications to the individual or, at the most, to the family. The process of voting, on the other hand, with all that it presupposes in the way of discussion and techniques of reciprocity, tends to broaden one's identifications beyond the individual and the family." (Torchbook ed., 1963, p. 422). In the further development of this line of analysis, in Anthony Downs, *An Economic Theory of Democracy* (New York: Harper and Row, 1957), and James M. Buchanan and Gordon Tullock, *The Calculus of Consent* (Ann Arbor: University of Michigan Press, 1962), any such distinction had disappeared. The political arena was merely an alternative to the market mode for the satisfaction of private wants, and the problem was to find the areas in which, and methods through which, it was a superior mode in this respect.

undersell the rest of the street.[20] The alternative view sees popular participation as embedded in the democratic process, and crucial for its
outcome. Without it, insufficient support will be forthcoming to sustain
the democratic method from a variety of potential threats. These threats
range from jeopardy of procedural safeguards by governing elites seeking
to perpetuate their power, to the pressing of popular demands that exceed
what the system can provide.[21] The "economic" approach to politics neglects both the conditions in which the end products of democracy, that
is, policies resulting from the democratic process, are provided; and the
influence of these conditions on people's behavior. As a consequence, it
misdefines the objective of the process and omits a constraint that helps
determine whether the process keeps going. It could therefore more properly be called a commodity approach to politics.

Sociologists cast essentially similar doubts on the validity of ignor-
ing the process by which social services are made available. Richard Titmuss, in a striking empirical investigation of the supply of blood under
different arrangements in different countries, produced strongly sug-
gestive, if not decisive, evidence that reliance on commercial motivation
rather than on altruism and mutual obligation had negative effects on the
quality of the product and the efficiency of its provision.[22]

For these various reasons, therefore, an extension of the process of
commercialization in our economy, substituting explicit exchange for informal exchange, is in some sectors not an efficient means of meeting individual preferences.[23] It represents not what people want, choosing
among all potential alternatives, but merely what they get when inadequate special provision is made for satisfying individual demands that
the market is technically unsuited to fulfill. Commercialization feeds on
itself in a way that may retard rather than advance social welfare, meaning by this no more than some aggregate of the satisfactions of individuals.

[20] More formally: "parties formulate policies in order to win elections, rather than
win elections in order to formulate policies" (Downs, An Economic Theory of Democracy, p. 28); this follows from the primacy accorded to the self-interest axiom, under
which both voters and politicians seek to maximize their own incomes, prestige, and
power.

[21] See in particular Peter Bachrach, The Theory of Democratic Elitism (1967) (London: University of London Press, 1969). See also T. B. Bottomore, Elites and Society
(1964) (Harmondsworth, Eng.: Penguin, 1966), chap. 6; and John Plamenatz, Democracy and Illusion (London: Longman, 1973), chaps. 4 and 6.

[22] Titmuss, The Gift Relationship. See also Arrow's discussion, "Gifts and Exchanges," in Philosophy and Public Affairs (Summer 1972), referred to in the following chapter. A less discerning and more combative reply to Titmuss is by Michael H.
Cooper and Anthony J. Culyer, "The Economics of Giving and Selling Blood," in
Armen A. Alchian and others, The Economics of Charity (London: Institute of Economic Affairs, 1973), pp. 109-143.

[23] When efficiency is related to the "broad" concept of the characteristics of goods
and services in their environmental conditions of use.

Appendix

The Commercialization Effect: The Sexual Illustration

The influences involved in the commercialization effect can be seen in strongest relief in what may be regarded as the polar case, namely, sexual relations. The view that commercialization of sexual activity affects the quality of the product is pervasive and deeply entrenched in the mores of many societies. Examination of the basis of this position in the context of my approach toward the characteristics of commodities in their environmental use exposes an economic rationale that is hidden by the narrower focus on the specific activity.

Until recently, economists assumed—though I am aware of few explicit discussions of the question—that sex and its correlates of love and marriage were *sui generis* in human activity, elevated from the plane of material wants. Love, in the famous and influential formulation of D. H. Robertson, is the ultimate scarcity which economists economize.[1] This view is fully consistent with recognition of a strong commercial element in marriage and sexual activity in some cultures, as evidenced by the function of the marriage broker and the gifts and money payments often accompanying the taking or offering of brides.

Economic analysis can have little to say about Robertsonian love, which appears as a nonoperational maximand: our ultimate objective,

[1] D. H. Robertson, "What Does the Economist Economize?" in his *Economic Commentaries* (London: Staples, 1956). In the same spirit, Arrow has written: "We do not wish to use up recklessly the scarce resources of altruistic motivation." "Gifts and Exchanges," p. 355. This conception rests on the questionable premise that altruism is a depleting stock rather than a self-generating flow feeding partly on itself. Contrast John Stuart Mill, a propos unselfish feelings: "the only mode in which any active principle in human nature can be effectually cultivated is by habitual exercise." "Utility of Religion" (1874), *Collected Works*, X (Toronto: University of Toronto Press, 1969), p. 423. The Titmuss school in Britain a century later took essentially the same view.

which we can do little to expand and must therefore do everything to preserve. But in recent years economists have found a way into this citadel, previously resistant to their incursions, by taking a more specific and essentially narrower view of what families are and what they do. The conception rests on Samuelson's view of the family[2] as a realm of altruism; each family member includes the utility of other members in his own. This "quasi-interdependence" of family utilities—with the individual utilities interdependent but separate, rather than truly joint—has been criticized as "applying economic analysis to the family by destroying it."

According to this criticism, personal relationships involving elements such as love, trust, and mutual obligation, have qualities and characteristics distinct from decisions on individual consumption. But when, in the approach taken in this book, utility from individual consumption is itself seen as derived in some combination from characteristics of the goods or services themselves and of the relevant environmental conditions, the distinction between transactions involving personal or social relationships on the one hand and material consumption on the other is no longer hard and fast. New dividing lines then exist between (1) market goods and services that are purely "private" in the sense that their use affects only the purchaser and is not significantly affected by environmental conditions; (2) market goods and services with a "public" aspect, for which satisfaction depends, to some degree, on the social context of use; and (3) other aspects of human desire. For some characteristics, such as the commercialization effect, it is the last two categories that can usefully be analyzed together (see figure). This is illustrated in the remaining portion of the appendix, which takes a sexual illustration from (3) to illuminate similar influences operating in (2).

Imagine, first, a visitor from the planet Chicago dropped into a typical mating selection area of the human zoo. Not since the sorting out of primitive barter has our visitor had such scope for his talents. He observes the latent demand for pairing, his magic eyes discerning different utilities (from large positive through to large negative) attached by individuals to different partnerships. In this way the possibilities conform to other observed bilateral transactions in which either (a) each partner has something the other wants, leading to a barter exchange of goods or (b) one partner is induced to give up something he values by a money payment of at least that amount. The actual terms of the exchange are determined by bargaining or market opportunity within the range of the reservation prices at which buyer and seller are willing to deal. Our observer has noted the role of market prices in conveying in-

---

[2]Paul A. Samuelson, "Social Indifference Curves," *Quarterly Journal of Economics* (February 1956).

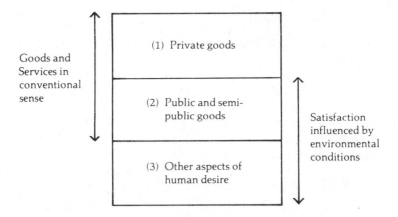

formation on optimum opportunities for buyers and sellers, and he has noted the informational and mediatory role of money in effecting gains from a move from bilateral barter to mutilateral exchange.

Yet astonishingly these sophisticated tools of exchange seem forgotten when it comes to sexual pairing. Transactions here are predominantly in *same kind*. Tremendous restrictions are thus imposed on pairing. It requires the double coincidence of pure barter in which the buyer has to find a seller who not only has what he wants but also wants what he has; and it imposes the additional restriction that the coincidence must occur within one category of demand, namely, for sexual union. The absence of the usual scope for offsetting an imbalance of satisfaction by compensation in money or other kind involves a huge increase in search and transactions costs. Peripheral market institutions such as marriage bureaus and dating services do little to help, since the information in which they trade is notoriously unreliable—people giving still less accurate information about their own personal qualities than about their used cars.[3]

The result, on the basis of conventional economic analysis, appears to be both a suboptimal aggregate volume of the activity (the optimal level being that resulting from compensated multilateral exchange) and inefficiency in the pairings that are accomplished. The lost transactions include (1) a denial of opportunities to all who could not find partners to whom they gave positive satisfaction (as if the sick could be tended only by Good Samaritans, as if the man who needed a spade could get it only from someone who enjoyed making one) and (2) artificial matching of specific-good satisfaction: only the beautiful make it with the beau-

[3]G. A. Akerlof, "The Market for 'Lemons': Qualitative Uncertainty and the Market Mechanism," *Quarterly Journal of Economics* (August 1970).

tiful (as if only the strong could acquire personal security and only the green-fingered acquire flowers).

Stumped for an explanation in their own terms, the local economists refer our observer to exogenous influences of sociological character. They cite the historically destructive implications of free sexual exchange for continuation of family life and perpetuation of the species. Functional necessities for society therefore became internalized in individual behavior responding to social norms. As these functional necessities change, for example, through improved methods of birth control, sexual restraints are expected to ease. And on their own ground, economists expect this tendency to be reinforced by several endogenous influences, one of which is the increasing general productivity of the economy, heightening the value of time. Accordingly, an increasing loss is involved from a given volume of search activity in nonmarket sex. Personalized seduction involves growing opportunity cost, in the sense of alternative opportunities foregone,[4] as does child rearing.

An additional influence is a differential increase in market productivity of women which, by reducing the typical differential between the potential earnings of the two partners in the market sector, reduces the "marriage gain from trade." This gain results from the partner with smaller *comparative* advantage in market activity renouncing this in favor of doing the other partner's housework.[5] On all these grounds, conventional economic analysis predicts a continuing reduction in the longevity of sexual unions, with their term being tailored more closely to current mutual satisfaction; perhaps accompanied by an increase in sexual activity on explicitly commercial terms. Either way, piecemeal calculation is expected to play an increasing role in the sexual decisions of individuals. Commercialization may, for special reasons, be shunned in explicit form, but optimization of individual opportunities is seen as demanding an implicit analogue to commercialization.

The limitation in this analysis, in the approach suggested here, is that it focuses only on the narrow commodity or activity—sexual union of whatever longevity—and not on potentially relevant environmental characteristics. Thus sexual unions, following established social conventions, may offer two characteristics which distinguish them from com-

[4] Compare Staffan Linder's lament for the passing of the *cinq à sept* (Linder, *The Harried Leisure Class*, p. 85) and Wilfred Beckerman's economic explanation of ministerial demand for call girls ("Sex and the Falling Rate of Profit," *New Statesman*, July 20, 1973).

[5] Becker, "A Theory of Marriage." Becker cites this influence as an economic explanation of the greater instability of marriages of blacks in the United States, as against Moynihan's more familiar cultural/historical explanation. Rather than as cultural hangover for a deprived group, the more frequent break-up of black families appears on this analysis as a precursor of what economic advance and reduced sexual discrimination has in store for us all.

mercial arrangements or unions subject to dissolution once the contemporaneous perceived utility of either partner falls to zero. These additional characteristics are:

(1) *Romance/antimaximization.* The love marriage in the form that developed in northwest Europe and North America with the commercial and industrial revolution has been seen by some sociologists as related to the pressures of industrialism itself; the integration of love with marriage provided "an antidote to the insecurity produced by social and technological changes," and met the accompanying demand for emotional instead of rational evaluation.[6] Now, one ingredient in romance is undoubtedly an antidote of individual maximization—the deliberate, cavalier sacrifice of immediate self-interest for some subjectively higher cause. In this aspect, the contingency of sacrifice in individual utility as a result of the sexual union itself becomes an attraction. "For better, for worse" is seen as a benefit, not a cost.

The deliciousness of such romantic merger of utilities lies in the relief from preoccupation with self, perhaps from the very jettisoning of individual calculation. "For richer, for poorer" also adds luster to the deal. The capture of these particular romantic utilities is, however, clearly inconsistent with a prominent "break" clause in the terms of the union. Divorce, in western marriage, remains a retrospective abandonment of a contract in which the contingency of separation remains formally unmentioned and unmentionable. Of course, the optimum for the individual through time is the undefiled romantic initial commitment, supplemented by a de facto but suppressed "break" possibility. The trouble is that the more the possibility is activated in practice, in response to individual assessment of the continuing benefits of sexual union on a contemporaneous basis, the more the romantic potentiality—the idealistic belief or illusion in a permanent union—is deflated. There is a dynamic externality: my divorce damages your children's illusions or life dreams. Individual expectations and hopes are built on the standards of behavior prevailing in the community. This general standard is a collective good in which all have an interest but which none will affect perceptibly through their own actions. People looking individually to their own situations will therefore tend to neglect this collective interest.

(2) *Insurance/trust.* A presumption of permanence in sexual union involves an implied exchange contract of mutual support, offering each partner security of a kind that is unavailable from institutions in the market. Its essence is a built-in principle of redistribution according to relative need (a principle interestingly discussed by Amartya Sen.[7] An attempt to do the same by formal contract, even where it can be enforced through the special laws applying to alimony, cannot approach the so-

[6] Hugo G. Beigel, "Romantic Love," *American Sociological Review* (June 1951).
[7] Sen, *On Economic Inequality.*

phistication of this implicit mutuality. The vague character of the criteria of relative need (how to decide which needs are truly more pressing) and the subjective character of the relevant information (who knows what state both partners are really in) makes the objective criteria required for market contracts unsuitable as well as unavailable for the purpose. The only satisfactory basis for such an arrangement is therefore the self-enforcement that can be expected from individuals' feelings of mutual interest or mutual obligation.[8]

The characteristics of both romance and insurance in sexual relationships are therefore dependent on the absence of piecemeal individualistic calculation. Attaining them is partly a matter for the particular people concerned (who can follow their own preferences) and partly a matter of what others do. To the extent that individuals' expectations and their associated behavior are set by what others do, increasing commercialization of sexual unions, whether explicit in the market or implicit in limited-period quid pro quo relationships outside the market, carries negative externalities for the romance and insurance aspects of sexual union. To be set against this, however, is the benefit from greater freedom to pair up according to one's inclination at the time. This benefit is equivalent to improved allocation of sexual union in its narrow commodity aspect. The benefit from greater piecemeal choice is achieved at the expense of losing wider characteristics that are dependent on general restraint of piecemeal choice. The net balance of advantage from these conflicting considerations will vary for different people, according to the weight they attach to each.

The fact that social restraints on casual sex and divorce remain considerable, and that prostitution may be declining rather than increasing with affluence,[9] may, to some extent, represent merely a legacy from the past; but it may also mean that the above externalities have been internalized in part through social controls or instincts. People instinctively feel that their behavior in these matters should be governed by more than their own calculated advantage. The basis for such social restraints is now being weakened by two general forces. First, by the technological and sociological influences making it easier for women to regulate their childbearing and to reduce further their commitment to child-rearing activities. Second, by the economic influence of "consumerism"—meaning

[8] One of the few references to this aspect that I have found in the literature occurs as an endpiece to Arrow's well-known analysis of the inefficiency of commercial provision of health insurance: "The economic importance of personal and especially family relationships . . . is based on non-market relations that create guarantees of behavior which would otherwise be afflicted with excessive uncertainty." Kenneth J. Arrow, "Uncertainty and the Welfare Economics of Medical Care," *American Economic Review* (December 1963), pp. 941-973.

[9] John H. Gagnon, "Prostitution," *International Encyclopaedia of the Social Sciences*, vol. 12 (London: Macmillan, 1968), pp. 592-597.

by that the daily assault on the individual, from advertisers and consumer watchdogs alike, to be ever aware of material possibilities and personal advantage: "Are you being fair to yourself?" It is not an ambience favorable either to romance or to implied contracts of long-term give and take. The highly specific marriage agreement proposed in *Ms.* magazine is a precise parallel to this consumerist approach. This explicit arrangement sees marriage as a narrow commodity, rather than embodying characteristics that include unspecific social ethos. So this calculative approach, with its determination to secure fair exchange, risks losing the antithesis of exchange. Orgasm as a consumer's right rather rules it out as an ethereal experience.

7 A First Summary: The Hole in the Affluent Society

The main implications of the analysis sketched out so far can now be drawn together. The concentration of economic growth in the material sector of the economy increases the relative price or reduces the unit quality of goods and facilities available in the positional sector. This tendency makes one's place in the distribution of income, wealth, and economic power a determining factor in providing access to goods and facilities that are socially scarce. Because they are allocated by an auction process or its equivalent, relative rather than absolute command over economic resources deployed in the auction will determine one's take. This struggle for relative shares, or positional competition, will also absorb real resources that add to the consumption expenditures necessary to achieve given ends, and in this sense add to "needs." So, if one's own income remains unchanged while the income of other people rises, one's command over the positional sector will fall. The income that earlier supported a downtown apartment, a country home, the acquisition of elite educational qualifications, or simply an active life protected from the crowds, is no longer sufficient.

There is therefore a connectedness in the income distribution as a whole. It makes a difference if others earn more than you, even if you are interested exclusively in your own consumption possibilities. That is to say, even those who are uninterested in their place in relative *consumption* must nonetheless be interested in their place in relative *income* since this factor, rather than absolute income, will govern their absolute consumption of positional goods.

The fall in relative prices of material goods resulting from the growth process will permit more of them to be acquired at the expense of positional goods. Those prepared to make this exchange will gain. Those reluctant to do so, as well as others who are caught in the mesh of additional needs resulting from positional competition, will have an incentive to maintain or improve their relative position. This will normally involve

102

increased market activity, for example, through taking an additional job, working longer hours, or exchanging job satisfaction for cash income. Thus, the more that high salary occupations such as banking or advertising dominate areas such as Manhattan or central London, the less feasible it becomes for those in low salary or high satisfaction occupations—teaching, for example—to live there. Additional money earnings will acquire extra importance. Time will be more carefully budgeted. This increase in the area of commercialization will further enhance the importance of relative position by restricting the economic and social facilities attainable without cash income.

Increasingly, social contact, relaxation, and play become "bought" commodities. This is what is involved in a general privatization of facilities earlier available through common access or informal exchanges, for example, in the substitution of the country club for the village common or city park, or of the effectively private school for the effectively public school. The effectively private school is regarded here as one to which entry is regulated either by specific charges (as in private schools in the United States and "public" and other independent schools in Britain) *or* indirectly in the form of relatively high local taxes and other costs; indirect charges of the latter kind occur where the school district is made up of a homogeneous upper income group and school financing is drawn predominantly from local sources. A nominally public school of this type no longer involves the cross subsidization of low income parents by the more wealthy (though it would still imply a subsidy to parents from nonparents). As noted in Chapter 3, formation of new suburbs with homogeneous residents has been a well-documented means for richer residents of big cities to escape from supporting less fortunate citizens.

Pressure to avoid subsidies of this kind will increase as positional competition intensifies, necessitating additional private expenditures by the individual who seeks a given degree of access to superior jobs or wants to live in a given favored area. A lessening of community ties as a result of increased geographical mobility works in the same direction.

This way of looking at the problem explains what is otherwise a strange irony: that as general prosperity grows, the diffculty of arranging redistributive transfers through the national or local fiscal system does not diminish. On the contrary, it may even increase, notwithstanding the large expansion that has taken place in public expenditures in all major countries.[1] Public policy in the United States has attempted to counter

[1] Reviewing twenty-two papers on various aspects of fiscal redistribution in the United States through both taxes and grants, Boulding and Pfaff stated the basic conclusion of these papers as follows: "redistribution toward the poor has increased through the effect of some components of the *explicit* grants economy, but despite this increase the actual distribution of income seems to have changed little, even though the number of poor has diminished, as we have all gotten richer together. On the

fiscal segregation, notably in political and judicial decisions to equalize resources available to local school districts. But these policies have encountered strong popular opposition. This resistance to redistribution in itself can be considered perverse, since in western civilization one would not expect either altruism or concern for the community to be inferior goods, diminishing in demand as income rises. Common observation of the frequency of laments for the decline of both these attitudes suggests they are not. One possible explanation is that the lamentations are really hypocritical airings of conscience that are cheap substitutes for altruistic or commercially oriented action.[2]

An alternative explanation focuses on two interacting accompaniments of increased prosperity: intensified competition for positional goods and privatization of common access facilities. As cash income becomes increasingly dominant in governing consumption activities and attainment of social and economic position, so it must increasingly dominate productive activities. If we grow more dependent on money for our life and leisure, we will also grow more dependent on money earnings. This is the internal logic in the process of privatization and more generally of commercialization.

The interacting process by which increased productivity intensifies commercialization is depicted in the following schema. The process is shown as operating through two channels, with some positive feedback (the lower loop). This schema summarizes the influences and relationships that have been discussed in detail in earlier chapters.

Thus, the juxtaposition of a growing material economy with a static

---

other hand the 'perverse effects' of implicit public grants, conveyed either through special provisions of the tax laws, public policy, or administrative practices, tend toward *greater inequality:* they help the rich and propertied more than the poor. Furthermore many public expenditures aimed at improving economic and social well-being in a particular area—for example, education or agriculture—tend to reinforce income disparities or even to augment them." Kenneth E. Boulding and Martin Pfaff, eds., *Redistribution to the Rich and the Poor* (Belmont, Calif.: Wadsworth Publishing Co., 1972), p. 2. In both the United States and Britain, taxation taken as a whole has been estimated to be broadly proportional to income. Public expenditure is progressive (that is, benefiting the poor disproportionately) for cash transfers and specific goods such as health and education; but assessment of the imputed benefit from public spending as a whole depends especially on treatment of general expenditures such as defense. Joseph A. Pechman and Benjamin Okner, *Who Bears the Tax Burden?* (Washington, D.C.: The Brookings Institution, 1974); Henry Aaron and Martin McGuire, "Public Goods and Income Distribution," *Econometrica* (November 1970); A. B. Atkinson, "Poverty and Income Inequality in Britain," in Dorothy Wedderburn, ed., *Poverty, Inequality and Class Structure* (Cambridge, Eng.: Cambridge University Press, 1974).

[2] This, for example, is the view taken by Gordon Tullock, "The Charity of the Uncharitable," in Armen A. Alchian and others, *The Economics of Charity* (London: Institute of Economic Affairs, 1973), pp. 16-32.

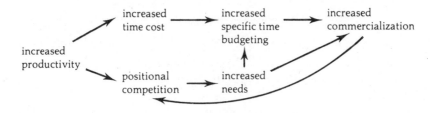

positional sector helps tip the commercialization process into a dynamic expansion. The upshot is a commodity bias. The economy as a whole becomes more commodity oriented than individuals would choose if they were confronted with the full consequences of their preferences in the context of the economy's capacity to deliver: and, in particular, of the incapacity to expand those facets of individual welfare that essentially depend on relative position, rather than on individual productivity. The issue posed is not merely to delineate the particular sectors in which the commercialization effect is damaging:[3] it is, rather, to find means of countering a general bias in the market system, a bias that will persist in some degree in any system responding to isolated individual wants. The incentives given at the personal level, where improvement in relative position remains possible, involve, for society as a whole, additional costs and distortions that are external to the individual and that will, therefore, not be taken into account in the absence of deliberate correctives. The perverse result is to encourage further the expansion of material production, while worsening the environmental conditions in which the products are used.

Marxists would doubtless see this commodity bias as a further and inexorable extension of the exchange relationship which Marx regarded as the essence of the capitalist mode.[4] There is an obvious sense in which this is true. If economies that are driven by private investment opportunities turn their backs on commercialization, they invite stagnation and depression. Britain's recent economic plight reflects this problem in some degree. The usual diagnosis of outright economic failure skims over the general problem embodied in this experience—that piecemeal attempts to

---

[3] The issue was posed in this way, though in different terms, in the reviews of R. M. Titmuss, *The Gift Relationship*, by C. J. Bliss, *Journal of Public Economics* (April 1972), and by Arrow, "Gifts and Exchanges."

[4] "Finally, there came a time when everything that men had considered as inalienable became an object of exchange, of traffic, and could be alienated. This is the time when the very things which till then had been communicated, but never exchanged; given, but never sold; acquired, but never bought—virtue, love, conviction, knowledge, conscience, etc.—when everything, in short, passed into commerce. It is the time of general corruption, of universal venality." Karl Marx, *The Poverty of Philosophy* (London: Lawrence and Wishart, 1955), p. 29.

counter the commercialization bias run against the grain of an economy dependent primarily on private enterprise in its productive sector.

Yet the public goods problem, which is at bottom a technical problem of social organization, is not restricted to capitalist society. It could be equally serious in an economy with decentralized common ownership of the Yugoslav type. Furthermore, centrally controlled economies of the Soviet type have found the problems of coordination so great that incentives given at the local level have often replicated the myopia of market incentives in the presence of externalities. The pollution of Lake Baikal and the manipulation of norms by Soviet factory managers to establish nominal at the expense of real improvements in productivity are well-known examples.

The central issue discussed in this book is an adding-up problem: what individuals want and what individually they can get, society cannot get; and society has to find some means for determining how the difference should be reconciled. This problem is a fundamental one for all social organizations predicated on fulfilling the wants of the individual. An economy responding to isolated individual wants registered through political channels would be subject to the same deficiencies, in this respect, as one responding to individual choice registered through the market; for well-rehearsed reasons, the former would detect and implement specific choices less efficiently. The problem is more prominent in the context of market capitalism, primarily because that system has been most successful at raising material productivity to the high levels at which positional competition and other externalities move from side issues to center stage, but also because, as has been discussed, orientation of the market economy is institutionally focused on the wants of the individual in his isolated capacity. These are the wants it satisfies best and these are the wants it explicitly encourages.

This institutional bias of capitalism is in the "wrong" direction, but the bias may nonetheless be the smaller part of the problem, which derives essentially from the individualistic orientation of the allocation of resources. Public expenditures responding to the same stimulus are in this sense a part of the problem rather than its solution. An obvious example is provided by the vast increases in public expenditure on higher education in all advanced countries in the 1960s, reacting essentially to potential opportunities perceived by and for individuals in the situation currently facing them. Public expenditures on highways to meet rising demand from motorists is another major example of this phenomenon. The tyranny of small decisions is then carried over into the sector that is supposed to surpass and offset them.

The substantial increase in the share of public expenditure in the economies of all industrial countries since about 1960 should be seen as a response to the frustrations of unbalanced growth in consumption opportunities. Imbalance between private affluence and public squalor was graphically depicted by Galbraith in *The Affluent Society*. But that analysis, discussed in more detail below, saw the distortion merely as a misallocation of resources through neglect or mistaken priority. The inference was plain—to channel a larger share of resources into the public sector—and governments in all advanced countries were quick to act on it. The analysis in this book suggests that the imbalance is more deeply entrenched in underlying opportunities. Goods and facilities provided directly or indirectly through the public sector fail to meet our individual demands partly because these cannot be met for all or most people together. It follows, on this line of thought, that blowing up the public sector may, by itself, do little to correct the distortion. The upshot has been frustration with the fruits of such expansion. This, in turn, contributes to inflationary pressures as individuals seek to satisfy their unmet demands either through increased private spending or by calls for still more public spending. A sequence of this kind has been one element in the deterioration of western economic performance since the mid-1960s.

The approach developed in this analysis therefore offers some new insights on certain tendencies in advanced economies which remain subject to sharp controversy. The remainder of this chapter suggests how the concept of social scarcity can bring a different perspective to two such issues: (1) the major Galbraithian theme of distortion in the pattern of output of the new industrial state and (2) the variety of evidence that economic growth is at once in acute popular demand and yet fails to increase the overall level of satisfaction when it is achieved. Both aspects have been touched on briefly in the earlier discussion.

I

The deservedly famous quotation from *The Affluent Society* encapsules the primary theme that Galbraith has followed up in various aspects in subsequent books:

The family which takes its mauve and cerise, airconditioned, powerbraked car out for a tour passes through cities that are badly paved, made hideous by litter, blighted buildings, billboards, and posts for wires that should long since have been put underground. They pass on into a countryside that has been rendered largely invisible by commercial art . . . They picnic on exquisitely packaged food from a portable icebox by a polluted stream and go on to spend the night at a park which is a menace to public health and morals. Just before dozing off on an air-mattress, beneath a nylon tent, amid the stench of decaying refuse, they may reflect vaguely on the curious unevenness of their blessings.[5]

[5] John Kenneth Galbraith, *The Affluent Society* (London: Hamish Hamilton, 1958), pp. 196-197.

The extended criticism that Galbraith's work has attracted from professional economists[6] has, for the most part, not seriously questioned the accuracy of the trends he has portrayed—the poignant contrast between private affluence (for many if not all) and public squalor; the greatly increased concentration of power in the corporate sector; and the insensitivity of corporate giants to the gripes of consumers. What the economists have questioned is Galbraith's interpretation of these phenomena. Galbraith provides no satisfactory basis for assessing what it is that consumers really want: his critique rests on the contention that consumers are dissuaded from whatever that is by advertising and by the lack of real alternatives to the offerings provided by the big corporations in their marketing decisions. There may clearly be something to this, but it does not explain why the corporations that come closest to matching the consumer's "true" wants do not outperform, and eventually dominate, their less responsive rival corporations, whether by takeover or by attrition. Galbraith has never adequately answered his critics' charge that the corporations are in a world of "planning *and* the price mechanism."[7] Nor has Galbraith provided any convincing reason why the massive structural distortions suggested by his diagnosis would be corrected by the main institutional remedies he proposes—euthanasia of the stockholder, nationalization, and stiffening of the noncorporate sector by the support of the state.[8] The criteria that are to guide the new controllers in determining the pattern of output are left in the air.

Yet the essence of what Galbraith has been describing can be given a firm conceptual grounding in the terms of his critics' models by viewing it as a case of market failure—failure of the price mechanism to reflect the choices available to individuals as a whole.

Suppose corporations *do* provide individual consumers with what they truly want in the market situation and the environmental situation in which they find themselves. Suppose also that each consumer, obliged to take this existing framework as given, makes a discerning choice among the corporate offerings, influenced by advertising only in the absorption of straight information; the corporations that serve best these discerning consumers are then the ones that grow and prosper. This hypothetical conformity to the orthodox economic model may yet be consistent with the Galbraithian diagnosis of misallocation. That is because, in the approach outlined earlier, what is sought by the consumer is not the product in isolation but the product with certain characteristics and

[6] See particularly Robert M. Solow, "The New Industrial State: A Discussion," *Public Interest*, no. 9 (Fall 1967); Scott Gordon, "The Close of the Galbraithian System," *Journal of Political Economy*, 76 (1968); and James E. Meade, "Is 'The New Industrial State' Inevitable?" *Economic Journal* (June 1968).

[7] See particularly Meade, "Is 'The New Industrial State' Inevitable?"

[8] John Kenneth Galbraith, *Economics and the Public Purpose* (London: Andre Deutsch, 1974), part five.

in a certain environmental framework or conditions of use. This latter framework is not part of the package supplied by the corporations. Moreover, the fact that their products, in the aggregate, may damage the conditions of use does not lessen their attraction to the individual purchaser. Rather, it may increase their attraction. The effect of private transport in stifling public transport makes a car more and not less essential to each individual. The spoliation of accessible countryside by suburban enclosure turns the excluded into potential customers.

More generally, the effect of privatization of facilities previously outside the strict commercial domain, and of substitution of commercial exchange for social convention in the way that has been described, tends to have a cumulative effect. It makes privatization more attractive or more necessary to those who have still to adopt it. The outcome of the chain of private market decisions will not conform to what consumers sought in their individual purchases; yet each individual consumer will come out even worse himself unless he acts in what, collectively, is a self-defeating way.

In sum, profit-seeking corporations may excel in discovering what we individually want, within some given social context. They may even excel in executing our order for what we want. But where this is also what we cannot all have, this attention to our irreconcilable demands may be exactly the trouble. The corporations then do their jobs too well. Switching the order to the government sector will merely shift the locus of the misassignment.

This is the lacuna in both the Galbraithian and the Nader critiques. The life depicted in the glossy magazines clearly is attractive to many of us, and no higher code of morality need be invoked to say that it ought not to be. The snag is that much of it is unavailable to very many of us at once, and its diffusion may then change its own content and characteristics. Which is to say that private goods have a public context, in the broad environmental conditions of their use; a context that their private marketing does not take properly into account. What is then wrong in the industrial system is not the delivery but the order: to meet consumers' *individual* wants.

In these circumstances, no assurance remains, by the canons of orthodox economic analysis, that the privately marketed product will best meet the needs of the set of purchasers who together are influenced by the consequential effects of their purchases. To the extent that marketing and advertising appeal to individuals to isolate themselves from these group or social effects—to get in ahead or to protect their positions—they are socially wasteful. They are then also socially immoral on the mundane level of the morality concerned with social stability and consistency. If all are urged to get ahead, many are likely to have their expectations frustrated.

The limitations on the reproduction of the kernel of traditional affluence—place and position—are the more daunting because they are inherent in the social situation; there is no analogue to the technological advance that keeps physical limitations at bay in the material sector. On this view, therefore, the social imbalance which Galbraith correctly diagnosed is grounded more deeply than in the excessive dominance of corporate oligopolies with their myopic vision. The flaw in the affluent society lies not in the false values of affluence but in its false promise.

In a relatively sympathetic critique of the Galbraithian position from the neoclassical standpoint, Harry G. Johnson succinctly formulated his point of basic agreement as follows: "we live in a rich society, which nevertheless in many respects insists on thinking and acting as if it were a poor society."[9] This was the heart of Galbraith's thesis: with plentiful production, more is less urgent than it was. The key difference between Galbraith and his orthodox critics concerns the capacity of conventional private enterprise institutions to harvest the new affluence. Neither point of view questions that the fruit is there. Both have thereby missed an important source of contemporary economic frustration.

A similar institutionalist optimism underlies much Marxist criticism:

> Contemporary capitalism generates a tension between aspirations increasingly widely shared and opportunities which, by the very nature of the class structure, remain restricted and unequally distributed.

In this quotation from a perceptive essay by J. H. Westergaard,[10] I would make the following substitution:

> Contemporary capitalism generates a tension between aspirations increasingly widely shared and opportunities which, by the very nature of the *things aspired to*, remain restricted and unequally distributed.

The point is vividly illustrated by Mao's cultural revolution in China, which to an important extent was designed to stifle the emergence of an elite enjoying superior jobs.

The singular feature of liberal capitalism has been to raise expectations—partly by its record in raising performance—and then to be inhibited by its individualistic ethos from distinguishing those aspirations that cannot be widely satisfied from those that can. But the problem itself is a product of material affluence—which, by dint of this problem, does not make an affluent society.

---

[9] "The Political Economy of Opulence," in Harry G. Johnson, *Money, Trade and Economic Growth* (Cambridge, Mass.: Harvard University Press, 1967), p. 166.

[10] J. H. Westergaard, "Sociology: The Myth of Classlessness," in Robin Blackburn, ed., *Ideology in Social Science* (London: Collins Fontana, 1972), p. 133.

II

The concept of social scarcity, as developed in our analysis, also helps to explain the full significance of relative incomes in economic welfare. The fact that most people's concern with their income is at least as much with how it compares with the income of others as with how big it is in itself has been observed by a long line of economists and philosophers. A "relative income hypothesis" was formulated by James Duesenberry after World War II in stronger form, contending that relative income was the dominant influence on the proportion of income spent rather than saved.[11] Although statistical tests of this proposition have been inconclusive, Duesenberry's focus on people's relative income position in setting the goals and reference points of individual economic behavior has remained of central concern. Sociologists have developed a concept of "relative deprivation" to explain the subjective character of felt discontent, and economists have come increasingly to look on poverty as a relative concept.

Perhaps the most striking indication of the significance of relative income has been presented by Richard Easterlin in a review of existing empirical evidence on the connection between income and expressed satisfaction with life, in the sense of happiness.[12] Ten surveys taken in the United States between 1946 and 1966, and a further nineteen surveys in other countries around the world, showed a remarkable consistency in one major respect. In every single survey, those people in the highest income group or broadly defined socioeconomic status group declared themselves happier, on the average, than those in the lowest group. Similar findings were reported in a subsequent survey undertaken in Britain by Mark Abrams.[13] The evident explanation is that while happiness is a mixture of complex and subjective factors, nonetheless the wealthier have, systematically, one less problem to worry about—financial security; and financial security is important enough to make the decisive difference.

At the same time, there is no comparable correlation between income and happiness *between* countries at given times. Americans show themselves no happier than Cubans, nor Germans than Nigerians. Nor is any similar correlation shown between average income and happiness within the United States over time. Although Americans in 1970 had real

[11] James S. Duesenberry, *Income, Saving and the Theory of Consumer Behavior* (Cambridge, Mass.: Harvard University Press, 1949).

[12] Richard A. Easterlin, "Does Economic Growth Improve the Human Lot?" in Paul A. David and Melvin W. Reder, eds., *Nations and Households in Economic Growth: Essays in Honor of Moses Abramovitz* (Stanford, Calif.: Stanford University Press, 1972).

[13] Mark Abrams, "Subjective Social Indicators," *Social Trends*, no. 4 (1973).

incomes per capita 1.7 times greater than in 1947, they nevertheless declared no increase in their felt happiness.

Easterlin's explanation is essentially in the dominance of relative standards and reference points as the basis of individuals' expectations of what they should have. At any given time, "the dispersion in reference norms is less than in the actual incomes of rich and poor."[14] So the poor get less than they expect and feel to be their due, and are accordingly aggrieved, while the rich get more, and are accordingly contented.[15] But over time, general economic growth raises the whole set of norms. Wants grow with availabilities, and neither content nor discontent show any marked trend.

Strong confirmation of the significance of relative income has been provided in a study by the sociologist Lee Rainwater, based on qualitative data from extended interviews in the Boston area in 1971. Rainwater's respondents sensed both a growth of income in constant dollars and a growth in the felt cost of living that substantially matched their increase in real income. This perception, commonly voiced and normally regarded by economists as inconsistent, is interpreted by Rainwater as reflecting the primacy of one's position relative to the contemporary

[14] Easterlin, "Does Economic Growth Improve the Human Lot?" The role of sociological reference groups is discussed by Harvey Leibenstein in a paper that confronts the usually neglected fact that the unit of personal consumption is the family rather than the individual. "Toward a Significantly (But Not Radically) New Theory of Consumption," Harvard Institute of Economic Research Discussion Paper 343, February 1974. Consumption standards are seen as being governed by standards prevailing among others in the same social income groups, partly because this provides an objective criterion for allocation of spending power within the family, through transfers to children that are akin to budgetary grants. Rising general standards raise the norm for these grants and thereby prevent a relaxation of pressure on the family budget. The concept of positional competition may be seen as providing a stronger version of this analysis since it does not lean in the same way on the existence of separate social reference groups.

[15] This general conclusion is broadly confirmed in an analysis by Julian L. Simon, drawing on a wide range of social indicators, including rates of suicide, murder, and mental illness ("Interpersonal Welfare Comparisons Can Be Made—And Used for Redistribution Decisions," Kyklos, 1974, pp. 63-98). Thus, suicide shows a clear inverse correlation with income in cross section studies when other variables—particularly education—are held constant: among people of given education, the poorer commit suicide more than the richer. From this it may be inferred that the short-run effect of more income, or the effect of more income with no change in "tastes," is to increase satisfaction (or at least to reduce suicidal despair). But higher suicide is associated with *higher* income when no other variables are held constant: education adds to anxiety (as well as wisdom), and higher income people have more of it. ("If you're so enlightened, why aren't you happy?") From which Simon infers that the long-run effect of higher income, over the period in which it must be expected to change people's taste (and capacity) in the direction of acquiring more education, is to make people more suicidal. From the various other social indicators or proxies for happiness, Simon contests the old view that the poor are happy in their poverty.

mainstream. Rainwater focuses on "the relative cost of participating in the validating activities that define a full member of society"; he concludes from his respondents that this relative cost does not really change from one decade to another.[16]

The present analysis suggests a further explanation of the primacy of relative incomes and one that need not be grounded in comparisons at all. What individuals actually get, in important aspects of their consumption and job satisfaction, has been seen to depend on their relative income position rather than on their absolute income.[17] This aspect is obscured in the conventional analysis of consumption that makes no distinction between intermediate and final consumption goods, and no allowance for the effect of environmental conditions on ultimate consumer satisfaction.

On this latter view, a feeling that a two-car household in an outer suburb entailing high commuting costs gives no more satisfaction than was provided by a materially more modest suburban life ten years earlier, necessarily implies a comparative standard, involving sociological concepts such as relative deprivation. But the alternative view of the same phenomenon suggested here rests on the interpretation that net consumption may not have increased. The characteristics sought from the suburb and the transportation facility may not have improved: more cars and more distant suburbs may have been necessary to offset a reduction in efficiency in processing or transforming these goods and facilities to the characteristics the consumer seeks. Unchanged satisfaction then needs no special explanation. Relative income is still the key, but now in interpreting how much (net) consumption the individual has rather than how the individual assesses it. The two explanations are complementary: it may be recalled that a part (but only a part) of satisfaction from positional goods relates to their scarcity as such, implying criteria of status that are inherently comparative.

In sum, rising national productivity entails an increase in individual need for income to secure certain satisfactions earlier attainable with lower income. Admittedly, rising national productivity will also add unequivocally to availabilities of other kinds, specifically of material goods. But this increase in material goods will be accompanied by frustration of rising demands for satisfactions dependent on relative position.

[16] Lee Rainwater, *What Money Buys: Inequality and the Social Meaning of Income* (New York: Basic Books, 1974), p. 93.

[17] A similar and more direct explanation of the Easterlin findings suggested by Tibor Scitovsky is that "correlated with the distribution of income there also exist inequalities in some other source of satisfaction, such as the enjoyment of work, inequalities that have persisted over time, and whose contribution to happiness is much more important than that of income." "Inequalities—Open and Hidden, Measured and Immeasurable," American Academy of Political and Social Science, *Annals* (September 1973), p. 119.

It may be that the frustration has offset the extra commodities. In any case, this interpretation can explain why climbing the ladder would yield more satisfaction than staying on the same rung of a rising ladder even if people's expectations were entirely isolated from those of their fellows. Relative position affects what we get, as well as what we feel.

part three

The Depleting Moral Legacy

From the standpoint of evolution, it seems plausible to say that ideology is a substitute for instinct.

—Joan Robinson,
Economic Philosophy

Virtue may be its own reward, but the reward is too often a collective good, shared only minutely by the virtuous individual.

—Thomas Schelling,
"On the Ecology of
Micromotives"

8 An Overload on the Mixed Economy

Social limits to growth, analyzed in the preceding chapters, are the problem—or problems—of success. The vast increase in material productivity has pushed the frontier of mass demand into terrain where there is no longer more for all. Once again, as in the pregrowth era, one man's gain is often another's loss; and both may lose from the struggle. This class of problems is at points exacerbated by the institutional mechanism of the market economy, as it has emerged under the drive of capitalist development as modified by a liberal-democratic state. But the essence of the problem has been seen to reside in a rather general influence, in the response by the economic mechanism or by political controllers to demands registered by individuals looking to their own immediate situation.

This individualistic orientation has impaired the smooth operation and continued growth of economies under a predominantly capitalist drive in a second way, which is the main concern of the present series of chapters in Part III. This limitation stems not from the achievements of past capitalist growth. Its roots lie, rather, in the essence of capitalism as a value system. The problem here is that the pursuit of private and essentially individualistic economic goals by enterprises, consumers, and workers in their market choices—the distinctive capitalistic values that give the system its drive—must be girded at key points by a strict social morality which the system erodes rather than sustains.

The social morality that has served as an understructure for economic individualism has been a legacy of the precapitalist and preindustrial past. This legacy has diminished with time and with the corrosive contact of the active capitalist values—and more generally with the greater anonymity and greater mobility of industrial society. The system has thereby lost outside support that was previously taken for granted by the individual. As individual behavior has been increasingly directed to individual advantage, habits and instincts based on communal attitudes

117

and objectives have lost out. The weakening of traditional social values has made predominantly capitalist economies more difficult to manage, that is, to guide by indirect state intervention. Yet at the same time, the continued expansion of material output in response to autonomous market forces brings increasing problems in its wake, predominantly of social crowding and intensified positional competition. Thus, the responses of isolated individuals to the situation that faces them have become a less sure guide to promoting the objectives of individuals taken together. Management of the system has become more necessary, but the entrenchment of the individualist ethos makes it more difficult. The problem of success joins and exacerbates the problem of the depleted legacy. The two problems interact so as to make each other worse.

This interaction also heightens tensions about the distribution of welfare. The traditional neutrality of the market system, in which the distribution of rewards is legitimated by the operation of autonomous and seemingly ineluctable market forces, is disturbed by the increase of collective bargaining power and by the larger role of collective activities. Validation of the outcome by some explicit criterion is increasingly called for, which poses additional problems for management of the economy. In all advanced countries in the past decade, governments have faced a deteriorating choice between rising unemployment and rising inflation. The classical counterinflationary instruments of monetary and fiscal policy then entail high costs in real output and employment. The heart of the problem is how the collectivist forces are to be tamed. It remains unclear whether economic and financial stability can be restored short of the fundamental step of validating the distributional outcome by some ethical criterion, striking at the roots of an individualist market economy. Meanwhile, the pressures on social scarcity—positional competition—exert a malign influence on the distributional struggle in two ways. They increase its intensity, from the standpoint of each individual alone (because relative position becomes more important), while increasing its cost for all individuals together.

I

Market capitalism has never been the exclusive basis of the political economy in any country at any time. That has been its strength. It was the marriage of market capitalism with state regulation that produced a hybrid politico-economic system with the necessary resilience and plasticity to survive. But the new skin grafted on to western capitalism to provide it with stability and support appears to have papered over a continuing and perhaps growing stress in the foundations of the system.

This stress has appeared in the protective cover itself; the control devices in this half century of managed capitalism have been unequal to their task. The natural response has been to perfect the devices—to make better mousetraps. Some critics have argued for greater emphasis on control of monetary aggregates and less resort to discretionary fiscal adjustments, others for new kinds of controls on wages and perhaps prices, others for a comprehensive use of all these instruments in harness. An underlying question, explored in this chapter and in the next, concerns stress in the general process of regulation of a market economy: a kind of economic management fatigue, comparable to the fatigue induced in conventional metals by conditions that make excessive demands on them. More precisely, the limitations that have been experienced in economic management may reflect not technical deficiencies of particular instruments but a pervasive flaw in the strategy by which they are supposed to be applied.

The essence of this strategy is to impose the necessary minimum of central control and guidance on an economy whose operating units remain motivated by individualistic aims and horizons and are guided by these individualistic aims in everyday behavior. In this way, the system is supposed to get the best and avoid the worst of both central control and individual initiative in the economic sphere. Eclectic and pragmatic, the intellectual model of the system is of largely English construction. The foundations were laid by Alfred Marshall and A. C. Pigou, drawing significantly on John Stuart Mill, but it was the work of John Maynard Keynes that opened the way to its practical application. The relevant policies extend far beyond what are usually thought of as the Keynesian instruments—budgetary adjustments to influence the level of monetary demand. Fiscal policy, monetary policy, and conventional incomes policy are all components of what can be thought of as the broader Keynesian system of continuous central guidance of an otherwise individualistic decentralized economy. Although often presented by contemporary critics as in conflict with the earlier tradition of economic liberalism, the complete Keynesian program can, instead, be regarded as its culmination. The stresses now being felt by the broader Keynesian system go correspondingly deep.

A key feature of this wider system was that motivation could be subordinated to results. This characteristic preserved the central aspect of the system celebrated by the classical economists in the heyday of unmanaged capitalism, the mobilization of the self-interest of the butcher and the baker to provide the public with its dinners. The presumption was that self-interested actions had socially benign results. The invisible hand of Adam Smith's *Wealth of Nations* was not to be abandoned, but merely guided by the Keynesian economic controllers. In the modern liberal view, the socioeconomic system is seen as amoral. This view does not of course imply that the individuals within it are amoral; but that in an individualistic society, morality is for the most part an individual matter.

But the benign neglect of individual motivation in the sense of morality, as celebrated in the received doctrine of the invisible hand,[1] occurred when capitalism was young, essentially unmanaged, and still facing an evenly expanding economic frontier. The Keynesian fire brigade arrived on the scene when all of these conditions had passed. They had given way to a ripely mature, managed capitalism, in which precapitalist morality had atrophied and the expanding frontier in material goods was juxtaposed with growing pressure on the confined frontier of positional goods. This evolution made the economic system less anonymous, less automatic in operation, and less benign in its growth.

To maintain the traditional separation between individual motivation and social result in these circumstances was a different matter. It involved the progressive extension of explicit social organization without the support of a matching social morality—more rules for the common good, having to be prescribed and adhered to in a culture oriented increasingly to the private good. The burden placed on individual morality has in this way been greatly increased. It can be seen in the context of our analysis as an overload on the modern mixed economy. The connection between the transformation that has taken place in the characteristics of the market system and the role played in that system by individual motivations has received inadequate attention.

II

The capitalist economy comprises the organization of production, accumulation, and exchange by private individuals, operating singly or in corporate groups and acting freely on the basis of commercial contract and motivated by their own pecuniary benefit. As such, market capitalism has been conditioned, confined, and supplemented by social controls of a variety of kinds. These controls, operated by the state or embodied in social conventions or instincts, have three major functions.

First, they soften the burdensome impact of capitalist market forces on those individuals or groups with least economic power. This is the "distributional corrective" which has always been recognized as necessary in some degree since the enactment of the Elizabethan Poor Law in the sixteenth century.

Second, controls are needed to make the market process efficient in its own terms—to ensure that private market choices reflect social benefits and costs as far as possible and to provide necessary correctives from outside the market system (at the minimum, central control over the

[1] Summarized as follows in the most widely used economics textbook: "every individual in pursuing only his own selfish good, was led, as if by an invisible hand, to achieve the best good for all." Paul A. Samuelson, *Economics*, 9th ed. (New York: McGraw-Hill, 1973). This received doctrine, as noted in Chapter 4, section IV, omits the original moral context of Smith's formulation. See also Chapter 10.

supply of money, supplemented in practice by fiscal and administrative regulations of a variety of kinds). The "efficiency" need for these departures from laissez-faire has long been recognized by mainstream economists, though often *sotto voce;* the scope for state regulation on this ground was greatly extended by the theoretical structure built between the two world wars by Pigou on the one hand and Keynes on the other.

Third, informal social controls in the form of socialized norms of behavior are needed to allow the market process itself to operate. These range from personal standards such as telling the truth to acceptance of the legitimacy of commercial contracts as a basis for transactions. An important aspect is implicit agreement on the sphere of market behavior: on what can be bought and sold, what interests may be pursued individually and collectively. These matters are recognized as of crucial importance in the establishment of a market economy, but as an underpinning for existing market practices they have been neglected in modern economic analysis. The social prerequisites of markets have been studied by sociologists rather than by economists, who have been generally content to leave it so.

Traditional social norms have necessarily been transmuted by the modern evolution of the economic system. The transmutation is well captured in the phrase "from status to contract," introduced by that characteristic Victorian Sir Henry Maine.[2] The essence of the change is the extension of choice at the individual level, exercised through market exchange. The depth of this individualist penetration is most clearly seen in its extension into its antibody, the sphere of collective action. The increasing extent of centralized intervention in the market economy, concerned with "distributional" justice and "efficient" allocation of resources (as in the first two categories mentioned above), has been seen by its liberal protagonists as subject to the overriding principle that personal behavior remains guided by an individualistic rather than a group calculus. This principle is sometimes seen as a desideratum in itself. In any case, it appears as a practical constraint: the individualistic calculus is what guides behavior in fact. A prime purpose of central economic management in a liberal order has been to create the conditions in which individualistic calculation can continue to operate in a socially benign way.

In this sense, Keynes completed the corrections to laissez-faire that were needed to validate what laissez-faire was designed to do. Subject to specific exceptions, which in greater or lesser degree had been admitted by all academic expositors of classical economics, the individual was left to pursue his own economic goals. The support added to the system by the guiding hand at the center opened up the full possibilities of maximiz-

[2] Sir Henry Maine, *Ancient Law* (1861) (London: Murray, 1894).

ing individual freedom along with economic prosperity. In this broad sense, the Keynesian contribution can now be seen as representing the high water mark of secular liberalism, attempting the ultimate in privatization—the addition of morality to the sphere of individual choice. Yet, as will be more fully discussed in the following chapter, the crucial social underpinnings of the market process are themselves weakened by the full permeation of an individualistic calculus.

The resulting deficiencies in this individualistic approach were obscured for a long time by the special, and largely unconscious, influence of the English tradition of enlightened paternalism. This paternalist cover has been removed in the formulation of market liberalism that has been developed most thoroughly in the modern Chicago tradition.[3] But Keynes's interpretation of managed capitalism retains a vital importance precisely because of its unquestioning reliance on obligations and instincts deriving from an earlier preindustrial culture. It is in the complete Keynesian system that we can best observe the limits of the guided market, because Keynes took for granted supportive characteristics that his own system could not preserve but that the purer system of his successors in economic liberalism ignored.

[3] See in particular Milton Friedman, *Capitalism and Freedom* (Chicago: University of Chicago Press, 1962); Johnson, "The Economic Approach to Social Questions."

9 Political Keynesianism and the Managed Market

The essence of Keynes's economics, as seen by one of his most perceptive interpreters,[1] was to save capitalism from the stupidity of its managers—and, one might add, of Keynes's ultraliberal critics. Keynes perfected the concept of an economic system serving the separable, and ultimately noneconomic, goals of men: notably, personal relations, appreciation of beauty, contemplation. These goals were treated as ultimate data, atomistically determined by each individual. They existed apart from the processes of economic effort—apart, that is, from what Marx saw as the social conditions of production. Such processes, according to Keynes, were no more than the means to the attainment of individually chosen goals. Equally, the prevailing social standards or norms comprised no more than the aggregation of individual goals and standards. For fulfillment of their objectives, individuals were to be provided with the fullest available choice that the department store could provide. The economic system, stripped down, was that department store. What use each individual made of his material possibilities was a matter for him alone. Equally, the means and motives through which the material cornucopia was achieved were a matter for individual rather than social choice. Echoing Adam Smith almost to the word, Keynes declared consumption to be "the sole end and object of all economic activity."[2]

---

[1] Harry G. Johnson, "Cambridge in the 1950s," *Encounter* (January 1974), p. 33. Johnson refers here to "Keynesian economics" rather than the economics of Keynes, but since he is concerned with the origins of the school, the distinction in this instance is probably not significant.

[2] "The General Theory of Employment, Interest and Money," *Collected Writings*, VII, 104. Compare Adam Smith: "Consumption is the sole end and purpose of all production; and the interest of the producer ought to be attended to only in so far as may be necessary for promoting that of the consumer." *The Wealth of Nations*, Book IV, Chapter VIII. The standard economic postulation of consumption as the sole end of production was assailed by Gunnar Myrdal in 1928: "Most people who are reasonably well off derive more satisfaction in their capacity as producers than as con-

In effect, the utilitarian-consumerist view of man banished from the social plane the explicit moral content that was embodied in Christian philosophy and sought after in Marxist and other socialist thought. This banishment was fully consistent with individual objectives: morality was a personal, individual matter, representing the individual's highest goal. But in so doing, liberal philosophy had an unintended side effect. It undermined its own mechanistic instrument for attainment of individual goals. For the efficient working of the market itself rests on certain aspects of social morality that are affected by the means and motives prevalent in the economic system. As capitalism has become more mature and more managed, the stresses resulting from the social dichotomy have grown.

I

In *The End of Laissez-Faire* (1924-1926)[3] Keynes attributed the popular hold achieved by that doctrine in the nineteenth century to a convergence of intellectual and administrative currents. Laissez-faire fitted the individualism of the political philosophers and the harmony seen by both the economists and the theologians; at the same time, it fitted the instincts of the practical man confronted with the ineptitude of public administrators and the contrasting initiative and achievements of the entrepreneurs of the industrial revolution. But this combination of influences was a product of its time. When it passed, the latent conflict between individualist and collectivist outgrowths of the Enlightenment became exposed. In blowing the whistle on laissez-faire as strongly as he did, both in this essay and in his wider works, Keynes acknowledged some key elements in this conflict. Yet from the hindsight of fifty years, his dominating part in engineering a middle way, in the shape of a managed (or attemptedly managed) market economy, may be seen as having obscured rather than alleviated the individualist-collectivist conflict in one central aspect.

Keynes assumed that the managers of the system would be motivated by higher goals than maximization of their private interests and that standards of public behavior would progress in a way that gradually put less rather than more emphasis on maximizing monetary gain. These noble and for the most part implicit assumptions enabled Keynes to bypass the *implementation* problem of superimposing collective objectives on an individualistic calculus. In the American liberal tradition, which for historical reasons has been disinclined to lean on similar assumptions of enlightened paternalism, the potential conflict is more apparent.

---

sumers. Indeed, many would define the social ideal as a state in which as many people as possible can live in this way." *The Political Element in the Development of Economic Theory* (New York: Simon and Schuster, 1969), p. 136.
  [3] *Collected Writings,* IX.

Keynes opposed extreme laissez-faire by an essentially technocratic, pragmatic, empirical, apolitical, and counterphilosophical approach.[4] His strictures on, and partial turn against, laissez-faire brought consternation among those for whom laissez-faire had itself been an ideology, of individualism safeguarded by capitalism.[5] In their eyes, Keynes had sold the pass, on the basis of his superficial underestimation of the true springs and necessary foundations of liberalism. Thus Keynes was seen as repeating the Benthamite sin of opening the way to collectivism via a careless pragmatism and an unrealistic faith in the capacity of legislation to improve social welfare.

But the consensus of philosophical agreement which Keynes saw as having ruled England for a hundred years[6] had never rested on the rigid interpretation of minimal state intervention. This is one clear conclusion that emerges from the swaying debate among economic historians on whether and in what sense there was an age of laissez-faire.[7] There were

[4] This was foreshadowed in "The End of Laissez-Faire" and "Am I a Liberal?" In the latter, the technocratic-elitist element was made explicit: "I do not believe that the intellectual element in the [Labour] party will ever exercise adequate control [of the party program]." *Collected Works,* IX, 296. For a discussion of Keynes's disdain for both politicians and mass opinion see Donald Winch, *Economics and Policy* (London: Hodder and Stoughton, 1969), and particularly the appendix on "Keynes and the British Left." Harrod summarizes an underlying assumption in Keynes's life view—one of the "presuppositions of Harvey Road," so named after the roomy, solid Cambridge house in which Keynes's parents lived for all his life—as "the idea that the government of Britain was and would continue to be in the hands of an intellectual aristocracy using the method of persuasion." Roy Harrod, *The Life of John Maynard Keynes* (London: Macmillan, 1963), pp. 192-193. On Keynes's elitism see also Elizabeth Johnson, "The Collected Writings of John Maynard Keynes: Some Visceral Reactions," in Michael Parkin and A. R. Nobay, eds., *Essays in Modern Economics* (London: Longman, 1975).

[5] The intellectual home of the defenders of the ultraliberal faith was at this time the London School of Economics. Its economics department, under the leadership of Lionel Robbins and powered by the formidable intellect of Friedrich Hayek, gave continuous battle with the interventionist pragmatism of Keynes's Cambridge and with the outright socialism of the London School of Economics's own Harold Laski. Criticism of Keynes by name was more widespread in private talk and correspondence (as partly reflected in subsequent memoirs) than in the contemporary economic literature. A significant exception was the publication by a group of LSE economists of William Beveridge, ed., *Tariffs: The Case Examined* (London: Longmans Green, 1932). Here Keynes was treated with courtesy and still with outward deference—the master who had lost faith in his own earlier teaching (see especially p. 242). The danger that many contemporary liberals saw in Keynes's interventionist turn did not surface fully until the reappraisal of the Keynesian revolution which began in the 1960s.

[6] "The End of Laissez-Faire," p. 272.

[7] Represented and summarized in A. W. Coats, ed., *The Classical Economists and Economic Policy* (London: Methuen, 1971), and Arthur J. Taylor, *Laissez-Faire and State Intervention in Nineteenth-Century Britain* (London: Macmillan, 1972).

deep-rooted "Victorian Origins of the British Welfare State."[8] In the assessment of Professor Scott Gordon: "Laissez faire was not a maxim which determined the issue in any instance, but it played a notable role in the contemporary lobbying and propaganda."[9] Laissez-faire has been aptly described as "the philosophy in office," but the *governing* philosophy of the age of laissez-faire was supremely pragmatic. Its strength lay in its nonideological capability.

Was it not these same characteristics within Keynesianism that made for its political appeal to the British (and to a lesser extent the American) liberal elite in the middle third of the twentieth century? Political Keynesianism of the 1930s, its program written by Harold Macmillan, Evan Durbin, and Geoffrey Crowther, as well as by Keynes himself,[10] provided an apolitical alternative to the polarized political choice of the time. To those equally repelled by the politics of Stalin and Hitler, and by the economics of John Strachey's communists and Montagu Norman's bankers alike, the Keynesian middle way came almost as deliverance: promising full employment and J. S. Mill too.[11]

After World War II, Britain's ruling establishment, which may be called such in the sense that political and administrative leaders continued to be dominated in their decisive actions by a common liberal ethos, was under ever-increasing pressure to legitimize itself as serving the interests of all classes and groups, from the meritocracy to its counterpart, which must necessarily be the idiotariat. The pragmatic, anti-ideological,

---

[8] David Roberts, *Victorian Origins of the British Welfare State* (New Haven: Yale University Press, 1960).

[9] Scott Gordon, "The Ideology of Laissez-Faire," in Coats, ed., *The Classical Economists*, p. 189. See also the same author's "The London *Economist* and the High Tide of Laissez-Faire," *Journal of Political Economy* (December 1955).

[10] Harold Macmillan, *The Middle Way* (London: Macmillan, 1938); Evan Durbin, *The Politics of Democratic Socialism* (London: Routledge, 1940); Geoffrey Crowther, *Economics for Democrats* (London: Thomas Nelson, 1939). A key postwar work in the same vein was J. E. Meade's *Planning and the Price Mechanism* (London: Allen and Unwin, 1948). A quarter century later, Meade wrote the still more elegant sequel: *The Intelligent Radical's Guide to Economic Policy: The Mixed Economy* (London: Allen and Unwin, 1975).

[11] This political function can be seen as a support for the successful "taking" of the Keynesian revolution on the academic plane, supplementing in a perhaps crucial way the favorable intellectual conditions listed by Harry G. Johnson, "The Keynesian Revolution and the Monetarist Counter-Revolution," *American Economic Review* (May 1971). As Winch has put it: "Here [in Keynes's ideas] was an effective weapon for use against the Marxists on the one hand and the defenders of old style capitalism on the other; a real third alternative, the absence of which before the *General Theory* had driven many into the Communist camp." *Economics and Policy*, p. 349. Keynes wrote to Roosevelt in an open letter in December 1933: "If you fail, rational change will be gravely prejudiced throughout the world, leaving orthodoxy and revolution to fight it out" (quoted in Winch, *Economics and Policy*, p. 221).

and consequentially elitist inferences of Keynesianism helped this establishment to satisfy itself and the electorate of its legitimacy and of the soundness of its policies. These were contrasted with the destructive forces of outmoded political struggle over faded ideologies and falsely conceived class conflicts which the new managerial approach could surmount. Stupidity, not cupidity, was the besetting sin of those at the helm: to govern, it was not necessary to choose, only to think, to count, and to manage.[12]

With the Kennedy administration, this attitude crossed the Atlantic. Superpowered with the growth models of Harrod and Solow, Keynesianism was seen at the political level as opening the primrose path of self-generating growth, providing the means to attain economic objectives without absolute sacrifice. Controversy, other than on the Marxist-Hayekian fringes which were then seen as outmoded beyond the academic pale, was mostly limited to the form in which the fruits of growth should be plucked: private consumption (in response to individuals' market choices); public consumption (as urged by Galbraith); world development (aid lobby); guns and butter too (Vietnam as 1965's fiscal dividend, making the United States the first country in history to be able to contemplate a war without a bill).[13] There was broad agreement also on the basis of the politicoeconomic system, a market economy tempered by state correctives applied at limited points—a managed market.

II

A usually unstated but conscious assumption in Keynes's own view of the system was that the macromanagers, the overseers of the system,

---

[12] This technocratic strand was common to four different critiques of postwar British economic policy published by economic journalists, which together had considerable impact on the climate of policymaking opinion: Andrew Shonfield, *British Economic Policy Since the War* (Harmondsworth, Eng.: Penguin, 1958); Michael Shanks, *The Stagnant Society* (Harmondsworth, Eng.: Penguin, 1961); Norman Macrae, *Sunshades in October* (London: Allen and Unwin, 1963); Samuel Brittan, *The Treasury under the Tories* (Harmondsworth, Eng.: Penguin, 1964). Keynes's writings influenced a generation of economic journalists in Britain perhaps still more strongly than academic economists. The campaigning journalists would have been less than human not to have been attracted by Keynes's insistence that it was the leaders of opinion and the masters of pragmatic intellect rather than the men of party or the men of business—or even the academics who remained in the ivory tower—who truly ruled the world.

[13] For a thoroughly documented critique of the view that U.S. fiscal policy was transformed by intellectual enlightenment, and an exposition of the continuing role of ideology and interests, see Herbert Stein, *The Fiscal Revolution in America* (Chicago: University of Chicago Press, 1969). The fiscal dividend was a concept developed by administration economists in the mid-1960s to denote the additional resources automatically made available by economic growth through its expansionary effect on the

were likely to be cleverer than the micromanagers, the overseers of its individual business units.[14] A second underlying assumption was unconscious and taken for granted. This was the belief, alluded to earlier, that the macromanagers were guided by different, more elevated, motivations; and that these noble promptings would be reflected in the social environment in which their regulatory activities were conducted. Both assumptions were a product of the English polity in which those who challenged the old aristocratic legitimacy put at least equal emphasis on public service. American liberalism, by contrast, developed the doctrine of the interplay of plural and competing interests, which does not rest on these assumptions; it is thereby at once a more complex and a more exposed system. Chicago liberals join with American Marxists in questioning the inclination and capacity of the bureaucracy to serve national rather than particularist interests.

The Keynesian assumption about superior brains is not crucial to the success of managed capitalism, as clever controllers can set up a system that equally clever controllees will find it worthwhile to follow. But the second assumption, on the motivations of the controllers and their influence upon the social environment in which their policing is conducted, does have a critical place. It bears directly on the viability of the strategy itself. This problem has been curiously neglected.

The generally accepted concept of managed capitalism runs about like this. State intervention is to set appropriate "rules of the game" and deliberately alter both the law and the market choices facing individuals. In addition, collective restraint in the general interest is expected from trade unions and other collective bodies.[15] Within this framework, comprising market opportunities as limited and corrected by state action, pursuit by individuals of their own objectives is again made consistent with the general or social environment.

Yet the more a market economy is subjected to state intervention and correction, the more dependent its functioning becomes on restriction of the individualistic calculus in certain spheres, as well as on certain elemental moral standards among both the controllers and the controlled.

---

tax base. The fiscal dividend for 1964 was the tax cut; for 1965 it was increased military expenditures for Vietnam. The unforeseen size of these expenditures thereupon discredited the concept.

[14] Businessmen and bankers were not among the elite who earned Keynes's respect, even for their nonintellectual qualities. When asked how, if businessmen were as stupid as he believed, they succeeded in making money, Keynes is said to have explained: "by competing against other businessmen." And in 1931: "A bankers' conspiracy? The idea is absurd! I only wish there were one." *New Statesman* (August 1931).

[15] Keynes was among the first economists to formulate the rationale of collective wage restraint in "How to Pay for the War" (1940), *Collected Writings*, IX.

The most important of these are standards of truth, honesty, physical restraint, and respect for law.

Standards of behavior, then, become more important for the functioning of the economy in a number of ways. Central regulation will often be ineffective or extremely costly if behavior responds solely to piecemeal individual advantage. Controllers have a standing handicap in relevant information vis-à-vis the people whose actions they are trying to regulate or guide. There is a problem both in the measurement of output and in the identification of output. Perhaps the most dramatic and gruesome example occurred in the Vietnam war, in the development of a sophisticated set of incentives designed to by-pass the usual bureaucratic channels of subjective assessment by substituting "body count" and other tangible indicators of the effectiveness of individual U.S. military units. What was neglected was the encouragement thereby given to those in combat to switch field activity to the indicators themselves, as distinct from the military objectives for which they served as proxy, as well as the direct manipulation of the indicators through conscious or unconscious falsification. Both elements could be observed in the tragedy of Mylai.

Analytically similar problems have been experienced with performance contracting in schools and attempts to pay teachers according to output rather than input. Output is measured by indicators such as the improvement in pupils' test scores for reading. The objective can be defeated by the incentive such a system also gives to teachers to neglect those aspects of educational output that fall outside the measure and to manipulate the tests themselves by teaching how to pass tests or how to cheat without being penalized. Thus there are two potential deficiencies. The first is to bias the allocation of effort to sectors and activities that are amenable to measurement and rating.[16] These aspects of educational output are, so to say, technically suitable to "market" production, and reliance on market type incentives will bias activity against other sectors that are technically unsuited to specific measurement and consequential marketing. The phenomenon can be viewed as an instance of the "commodity bias" (see Chapter 6).

A second potential deficiency is that the process of production af-

---

[16] The conclusion of one study is as follows: "If as seems [more] likely, the outputs of a school or other public service are too numerous and too difficult to measure to make pricing of each dimension feasible, then by resorting to performance contracts the public authority may create large-scale shifts in resources it does not intend:" George E. Peterson, "The Distributional Impact of Performance Contracting in Schools," in Harold M. Hochman and George E. Peterson, eds., *Redistribution Through Public Choice* (New York: Columbia University Press, 1974), p. 134. See also E. Gramlich and Patricia P. Kushel, *Educational Performance Contracting* (Washington, D.C.: The Brookings Institution, 1975).

fects the nature of the product itself or has repercussions on other trans-actions: this is an instance of the commercialization effect (also discussed in Chapter 6). If teachers are paid according to the test results they pro-duce, then both what they teach and the way they teach it are likely to be redirected to the tests themselves. They may not only teach tests rather than subject; that priority may also be the more general message that they convey to their students. Neither of these considerations is a deci-sive argument since the incentives promoted by the tests may stimulate improvement in desired performance by bad or otherwise unmotivated teachers.

The point emphasized here is that any such improvement has a potential cost in weakening "internalized" sanctions of teacher, student, or both. Such weakening of the individual's sanctions from within tends to encourage response only against specific reward; and this constitutes an adverse externality. The classic example of the "buying out" of individ-ual responsibility is a system of money bribes and fines imposed by par-ents on their children: a system that few educated parents use themselves as the best means to good behavior or good performance. For them, the externality is internalized, as the effects of a future weakening of their children's internal sanctions will stay within the family. In contrast, for a performance contractor paid by specific results, the future drawbacks are externalized. If future citizens are discouraged from recognizing any obli-gation not compensated by direct reward, the rest of society bears the cost.

A further problem that arises from attempts to set up central control on the basis exclusively of private self-interest is: who is to set the per-formance indicators for the controllers? Presumably it will be other con-trollers. There is a problem of infinite regress. The distortion of output resulting from use of proxy indicators, which has been discussed above, may then grow cumulatively as a chain of such indicators interacts along-side the chain of command.

Use of the price mechanism in an imposed way therefore is not a sure safeguard of operational efficiency. It will have its best results where scope for manipulation is small and where the exercise of personal re-sponsibility in pursuit of the desired objective is least likely to be dam-aged by diversion of effort to achieve proxy results.

The analogy with the independent operation of the price mechanism in unregulated transactions undertaken by private parties therefore has only partial validity. Costs as well as output are dependent on the pro-cess by which economic activity is carried out. Costs are not objective phenomena, but can be established only by the actions of individual pro-ducers, and these actions in turn will depend on the incentives offered them. Managers motivated to maximize their own incomes will strive harder to minimize costs in producing a given product if they have a direct stake in the resulting profit than if they do not. The relevant cost then is the cost to the decision-maker.

It is not the price mechanism, as such, that teases out the relevant information in automatic signals to efficient production, but the harnessing of market prices with individual incentive.[17] Market prices will not do as well where they are partly or wholly divorced from producers' incomes or where they are open to manipulation by producers. This limitation is usually discussed as a weakness in the context of "market socialism," in the sense of a system of public ownership operating in response to private incentives. But a similar weakness applies in a different way to management of capitalism, through public regulation of private ownership and private trade.

Central guidance of the invisible hand is therefore subject to an internal snag. It wilts under the legitimized standard that covers the heartland of the market economy, the maximization of private interests and of command over economic resources. In principle, individual maximization can be held to its social purpose—making the best of the opportunities for all—so long as it operates on the basis of properly designed and implemented rules; yet individual maximization means manipulating these rules too.

At the individual or micro-level, therefore, motivation under managed capitalism has to be kept in compartments; but there is no obvious way of communicating to individuals just where maximization of private interests is to stop short. Business firms are to compete to the hilt to the point where successful competition produces its private jackpot, in the reward of monopoly; but are they thereafter to cooperate fully with the antitrust division? The trust-busting officials are to maximize their salaries and promotion prospects in all legal ways; but does this include the most lucrative way, which is to change sides? Individual taxpayers must not evade their legal obligations but are entitled to do anything to avoid them. The law has to be obeyed; the spirit of the law does not. Yet this ethos is itself likely to undermine the law, and thereby produces an unstable situation. More ambiguous still: individuals are to seek the maximum reward for their services, but individuals organized in trade unions are to exercise restraint. Corporations are to maximize profits, but to consider the national interest when setting their prices.

In principle, according to the conventional interpretation of the viability of managed capitalism, the conflict is to be avoided by soliciting

[17] The subjective nature of costs is developed at length in James M. Buchanan, *Costs and Choice* (Chicago: Markham Publishing Co., 1969). The locus classicus is Friedrich A. Hayek, "The Price System as a Mechanism for Using Knowledge," *American Economic Review* (September 1945), in Morris Bornstein, ed., *Comparative Economic Systems* (Chicago: Richard D. Irwin, 1965).

the desired changes in individual behavior through requirements of law (direct taxes and limitations of collective bargaining) or alterations in market opportunities (indirect taxes). The Hayek-Friedman school argues strongly that attempts to influence individuals and corporations should be strictly confined to statutory rules and incentives of this kind. Private parties can then continue to operate according to their own interests, as modified by these rules and incentives, leaving implementation of the public interest in the hands of the public controllers. In practice, reliance on these inducements alone, unsupported by adaptations in individual norms of behavior, is likely to ensure that the regulation is inadequate. Controllers will be unable to diagnose, implement, and enforce the intended correctives to individual behavior in response to the norm of private maximization in the underlying market situation.

A purely individualistic ethic will therefore weaken or impede the efficiency of these correctives themselves. The significance of the impediments will vary with different cases, being least where individual behavior, whether of controller or the controlled, can be directly observed (use of cars in congested city streets), and greatest where it is intrinsically subjective (telling the truth about one's own preferences). An intermediate case is that of control of litter, discussed below; tax morality is probably another.

III

Extension of state intervention in the market economy makes new demands on the morality of the system. More precisely, such intervention increases the need for a link between motives that operate at the individual level—"micromorality"—and the desired outcome for society. Individual motives cannot be ignored or assumed to be benign. The motive to accept and work within the spirit of the growing body of social rules becomes important, and perhaps crucial. Without it, more rules will be needed to enforce the primary ones. An increasing portion of resources then will be absorbed in enforcement and in the waste resulting from reliance on crude proxy targets for the collective objectives. The rising mass of codified petty regulation—swollen by the need for rules to enforce rules and to counter their avoidance—will increase public expenditure and cause frustration with its results.

Law and social obligations are complements rather than full substitutes. Social convention must rest on the needs of the economic system as well as on the demands of individual constituents. Yet individuals can be expected to go along with these conventions, and by so doing meet the needs of the system, only if they feel this to be their own interest, duty, or social obligation. With the atrophy of traditional social ties, including those stemming from active religious belief, the only remaining basis for social obligation has become civic duty to uphold a just society. Acceptance of the market economy as a just one thereby becomes a condition of its stability.[18] What may be termed the macromorality of the system thereby becomes integrally connected with the micromorality that is required for it to function smoothly.

This marks a major change. The justification for managed capitalism has always been a pragmatic one, residing in the overall results of the system *en large*. Its strength, as a system, has been precisely its presumed ability to do without ethical judgments and moral obligations based upon them.

Keynes's central judgment of the macromorality or general acceptability of capitalism is well known. Capitalism *was* morally objectionable, but could be made more efficient at attaining economic ends than any other system.[19] And although economic objectives must be kept in their place (and Bentham and Marx, in Keynes's judgment, did not do this), they still had their place for one or two generations more. Moreover, echoing Samuel Johnson ("A man is never so harmlessly employed as when making money") and J. S. Mill ("While minds are coarse, they require coarse stimuli"—the struggle for riches being the contemporary exemplar that had taken over from the struggle of war),[20] Keynes saw the unattractive individual goal of making money as a useful diversion from political tyranny ("It is better that a man should tyrannize over his bank balance than over his fellow citizens").[21] Or, in Paul Samuelson's later

[18] The point is discussed in more detail in Chapter 10.

[19] The best encapsulation of this point that I know is in an anecdote about Asquith in a Cabinet discussion in World War I, related by C. F. G. Masterman: "The question of large speculative profits being made out of shipping cargoes of food or munitions to England arose: 'Disgusting,' said Asquith. A minister at once protested. He declared that this was the normal operation of trade. He declared that if their men had not done it other men would have done the same. He declared that if they had chosen not to bring the stuff to England they would probably have attained as much or greater profit by taking it to neutral or allied countries. 'I can see nothing disgraceful,' he said, about the whole transaction.' 'I did not say disgraceful,' said Mr. Asquith with a characteristic shrug of the shoulders. 'I said disgusting.' " Quoted by Roy Jenkins, in his *Asquith* (London: Collins, 1964), pp. 238-239.

What would Keynes have said? Despite his frequently expressed distaste for the money motive, Keynes had no qualms about financial speculation. But he occasionally applied moral criteria of a kind that fellow economic liberals then and since would consider both quixotic and harmful rather than helpful to the community, by impeding the response of market forces to economic pressures. In 1931, despite the suggestions of O. T. Falk, he refused to manage the assets of the unit trusts and other funds for which he was responsible so as to take advantage of the likely depreciation of sterling in 1931—a depreciation that Keynes thought certain. I am indebted for this information to Dr. D. E. Moggridge, from his work on the Keynes papers in course of publication.

[20] John Stuart Mill, *Principles of Political Economy*, Book IV, Chapter VI (1848) (Harmondsworth, Eng.: Penguin, 1970), p. 114.

[21] "General Theory," chap. 24 ("Concluding Notes").

formulation of this strong second best argument for market liberalism, good clean money is better than bad dirty power. Keynes's a-Marxist and fundamentally apolitical predilection discouraged him from pursuing the question of whether money power and political power went hand in hand. The upshot was the view of managed capitalism as the unattractive system, with the least bad results.

This left the following moral problem at the microlevel: "Why should *I* adopt moral standards helpful to the system if the outcome of the system for me cannot be validated on moral criteria? True, the system is said to work out for people as a whole, compared with the alternatives. But I am not people as a whole, I am me; and unless the system can be shown to give me a fair deal in the only currency it deals in—material advantage—it can't ask me moral favors."

This microproblem was widely neglected by economists, at least until the issue was reopened by Rawls in *A Theory of Justice*.[22] The great significance of this work rests on its attempt to face the problem of political obligation within the context of a liberal market economy, and its acceptance that the basis of such obligation must be the justice of the politico-economic system, in the sense of fairness. The principles of justice that Rawls extracts have been challenged by critics from left, right, and center;[23] yet all are agreed on the importance of the undertaking itself. Rawls has brought the moral issue back to a system that had earlier hived off the issue as belonging to a separate and higher sphere. Morality of the minimum order necessary for the functioning of a market system was assumed, nearly always implicitly, to be a kind of permanent free good, a natural resource of a nondepleting kind. Beyond this, morality was a luxury not obtainable in the humdrum economic department. The position was neatly put in a much quoted aphorism by a specifically Keynesian prime minister, Harold Macmillan: "If people want morality let them get it from their Archbishops."

In his noneconomic writings, Keynes acknowledged a moral problem at the micro-level; but he too kept morality and economics in separate compartments.[24] As a result, he glanced over the economic aspect of the problem.

[22] John Rawls, *A Theory of Justice* (Cambridge, Mass.: Harvard University Press, 1971). The Rawls principle of maximizing the position of the least advantaged, whatever its difficulties and qualifications, provides the basis of politico-moral obligation which is lacking in a system that rests on its total or average performance, as under the utilitarian criterion of the greatest good for the greatest number.

[23] See, respectively, Brian Barry, *The Liberal Theory of Justice* (Oxford: Clarendon, 1973); Robert Nozick, *Anarchy, State and Utopia* (New York: Basic Books, 1974), chap. 7; and Kenneth J. Arrow, "Some Ordinalist-Utilitarian Notes on Rawls's Theory of Justice," *Journal of Philosophy*, 70 (May 1973). See also C. B. Macpherson, *The Political Theory of Possessive Individualism* (Oxford: Clarendon, 1962), chap. 6.

[24] The main text is in two "confessions"—his acknowledgment of the moral-religious attraction of communism (the joys of the noncalculative ethic, expounded in "A

IV

What Keynes in his maturity saw wrong with the Bloomsbury life view was its meliorist, rational base—"the eighteenth century heresy" that human nature is reasonable, that man is a rational being. It was this rationalist belief that "underlay the ethics of self-interest—rational self interest . . . it was because self interest was *rational* that the egoistic and altruistic systems were supposed to work out in practice to the same conclusions." Yet Keynes in these philosophical reflections had neglected his central contribution to economic policy. Rational pursuit of individual self-interest could *not* be expected to keep the economy at full employment; nor could it be expected to prevent inflationary wage bargaining in conditions of full employment. Keynes was also well aware of the other set of conflicts between private and social economic interest, developed by Pigou, in which costs and benefits resulting from a particular market transaction were not fully embodied ("externalities"). To tame the market, and to manage the market, explicit cooperation is required by individuals acting through the medium of the state or some other collective agency.

Such cooperation, if undertaken by all, could be shown to be in the interests of all. Bertrand Russell, echoing the predominant liberal view of the time, regarded rational social cooperation of this kind in the category of self-interest: "If men were actuated by self interest . . . the whole human race would cooperate."[25] But it would not. Russell here ignored the distinction between self-interest in an outcome dependent entirely on one's own actions and self-interest in an outcome dependent on the actions of others.

The rational individualist, in situations of social interdependence, knows that he does best when everyone *else* cooperates and he does not, for example, in ducking his contribution to a community project; he is then a "free rider," carried along on the cooperation of others. He does worst when only he cooperates, that is, when everyone else is trying to free ride. It follows that in the absence of coercive or self-enforcing arrangements to impose the cooperative lines of action on everyone except himself, or as a second best on everyone including himself, he will take the third best course, of noncooperation; this being individually rational (because it is superior to the fourth best outcome when only he cooperates), even though socially irrational.

Short View of Russia," *Collected Writings,* IX); and his repentance for the mistakenly amoral personal philosophy of his youthful Cambridge set: "We entirely repudiated a personal liability on us to obey general rules." "My Early Beliefs," *Collected Writings,* X, 446.

[25] From *Human Society in Ethics and Politics,* as quoted by Samuel Brittan (p. ix) as motif for his book *Capitalism and the Permissive Society;* the words I have omitted from Russell's quotation are "which they are not—except in the case of a few saints."

The rationale of collective action within a context of individually oriented objectives was formally analyzed after World War II in the framework of game theory and developed in particular by Mancur Olson.[26] The most evocative illustration of the issue is the parable of the prisoner's dilemma, in which each of two prisoners will fare worse when each seeks independently to maximize his own interests in doing a deal with the prosecutor.[27] Only cooperative action between the two can get the best result attainable for both. Since cooperation of this kind is normally difficult and costly to organize, latent collective interests, particularly of large groups, will not be mobilized by voluntary action unless particular private benefits can be built in as an incentive to participate (sickness benefits provided by trade unions to their members are one example).

This rationale is an inadequate explanation of collective action since it neglects individual objectives that are associated with group values or group processes. Most dramatically, it cannot explain the individual decision to vote, since the time and effort involved must virtually always outweigh the remote chance of the individual's vote determining the result.[28] The fact that the great majority of people do vote is one indication that the predication of private maximization cannot be easily transposed from its original market home to the politico-social arena. The narrow "market" assumptions that (1) individual objectives are directed only to private goals and (2) individual behavior follows these objectives, are insufficient to explain some critical collective activities. Something else is necessary to elicit independent support for society's rules and conventions.

[26] Mancur Olson, *The Logic of Collective Action* (1965) (New York: Schocken, 1971). An informal and early presentation of the problem of collective action is contained in the logical understructure of Joseph Heller's novel *Catch-22* (1955) (New York: Dell, 1970) in which the hero, Yossarian, draws a rational distinction between the effects on winning the war of what he might do and of the quite different and hypothetical situation of everyone else doing likewise. This is discussed further in chapter 10.

[27] I have always thought this standard example to be a rather curious one in the context, and perhaps indicative of the alien nature of collective action in the American polity. For if the objective is widened to the collective interests of society as a whole, rather than the prisoners as a pair, the best outcome is of course for them not to collude—provided the operations of prosecutor, judge, and jury system together can be relied on to get the just verdict, and thus to meet social rather than private interests.

[28] Brian Barry, *Sociologists, Economists, and Democracy* (New York: Collier-Macmillan, 1970), chap. 2. The point is discussed in Chapter 6 above.

10 The Moral Re-entry

If the rationale of collective action in an individualistic culture has been formalized only in recent times, this largely reflects the atrophy of the original foundations of economic individualism itself. Such atrophy can be seen as the nineteenth-century heresy. In its origins two centuries earlier, economic individualism was predicated on an underlying moral-religious base. Adam Smith's economic analysis in *The Wealth of Nations*, as has been widely discussed, rested to a substantial extent on his social analysis in *The Theory of Moral Sentiments*, even if the precise connection remains controversial. The complex relationship seen by Smith has been summarized as follows: "[Men] could safely be trusted to pursue their own self-interest without undue harm to the community not only because of the restrictions imposed by the law, but also because they were subject to built-in restraint derived from morals, religion, custom, and education."[1]

Smith's position is a far cry from some contemporary liberal celebrations of the dominance of self-interest. "What is important is that the pursuit of self interest has become institutionalized . . . this is of the greatest importance for the future of capitalism," proclaims Theodore Levitt, of the Chicago Law School, in celebration of "other directedness."[2] And as a sympathetic critic of Milton Friedman has put it: "The idea of bourgeois virtue has been eliminated from Friedman's conception of bourgeois society."[3] In discussing principles of income distribution, Friedman

---

[1] Coats, ed., *The Classical Economists and Economic Policy*, p. 9. Market notions of human society were equally antipathetic to Mill. 'The idea is essentially repulsive of a society held together only by the relations and feelings arising out of pecuniary interests." *Principles of Political Economy*, Book IV, Chapter VII, p. 120. Mill looked to the progressive advancement of public opinion and self-development based on a Religion of Humanity.

[2] "The Lonely Crowd and the Economic Man," *Quarterly Journal of Economics* (February 1956), p. 109.

[3] Irving Kristol, "Capitalism, Socialism and Nihilism," *The Public Interest* (Spring 1973), p. 13.

makes the point that a man who finds a sum of money in the street will not generally be expected to share his windfall with the less fortunate who have made no such find.[4] Two other possible courses of action that an earlier bourgeois virtue would have demanded—that the finder should take the money to a police station or else burn it—receive no mention. The individual, in effect, is invited to choose the morality as well as the God of his choice.

I

Modern economic analysis has kept religion firmly outside the economic sphere and has thereby obscured the role it has played in the economic system. The most widely discussed interconnections have been of a sociological-cultural kind. In Marx, religion was seen as the analog of the proletarian's alienation,[5] and as "the fantastic realization of the human being in as much as the human being possesses no true reality."[6] Weber and Tawney discussed the religious basis of the motivations of a rising class of capitalists, and Thompson of bewildered proletarians.[7]

The role played by religion in these various contexts is far from resolved. My concern here is narrower: to bring out the functional economic role for religious belief. This is the role of God-cum-Satan as the deus ex machina for the "prisoner's dilemma," the solvent for the needs of explicit or internalized social cooperation. The function of religion as "a supplement to human laws, a more cunning sort of police,"[8] has been discussed mostly as a means of making men better social beings. The

[4] *Capitalism and Freedom*, p. 165.

[5] Paris Manuscripts, in Karl Marx, *Early Writings*, ed. T. B. Bottomore (New York: McGraw-Hill, 1964), p. 125.

[6] Introduction, ibid., p. 43, Critique of Hegel's *Philosophy of Right*, italics omitted. Later in the same passage: "Religion is the sigh of the oppressed creature, the sentiment of a heartless world, and the soul of soulless conditions. It is the *opium* of the people." The famous last sentence can be understood only in the context of the earlier ones. Marx has been described as seeing religion as "an ideological cover either for the defense of the social status quo, or for protests against it." Robert N. Bellah, "The Sociology of Religion," *International Encyclopaedia of the Social Sciences*, vol. 13, p. 408. Religion for Marx was a matter not of the intellect but of social needs; as these were changed by the transformation of the structure of society, religion would become functionless and wither away. Alasdair MacIntyre, *Marxism and Christianity* (1968) (Harmondsworth, Eng.: Penguin, 1971), pp. 84-85. The approach discussed in this chapter also sees an essentially social role for religion, but one grounded on quite different factors, more humdrum and technical (in the form of organizational) than those with which Marx was concerned.

[7] Max Weber, *The Protestant Ethic and the Spirit of Capitalism* (1904) (New York: Scribner's Sons, 1958); R. H. Tawney, *Religion and the Rise of Capitalism* (1926) (London: Murray, 1964); Edward P. Thompson, *The Making of the English Working Class* (Harmondsworth, Eng.: Penguin, 1968).

[8] John Stuart Mill, "Utility of Religion," p. 415.

same function also serves the purely technical problem of organizing collective action.

The essence and subtlety of situations requiring such cooperation is that, while this is consistent with exclusively self-interested values or *objectives*, it is not attainable by self-interested *behavior* on specific actions; individuals can attain their self-interested objectives only if they behave *as if* they were altruistic.[9] This is so whether they take a short-term or a long-term view of the matter. If, in Sen's example, my objective is to minimize litter, and if I mind the mess that results from no individual restraints on littering more than I mind the discipline of not littering on my part, then it will be rational for me (along with everyone else) to behave as if I cared about the damage done by my own litter to others, and not to drop it. Only a comparable (as if altruistic) action on the part of all will meet my self-interested preference for no one littering, myself included, over everyone littering. While altruistic objectives would also work, they are not necessary. Provided everyone behaves *as if* he were really altruistic, no one need be: everyone's interest will be better served than if everyone behaved unaltruistically.[10]

Christianity sets great store by altruistic behavior. The point emphasized here is that if this is undertaken as a means to religious ends, it also acts as a means to functionally necessary social cooperation for individualistic earthly ends.[11] In this function, it is the altruistic behavior that counts and not what motives happen to underlie it—whether Christian values, social pressure, conformist cowardice, humanitarianism, or anything else. For while such cooperation can, in some cases, be replaced by coercive rules, or stimulated through collectively imposed inducements to individuals' private interests, this will rarely be as practicable and efficient as when it is internally motivated. The underlying problem (discussed in Chapter 9) is that the controllers usually have a large handicap of relevant information. Only *I* can see everywhere I litter.

Generally, restraints on individual behavior imposed in the collective interest can be enforced most effectively when the sense of obligation is internalized. These restraints grow more necessary as communities become physically larger and socially more transient. In the Athenian city-state and in many small communities even today, fellow citizens and neighbors observe one's social behavior and influence it through social

[9] Armatya Sen, "Behaviour and the Concept of Preference," *Economica* (August 1973).

[10] The point is taken up further in section IV of this chapter.

[11] As Joan Robinson has put it: "Religion is being recommended to us because it supports morality, not morality because it derives from religion." Joan Robinson, *Economic Philosophy* (1962) (Harmondsworth, Eng.: Penguin, 1964), p. 15. This can also be regarded as a "Schelling" problem (Chapter 6, section II).

pressure. These pressures, in themselves, can be oppressive. Their reduced force in larger and more anonymous communities is welcome to
many people and helps attract them to these communities; but this process in turn puts a greater burden on internalization of social obligations.
Without this internalization, and with reduced "neighborly policing,"
collective interests will be neglected.

Yet liberal market society has become accustomed to a different emphasis. Internalizing ad hoc *incentives* for people with privately oriented
norms so that they direct their self-regarding actions in a socially desirable way is easier and more practicable than attempting to internalize
social norms of behavior. In this approach, taxes, subsidies, and legal
restrictions are imposed to supply the necessary incentives. The carrot
and the fine get a more reliable response than the sermon. But this short-
term advantage is bought at the cost of an additional, and perhaps growing, policing problem, as discussed previously. In enforcement of collective obligations, "the mere existence of an effective sovereign, or even the
general belief in his efficacy, has a crucial role."[12] If the sovereign happens to be the spiritual Lord, we are spared the cost of enforcement.

All this was obscured by the logical error in utilitarianism, which
saw collective as well as private goods attainable through rational self-
interest.[13] The error has not been fully expunged from liberal thought,[14]
as the earlier quotation from Russell shows; many contemporary less-
elevated pronouncements could be cited in the same vein.

It should be emphasized that certain individual objectives of an altruistic as well as of a self-interested kind may be unattainable through
purely individualistic behavior. Thus, an individual's desire to reduce the
inequality in income distribution as a whole, backed by a readiness to
devote part of his income to this purpose, can be effected only through
organized collective action, through compulsory taxation. No action by
a single individual could attain such a goal or even be sure of contributing
toward it. Even if this goal were universally held, it could not be attained
through purely individualistic behavior. The same applies to a desire to
live in a community with a particular social or racial balance or to edu-
cate oneself or one's children in schools that have such a balance (see
Chapter 6). In these cases, internalized altruistic norms of behavior
would not be a substitute for the necessary central direction of individual
actions, although such norms are likely to help implement the necessary
collective policy, for example, to enforce tax collection and to minimize
adverse effects on work incentive.

[12] Rawls, *A Theory of Justice*, p. 270.
[13] But see footnote 20 below.
[14] Barry calls it "the standard liberal fallacy"—the statement or implication that if
something is a collective good it is ipso facto an individual good. Barry, *The Liberal
Theory of Justice*, p. 108.

Nineteenth-century critics of utilitarianism, such as Fitzjames Stephen, pointed to the religious underpinning of moral actions, but in considering the effect of a weakening in religious attitudes, focused on likely changes in the output of the economic system—thus more health might be obtained at the expense of less honesty.[15] The modern "public goods" approach, which looks to the effect that a loss of moral imperatives has upon the system, would emphasize the impact on *instrumental* means to final output: that is, less honesty, therefore also less health, because of a diminution in the trust necessary at various points of the doctor-patient-public relationship. This is the economic rationale that can be given to the Titmuss critique of commercialization of a variety of social relationships—a critique that, on a narrower economic view, appeared to be fallacious or at best irrelevant.[16] The point is that conventional, mutual standards of honesty and trust are public goods that are necessary inputs for much of economic output.

The functional aspect of religion has always been prominent in the sociological approach: Comte stressing the contribution of belief and ritual to social solidarity, and Durkheim the role of religion in inducing participation in social life.[17] The economic concept of public goods provides a tool for integrating moral-religious norms into the economic framework. It suggests religion as a behavioral standard supporting collective action and cooperative relationships. In this context, it should be stressed, these norms are needed not for the ambitious or optimistic objective of attaining some wholly good or fully rational society, but for the more modest and limited purpose of maintaining some key underpinnings of our existing contractual, market society.

II

Truth, trust, acceptance, restraint, obligation—these are among the social virtues grounded in religious belief which are also now seen to play a central role in the functioning of an individualistic, contractual economy.[18] To this extent, the payoff to religious belief is in earthly coin. The traditional concept of religion as insurance on the next world, which might or might not pay off in this one, is exactly reversed. One might or one might not go to heaven by loving one's neighbor as oneself (on cer-

---

[15] James Fitzjames Stephen, *Liberty, Equality, Fraternity* (1873) (Cambridge, Eng.: Cambridge University Press, 1967).

[16] See the discussion and references given in Chapter 6.

[17] Auguste Comte, *System of Positive Policy*, vol. 2 (1851) (New York: Franklin, 1875); Emile Durkheim, *The Elementary Forms of the Religious Life* (1915) (London: Allen and Unwin, 1971).

[18] John Goldthorpe has pointed out to me the affinity of this insight, fundamentally due to Arrow, to Durkheim's stress on the dependence of market relationships on nonmarket norms such as those mentioned: "All in the contract is not contractual."

tain days and for certain purposes). What was certain was that one would thereby get more worldly goods out of the market; provided that all one's neighbors did likewise. More exactly, the earthly payoff does not require neighborly love to exist, but only action *as if* it exists. And the religious belief, once adopted, operates conveniently as a private sanction, being seen to provide rewards and penalties directly in accordance with the individual's performance of his social obligations. A more effective inducement for cooperative action could hardly be devised deliberately.

Religious obligation therefore performed a secular function that, with the development of modern society, became more rather than less important. It helped to reconcile the conflict between private and social needs at the individual level and did it by internalizing individual norms of behavior. It thereby provided the necessary social binding for an individualistic, *non*altruistic market economy. This was the non-Marxist social function of religion.[19] Without it, the claims on altruistic feelings, or on explicit social cooperation, would greatly increase, as was foreseen, and to some extent welcomed, by a long line of humanists and secular moralists. Less love of God necessitates more love of Man.

Thus Mill's contention that "in its effect on common minds . . . religion operates mainly through the feeling of self-interest" was cited by him as demonstrating the inferiority of supernatural religion compared with the Religion of Humanity in the cultivation of unselfish feelings. In the approach put forward here, the same characteristic permits religion to perform its instrumental social function (inducing people to behave as if they were altruistic although they are not) where the higher goal might be unattainable.[20] I should emphasize that I am making no judgment on the superiority of the religious sanction or on the feasibility of its revival after a period of erosion. My focus rather is on the weakening of a traditional support for social cooperation.

[19] See footnote 6 above.

[20] It may be noted that Mill's faith in public opinion (as well as in education) as the effective element in the support given by religious teaching to morality implicitly assumed a "small numbers" state, or at least a community in which basic social values were uniformly and firmly held. An individual's failure to meet social norms would be noticed and would bring him social disapproval with resulting diminution in his private opportunities. In these circumstances, the collective good is indeed an individual good, and the "free rider" problem does not arise. Mill, "Utility of Religion," pp. 411 and 423. The same assumption underlies Mill's faith in public opinion as a partial restraint on excess population, expressed in his *Principles of Political Economy*, Book IV, Chapter VI, p. 113.

For a sensitive discussion of Mill's bold attempt to blend individual liberty and social duty via education and self-development see Graeme Duncan, *Marx and Mill: Two Views of Social Conflict and Social Harmony* (Cambridge, Eng.: Cambridge University Press, 1973). "Individual rectitude was to be maintained through the coercive use of social norms—though through habit and moral development they would

Although religiously based norms fulfilled a social-secular purpose by proxy, providing an outside support for the market system, this functional role had not, of course, been the original basis of religious obligation, which predated the market system. It was a fortunate legacy from a set of principles that was being replaced. Moreover, the functional rationale, because it was a social rationale that was not transmitted to the individual level, would tend to be weakened by the counterforce and strength represented by market values themselves.[21] The market system was, at bottom, more dependent on religious binding than the feudal system, having abandoned direct social ties maintained by the obligations of custom and status. Yet the individualistic, rationalistic base of the market undermined the unseen religious support.

This undermining left a vacuum in social organization. Social obligation of the most elemental kind lost its base. The market system, left to itself, tends to fill this vacuum in the same way as it fills others; but here it may sabotage its own foundations. An extreme but pertinent example illustrates the wider point. If judges were regularly to sell their services and decisions to the highest bidder, not only the system of justice but also of property would be completely unstable, as Arrow has pointed out. (In the post-Watergate era, one instinctively adds: or Presidents.) If everything can be privately appropriated, including the judge, then nothing can be—for who will save the system from the first entrepreneur to be able to raise enough credit to buy the judge and everything else through him? As Arrow put it: "Thus the definition of property rights based on the price system depends precisely on the lack of universality of private property and of the price system."[22] Some minimum area of social obligation therefore has to be held. The problem is how to reconcile this social responsibility with the opposing mainstream of the market ethos.

III

Why and when can individuals be expected to adjust their behavior to a social need—to restrain their pursuit of individual advantage, to join in a cooperative effort, to obey the spirit as well as the letter of the law?

The best statement of the problem that I know can be derived from Joseph Heller's *Catch-22*, which is not to say that the author was explicitly aware of it. The novel contains an apparent flaw: how does Yossar-

---

gradually lose their external character" (p. 255). Duncan's interpretation emphasizes Mill's "conception of man as an essentially social animal" (p. 273).

[21] This was foreseen by conservative opponents of nineteenth-century liberalism such as Fitzjames Stephen: "Duty is so very often inconvenient that it requires a present justification as well as an historical explanation," the only possible such justification residing in God as a legislator and "virtue a law in the proper sense of the word." Stephen, *Liberty, Equality, Fraternity*, p. 252.

[22] Arrow, "Gifts and Exchanges," p. 357.

ian, the American bombardier, reconcile his own social objective, that the Allies of World War II should win, with his individual objective, to stay alive? His "free ride" is individually rational for his individual-cum-social objective: but is it not immoral? Some critics have suggested that this apparent dichotomy made this book on World War II prophetically appropriate for a different, future, unjust war—Vietnam. Certainly the readers seem to have taken it that way, as the book, published in 1955, took off only in the early 1960s.

Yet the criticism misses the connectedness of Heller's system. Yossarian is placed in a world in which individual self-interest governs all private behavior (Milo Minderbinder's syndicate of food racketeering in which all sins are forgiven because "everyone has a share," and so no one has responsibility—a kind of microcosm of the joint stock capitalist system). It is a world in which the same individual self-interest governs political-bureaucratic behavior (the scheming generals and staff officers indulging their personal fancies and playing to the gallery of the personnel selectors with the blood of their own troops, in a show of bureaucratic-individualistic "rationality" that foreshadowed the more formal models of American economic analysis a decade later by Tullock and Niskanen).[23]

As explained by Olson, voluntary cooperative behavior cannot be rationalized as a means to a self-interested objective, at least as long as the individual can reckon on being able to reap the fruit of cooperation by others and/or cannot reckon on others following his example. Cooperation—foregoing the free ride—demands either compulsion or an internalized social ethic. Under the individualistic ethic which governs Yossarian's (capitalist) society, "the enemy is anybody who's going to get you killed, no matter *which* side he's on."[24]

What Heller exposes is that voluntary pursuit of a just war—and for this read individual behavior to further any other collective enterprise that overrides piecemeal individual advantage—is inconsistent *behavior* for an individualist who maximizes his private interest, even though he

---

[23] Gordon Tullock, *The Politics of Bureaucracy* (Washington, D.C.: Public Affairs Press, 1965); William A. Niskanen, *Bureaucracy: Servant or Master?* (London: Institute of Economic Affairs, 1973).

[24] Heller, *Catch-22*, p. 127. This definition follows the protest by the clever-silly intellectual, Clevinger, that Yossarian's doctrine that "It doesn't make a damned bit of difference *who* wins the war to someone who's dead" will give maximum comfort to the enemy. The sequence leaves it open whether Yossarian would still maintain the first doctrine, just cited, under different social arrangements in which his societal neighbors were not trying to get him killed (do him down). The book's widely criticized ending suggests not: Yossarian makes a specific distinction between personal sacrifice for his country and his comrades on the one hand and for his self-serving superiors on the other (p. 455).

shares the collective objective. That is to say, voluntary participation in the provision of a collective good (which will often be necessary for furnishing it efficiently, even under compulsion) cannot be expected to be induced merely by approval of the specific collective objective. For at the individual level, personal participation is neither sufficient nor necessary to secure the collective objective. This objective will normally be attainable by relying on others to do their share; the bad example set by the free ride on social morality taken by this one individual will normally be too small and inconspicuous to deter others, just as the good individual example will be too inconspicuous to encourage them. In the absence of a "private" sanction such as that furnished by religious belief, cooperation can be expected only on the basis of some directly "felt" sense of duty or obligation. This feeling, in turn, rests either on unthinking habit, or on a conscious acceptance of the wider system, within which cooperation is sought, as a just system. Voluntary cooperation is therefore dependent upon an internalized sense of social obligation—in a fair game, I obey the spirit as well as the letter of the rules.

An illustration of this proposition, at least in its negative side, is provided by attitudes of trade unions and shop stewards to social pressure for restraint of their power to achieve wage increases and otherwise use their potential for disruption to secure direct benefits. It can be easily demonstrated that use of such power is inimical to the general welfare (in the sense that greater welfare could be achieved at lower cost in other ways) and perhaps, when all repercussions are taken into account, that it eventually reduces the welfare of the group of workers concerned. Yet as long as the individualistic calculus remains, each group of workers will not rationally take such interactions into account; restraint from the exercise of full bargaining power is not in the group's self-interest, unless the group is sufficiently large to influence behavior by others. Thus John Goldthorpe has pointed out that in a society where individuals and groups "exploit as best they can their positions within a generally unprincipled structure of power and advantage," it is illogical to expect shop-floor workers to hold back their power to obtain piecemeal advantages for the general welfare, on the ground of agreed normative codes that have not been established.[25]

IV

The conventional response to this problem is to reconnect individual and collective rationality in one of two ways: through collectively imposed compulsion or through collectively imposed incentives (taxes and subsidies), both acting on individuals' private interests to secure the neces-

[25] John Goldthorpe, "Industrial Relations in Great Britain: A Critique of Reformism," Columbia University Conference, March 1974.

sary shift in behavior. Economic theories of bureaucracy and of political action, which have been extensively developed in Virginia and in Chicago during recent years, are built exclusively on the individualistic norm. Political and bureaucratic activity are seen, in the same way as market activity, as means to private ends. As such, they tend to be inherently inefficient. The inference drawn by the exponents of this approach is that the sphere of political action should be minimized.

An alternative inference flowing from the same analysis is that where individual preferences can be satisfied in sum only or most efficiently through collective action, privately directed behavior may lose its inherent advantages over collectively oriented behavior *even as a means to satisfying individual preferences themselves,* however self-interested. It follows that the best result may be attained by steering or guiding certain motives of individual behavior into social rather than individual orientation, though still on the basis of privately directed preferences. This requires not a change in human nature, "merely" a change in human convention or instinct or attitude of the same order as the shifts in social conventions or moral standards that have gone along with major changes in economic conditions in the past.

The issue can be illustrated by reference to the accompanying tabulation. It distinguishes between private and public orientations at the three successive stages of individual actions: starting from the individual's underlying objectives or preferences, proceeding to his behavior, and through to the results of his behavior.

	Orientation of		
Regime	Objectives (preferences)	Behavior	Results
(1) Invisible hand	Private	Private	Private
(2) Guided invisible hand	Private	Private (market correctives)	Public
(3) *As if* altruism	Private (social conventions)	Public	Public
(4) Full altruism	Public	Public	Public

The distinction between preferences and behavior, which has been developed by Sen and briefly discussed above, rests on the notion that the market behavior of individuals may not reveal their underlying preferences because of built-in social conventions or norms that are necessary to bring individually oriented behavior into line with individually oriented preferences. The necessity arises where the behavior of individuals without such conventions interacts in a malign way with the similar behavior of others. Sen's example of social restraints against littering is one illustration; another is the instance of sociability discussed in Chapter 5.

A market economy operating without state intervention—regime (1) in the tabulation—relies on the invisible hand to reconcile private and public interests; it is private in orientation at all three of our stages. The managed market economy, relying on the guided invisible hand, continues to assume that individual behavior is privately oriented, but by intervening on the terms of market choices or on the surrounding rules, produces behavioral results with the desired public orientation. The alternative method of achieving publicly oriented results has usually been assumed to be full altruism—regime (4)—requiring that individuals cease to put themselves above others—the change in human nature. The intermediate state—regime (3)—introduces a distinction between individual preferences and individual behavior by interposing social conventions that override individual preferences as such.

This intermediate standard requires the less fundamental change to socially influenced behavior, rather than to socially oriented objectives: doing our bit because we feel we ought to rather than because we want to. The distinction is meaningless in a purely individualistic calculus. It rests on a concept of implicit exchange between the individual and the community. The individual recognizes that he gets something out of some facility or characteristic of the community, for example, litter-free countryside, friendly people, and feels he "ought" to reciprocate with his own contribution, even though he may not "want" to. In the language of John Plamenatz, the individual's social aims may override his personal aims.[26] Although this concept is alien to the utilitarian element in orthodox economics and the economic approach to politics, in which social aims exist only as a means to fulfill individual aims, some bedrock of overriding social orientation has been seen to be essential to the fulfillment of individualistic objectives. This is the nettle that economic liberalism is so shy to grasp.

Yet reliance on socialized norms alone—on individuals directing themselves to do what the community expects of them—would be extremely inefficient as well as oppressive. As Kenneth Boulding has pointed out, the principles of altruism and of exchange are mutually supportive as well as antithetic.[27] Pushed to extremes, the principle of meeting the wants of others can be as alienating as the principle of acting only against fair exchange; and both principles can be inefficient in the sense of failing

---

[26] Plamenatz, *Democracy and Illusion*, pp. 159-168.

[27] Kenneth Boulding, *The Economy of Love and Fear* (Belmont, Calif.: Wadsworth Publishing Co., 1973).

to meet individual wants that could be fulfilled under alternative methods of organization.

The inadequacy of orienting individual actions to communal needs alone can be strikingly illustrated in the context of public expenditures. These expenditures have a cost in terms of other opportunities foregone, so the operative question is whether the benefits—summed in some way over all the individuals to whom they accrue—exceed the costs. Since each individual can accurately measure only the benefit to himself or herself, the relevant entity for purposes of this information is the individual's own private gain derived from the facility—the amount that he or she would be willing to pay to have the public good available for personal use. The snag is that to obtain this information and to hold individuals to paying up the equivalent of their benefit or some proportion of it to finance the collective project will be impossible while individuals seek to maximize their individual gains, since they will then have the incentive to dissemble.[28] If you pay what you say it is worth to you, you have an individualistic incentive to say it is worth little. Even the less ambitious task of collecting compulsory taxes for the public project on some objective basis of assessment becomes all the more difficult the more individuals seek to avoid or evade paying their due.

The prima facie division that suggests itself to meet these conflicting considerations is privately directed objectives for choices between alternative spending patterns, combined with socially directed objectives in following codes and rules of behavior. These codes and rules should, in principle, apply where cost of compliance to the individual is almost invariably disproportionately small compared with the benefit from observance of the collective convention or law by other people. Telling the truth, obeying the law, paying one's taxes are all prominent examples. Avoidance of taxes, in the accepted sense of arranging one's affairs with the deliberate objective of minimizing one's tax liability, would infringe this code, as would "strategic" voting or other distortions of one's attitudes on public policies. Avoiding litter, showing casual friendliness to strangers, and accepting a strong obligation to aid them in distress are further examples in which ratios of benefit to cost from observance of the social convention are likely to be sufficiently high to justify the patterning of individual behavior through such conventions. But this would not be true of other kinds of friendliness involving enforced camaraderie, which can have a proportionately large private cost.

A stronger criterion for collectively directed norms is that the collective benefits are judged to be large relative to the costs in the aggregate,

---

[28] For the classic formal analysis of this point see Paul A. Samuelson, "The Pure Theory of Public Expenditure," *Review of Economics and Statistics* (1954), in R. W. Houghton, ed., *Public Finance* (Harmondsworth, Eng.: Penguin, 1970).

even though they carry a substantial net cost for a significant number of individuals. A prominent example would be renunciation by the rich, the clever, or the beautiful of the additional pleasures gained by associating themselves, and their children, predominantly with their own kind. Such renunciation has traditionally not been a generally accepted norm of social behavior, although the idea has been present to some degree in certain traditions of service. The social demand for a norm of this kind may be increasing.

Suppose, for example, it were clearly demonstrated that society was becoming segmented on meritocratic-hereditary lines (elites being formed by merit groups that had a substantial hereditary component based on transmission of both genes and favorable environment); and suppose it were also clearly demonstrated that this segmentation induced frustration and anger among the less-favored groups herded increasingly together—the poor, the stupid, and the ugly, making up a ferment of continual rejection and violence. This is the warning delivered by Michael Young in *The Rise of the Meritocracy*.[29] The prospect remains in important respects a fantasy; it neglects the rule of chance in economic success, which has been emphasized in some major statistical studies.[30] But with a broad interpretation of merit—itself a subjective concept—the vision is today depressingly familiar. It takes the shape of a division between the successful and the unsuccessful in the economic stakes that is resented and resisted by many as unprincipled and, therefore, unjust. There is at least the possibility that society will be faced with the unpleasant choice between constant insecurity for all and a crackdown involving repression of the individual liberties of all. To avoid a choice of this kind, some of the favored groups would prefer to give up their isolation and perhaps also some of their advantages.

The organizational problem is how to keep that option open. Attempts to check tendencies toward social segmentation have been made through public policy in various spheres, for example, busing in school districts in the United States to achieve a greater degree of racial integration, and replacement of selective by comprehensive schools in Britain to achieve a greater degree of social and intellectual integration. In both cases, the policies have met strenuous and successful resistance from parents who judged that they and their children could lose out in the deal. Basically they have probably been right; for the important extent to which education is a positional good implies that wider extension of edu-

---

[29] Michael Young, *The Rise of the Meritocracy 1870-2033* (1958) (Harmondsworth, Eng.: Penguin, 1961).

[30] In particular by Christopher Jencks, *Inequality* (New York: Basic Books, 1973). The measurement of inequality by income alone, as well as other factors that have been extensively discussed, is widely believed to have somewhat exaggerated the role of chance in the Jencks analysis.

cation, even of unchanged quality, will leave the previous beneficiaries worse off. Their scarcity value declines. The school badge no longer distinguishes.

Although public policy and the law have increasingly treated racial and social integration as public goods, individuals are still generally expected to act within the law according to their private interest. Yet the side effects of such action may block certain choices available to others, for example, living in an integrated community, where polarizing or tipping effects of the Schelling type are operating. The interactions following a particular decision may then produce a result undesired by all, as long as individuals' decisions are motivated by the immediate and identifiable effects of their actions and determined on a purely individualistic calculus. And if someone orients his actions to the social interest rather than to his private interests, the effects of this action on his private interests cannot be determined on a piecemeal basis. It will depend on what other people do. Action that would entail a heavy cost to the individual if undertaken by himself alone could involve imperceptible costs, or even benefits, if similar action were taken by his fellows, because this would change the aggregate impact as well as affecting its apportionment. The classic example is the potential "run" by members of a particular social group out of a school or a residential community. For the individual contemplating his decision, the key factor is the decisions that other people make. The pressure to act defensively out of individual interest will be increased not only by the number of others who act this way but also by the uncertainty that they might.

In this sense, to act socially is less costly in a social setting. Where mutual interdependence is strong, the group is more efficient as a decision-making body than individuals acting in isolation. Differently put, there is an interdependence in social orientation itself. Its costs to the individual are indeterminate without knowledge of how other individuals act. This is what is wrong with the standard liberal presumption that the extent to which people want to act socially will be shown by the extent that they do. Independent decision-making will mean that a defensive policy of safety first will bias decisions in an antisocial direction.

This interdependence in social orientation will tend to become more widespread as one's relative position in the income distribution becomes more important in determining one's actual take, through the processes discussed earlier. A given tax or its equivalent is a smaller burden if it also falls on rival bidders in the auction room who are after the same scarce things one is after oneself. If such a tax is borne by only one man with a taste for vintage wine, he may find himself priced out; if it is borne by all who have such tastes, the scarcity prices will fall and the impact on each individual will be reduced. A reduction in relative income vis-à-vis people with similar tastes reduces disproportionately one's ability to indulge those tastes. The same influence will operate less visibly across the range of positional goods.

Thus the significance of a given decline in one's educational premium will depend on how many others face or accept a similar decline. Parents in central city areas feel deprived when integration is imposed on the city school districts but not on the metropolitan area. Their reaction is often attributed to envious or irrational concern with whether others are escaping a similar burden; but it may also show an instinctive recognition by the city dwellers of their positional relegation. Because relative as well as absolute position determines the absolute value of education, their deprivation is more than relative; they are made worse off than if integration were comprehensive. The natural response is defensive action to resist this loss. The loss entailed by a shared impost would tend to be more acceptable on two grounds: it would be smaller in size, and it would be seen to be more equitably spread.

Putting one's private interest ahead of social orientation, therefore, has some characteristics of a dynamic process, in which the drive is the social interaction between individual decisions. The process can be put into reverse. Public perception of the damage to society as a whole will help promote a social ethos, but will not be sufficient to secure it so long as individualistic behavior retains its legitimacy over the whole field of collective action. Once again, individualistic behavior can then be an obstacle to satisfaction of individual preferences. People may be willing to put social interests first at a modest sacrifice of their individualistic interests, but they cannot act out this preference on their own.

11 The Lost Legitimacy and the Distributional Compulsion

Managed capitalism, and more generally any decentralized economy subject to central guidance, faces an unfamiliar new priority: it is to resolve, or at least to confront, a hypothetical question about the springs of personal behavior. What conditions are necessary for individuals to guide certain key actions according to a social norm? The answer given in the major work of modern liberal philosophy by John Rawls is: the existence of justice, in the sense of fairness.[1] Individuals can be expected to restrain the exercise of their individual power in the interest of protecting the fabric of their society if, but only if, they believe the society as a whole to be a just one. This is an intuitively acceptable view—there is no independent criterion by which it can be said to be formally rational.

Translation of such a principle into practical terms raises two questions: what is justice, and what is power? It is the first question that is the central focus of Rawls's work and of the recent resurgence of analytical work and public debate on the normative aspect of welfare distribution —who should get what. This discussion is only beginning to grapple with the well-known conflicts between various desiderata, and between various ways of looking at inequality of reward. Resolution of these issues is almost certainly still far off. Their present intractability, however, does not mean that the distributional issue can be fended off. In this analysis, the issue has been dragged back on stage by two major structural developments of advanced economies: the growing importance of positional competition and the accompanying extension of the necessary sphere of collective action for which a basis of social consensus has to be found. Without the consensus, resort must be had to privatization that would otherwise be a second-best solution (see in particular Chapter 6); and the irreducible minimum of collective action becomes less efficient and more costly.

[1] Rawls, *A Theory of Justice*.

But agreement on what constitutes social justice—or, less demanding, a move toward social justice—is only one prerequisite for restraint by individuals of the exercise of their power and for the observance of social norms in the interests of preserving stability of their society. Agreement also is necessary on the relevant aspects and dimensions of power that call for restraint. This problem is much less discussed. Yet it reflects back on the determination of justice itself.

I

The key issue is whether account should be taken of ordinary market power as a component, often a dominating one, of total economic power. "Market power" is used here in the sense of command over economic resources *in* the marketplace, rather than in the sense of influence *over* markets (of a monopolistic kind). The latter usage, which has become the conventional view in economic literature, begs the question that is at issue here.

In the standard liberal analysis, economic power is regarded as essentially external to the competitive market outcome; this outcome, actual or hypothetical, provides the norm against which economic power is measured. Individuals or groups exercise economic power when they use either monopolistic advantages or political means of explicit organization to subjugate others to their own influence and/or to secure additional resources for themselves. Power is measured by distortion of free market forces; the outcome of these forces is the datum.

This conception was a natural analog to the view that no criterion for distribution of reward can be reached other than the competitive market outcome. This criterion has undoubtedly been greatly weakened as to both prescription and description. The view that the marginal productivity of labor, the sine qua non of the classical tradition for determining who gets what, has some ethical significance, that it indicates what rate of pay is deserved, has not been held by any major economist since J. B. Clark in the early twentieth century. There has been a parallel weakening, though a much less extensive one, in the view that marginal productivity is the major determinant of rates of pay. As the product of any one man's labor has become more difficult to isolate and to measure in organizationally and technologically complex processes (see Chapter 3), custom and bargaining power have become increasingly important in determining relative pay scales. Where marginal productivity undoubtedly retains major significance is in influencing levels of employment at these pay scales. Marginal productivity does not determine what airline pilots or teachers are paid; it does influence how many airline pilots or teachers there are.

The conceptual notion of "the" market rate of pay has been impaired therefore as a criterion for the distribution of reward in the competitive market. It has undoubtedly lost in determinacy and, thereby, in legitimacy. It appears manipulable. Economic forces set a wide range within which wage and salary rates can be set; no more. The way is thereby opened to alternative or additional criteria.

But once the distributional neutrality of the competitive market outcome has been abandoned, even for a relatively weak distributional criterion such as that the worst off should have more, then it is no longer meaningful to equate economic power with deliberate distortion of free market forces. The fact that some view is being taken about the desirability or acceptability of a particular pattern of economic rewards, whatever their source, removes the special significance for policy provided by the competitive market outcome. Thus organization of the market power of the weak, to the extent that it increases their take, can be approved, while the right to retain the full rewards of competitive market activity can be denied. This suggests an alternative, and more comprehensive, view of economic power as a resultant of all the influences affecting the economic push and pull that individuals and groups exert. Earning capacity of claims stemming from property rights are then seen as a part of economic power, whatever the degree of organization of the market in which they are exercised.

This approach also suggests that economic power has two forms. The first, which is the primary and direct economic form, is independent acquisitive power, or power within the market; this power is measured by the economic rewards of various kinds that individuals can attain in the market on their own. Independent acquisitive power results from market opportunities exercised in a competitive market. It flows from some combination of physical productivity, scarce talents, good contacts, scarce information, and good luck.

The second form of economic power results from some degree of collective organization or monopolistic domination; an important dimension is the economic disruption and hurt that can be caused to others. Power of this second form is typically exercised by political or quasi-political means of group organization, including trade union bargaining. Although the most important dimension of collective economic power of this type is disruptive, its exercise will usually be a means to acquisitive power. The fact that large disruptive power exists or is used by one group does not itself indicate that its members have more acquisitive power in total. This may turn out to be the case in a racketeering union, where a union boss converts the power under his control into a personal, blackmailing gain. Otherwise, the gains from the exercise of union power have to be spread over union members, and the exercise of even considerable disruptive power may leave members worse off than others with little capacity for such upheaval.

II

Once distributional objectives are admitted as a goal of policy and thereby as a criterion of successful economic and political performance, the exertion of disruptive power cannot itself be deemed to be inadmissible. Its exercise can be shown to be potentially inefficient for the community as a whole, in the sense that the same distributional outcome could be attained in other ways with no comparable loss or distortion in output. This reflects the fact that exercise of organizational power, unlike independent acquisitive power, acts directly on the volume and composition of output and not merely on distribution of consumption claims. But if the distribution that actually occurs without the exercise of disruptive power is different and inferior, then this result may outweigh the gain in aggregate output. Thus, rules or views about exertion of disruptive power involve views, at least implicit, about the validity of the apportionment of acquisitive power, that is, about the final distribution. More specifically, restraint of the exercise of political or monopoly power by or on behalf of those whose independent acquisitive power is weak involves an implicit obligation to achieve at least the equivalent distributional transfer in some other form.

In this approach, no unqualified distinction can be made between restraint of economic power that is explicitly exerted in some political or organizational form and direct economic power that flows from market opportunities. Rather, restraint over politically organized economic power, which is likely to take the form of disruptive power, has to be considered in the context of what restraint, if any, is exercised on independent acquisitive power in the sense of market opportunities. The relevant entity is the combination of direct (independent) and indirect (disruptive) acquisitive power. It is one-sided to expect those who command relatively great organizational or political power to restrain its exertion, in the collective interest, if no similar restraints are applied to the exercise of relatively great independent acquisitive market power by other individuals in the collectivity. Yet this asymmetry is endemic in almost all liberal discussion of the issue.[2]

This is the heart of the trade unionist's objection: "In a free-for-all, we are part of the all." Workers organized in unions are asked to restrain their use of disruptive economic power, while individuals who are able to exert greater acquisitive power without recourse to disruptive power remain free to do so.

A common argument among liberal economists is that power exercised collectively through unions is a socially unacceptable exploitation

[2] For a discussion of this asymmetry in Rawls see Barry, *The Liberal Theory of Justice*, p. 157.

of monopoly. But this contention rests on the implicit judgment that collective exploitation of the economic power of individuals, even if they are themselves relatively weak, can be ethically condemned while individual exploitation of the economic power of the independently strong cannot be. This is itself an ethical value judgment.

A stronger argument is that the process of bargaining between large groups or other concentrations of market power is inherently disruptive, because the outcome can be influenced by the exertion of bluff and blackmail. Bargaining between groups whose behavior influences the terms of the bargain itself involves a deadweight loss as compared with transactions in a market sufficiently competitive for each participant to be a price taker rather than a price maker. This is one classic argument in favor of atomistic competition. The indeterminacy of the bargaining solution is itself a source of disruption and, therefore, inefficient. Yet potential benefit for all is neither a sufficient nor a necessary incentive to persuade groups that are currently profiting from exercise of collective bargaining power to give it up. They need to be shown either that they could themselves benefit, or at least that cooperation in the general interest is warranted and called for by the just nature of the system their action will help to uphold.[3] If the groups with actual or latent bargaining power are not so convinced, because exploitation of individual bargaining power remains unprincipled, then it will be a false dichotomy to pose a contrast between the stability of individual exploitation of market power and the instability or disruptiveness of its collective exploitation, since the former will provoke and perpetuate the latter. Thus the empirical question of whether individual exploitation of market power is consistent with social stability while collective exploitation is not, will depend on how the unions and nascent unions see the matter, which in turn may depend on resolution of the ethical question, that is, on achievement of "justice" in Rawls's sense of perceived fairness.

Restraint of the use of available power by some can be validated only by reference to ethical principles within the society. No internal logic can be adduced to confine this ethical test to the primary area of respect of political obligations and to exclude it from apportionment of economic rewards. The liberal market economy, even as corrected on the principles stemming from Keynes and Pigou, has great difficulty in accommodating such a test for the distributional outcome.

The greatly increased and now very extensive fiscal operations of industrial states do not appear to have effected major changes in the distribution of income.[4] There is widespread doubt whether such changes

---

[3] It should be recalled that as discussed in Chapter 10, a preference for the fruits of general cooperation (over the alternative of no cooperation) is not sufficient to evoke such behavior by any one individual or group on grounds of self-interest.

[4] See Chapter 7, footnote 1.

could be effected under the ethos that individuals should seek to maximize their private interests in the market situation with which they are faced. An attempt to restructure the pattern of laws and choices facing "maximizing" individuals in a way that would secure major changes from the market outcome would impose great strains on the administration and enforcement of such regulation, for the reasons discussed in Chapter 9. The technical efficiency of the market mechanism in transmitting choices and preferences among many interacting individuals can be extended to only a limited degree to social choices, deriving from individual preferences. The limitation, it may be recalled, derives essentially from the associated deterioration in information about actual individual preferences and in the inefficient transmission of incentives to fulfill them.

III

Satisfaction of private wants can be achieved with technical efficiency by the maximization of private interests in a market process. The analog for the satisfaction of wants for collective goods is not an equivalent process of private maximization in a market process in which the parameters have been adjusted to reflect these collective wants. That is the modern liberal heresy. "An end which cannot be atomized cannot be dealt with by an atomic analysis. Such ends are common."[5] The analog in terms of efficiency is maximization of individually held objectives for the common end. In the language of neoclassical economics, this involves internalization of social norms, at least those concerned with behavioral standards, rather than merely a change of available opportunities. In its growing incorporation of collective goods of a variety of kinds—from views about the distribution of income to common access to parks or schools—the economy becomes more dependent on moral or conventional standards for its efficiency.

Thus the moral lacuna in the capitalist system no longer appears, in the traditional view of enlightened liberals, from Mill to Keynes, as a kind of esthetic blemish to be put up with for the sake of its superior efficiency compared to the alternatives. The absence of explicit moral justification and/or of specified moral obligations within the system is now seen as weakening its operating efficiency in the previously neglected problem of securing the necessary collective goods and socially functional individual norms. Yet dependence on these grows rather than lessens as economies become more interdependent and complex. Appeal to Marshall's "strongest motive" of private self-interest remains in many

---

[5] E. F. M. Durbin, "The Social Significance of the Theory of Value," *Economic Journal* (December 1935), as quoted by R. H. Tawney, *Equality* (London: Allen and Unwin, 1952), p. 126.

situations the most effective instrument available for attainment of the immediate objective. But by weakening the norms of deliberate cooperation and social restraint, reliance on this appeal as the dominant value of society produces an unstable system over time. The effectiveness of the miracle drug is eventually weakened by its side effects.

part four

**Perspective
and Conclusions**

12 The Liberal Market as a Transition Case

The contemporary impasse on who gets what and the associated impediments in the operation of the market economy can be seen as the surfacing of an embedded historical process. A long latent conflict is coming to a head.

From its seventeenth-century English beginnings, political liberalism was characterized by an ambiguity over the extent of its constituency. Essentially a movement of the middle classes, it nonetheless mobilized support from below in the struggle against the political power of crown and aristocracy and staked its claim in the popular cause. The fruits of the victorious bourgeois revolution in three main areas—civil liberty, political rights, and economic opportunity—were passed down the line in notably different degree and sequence.

Civil liberties were diffused first, with the major exception of non-white populations in the United States. Political rights followed, in the great nineteenth-century struggles. By the end of the century, it was clear that the extension of the franchise that liberalism had begun would have no class stopping point. The principles that had aided and legitimized the attainment of political power for the middle class had acquired their own momentum. So the triumph of bourgeois political power itself immediately undermined it. The final push to universal suffrage was provided by World War I, with its unprecedented call by the state on the active cooperation of working men, and of all women. Both world wars have been seen as involving in Britain a significant and lasting extension in the effective political constituency, in the wider sense of the section of the population which has a claim of right to participate in the state establishment.[1] In the United States, extension of full political rights to the adult

---

[1] Arthur Marwick, *Britain in the Century of Total War, 1900-60* (London: Bodley Head, 1968); Richard M. Titmuss, *Social Policy 1939-45* (1950) (London: Allen and Unwin, 1974).

population was effectively completed with the redistricting legislation of the 1960s and the Voting Rights Act of 1965.

For the middle class, political enfranchisement had followed economic advance. It had been more or less the result of economic strength, the political recognition of economic reality. For the working class and poor or handicapped ethnic groups, acquisition of equal political rights has run ahead of economic advance. Full equality of civil rights and of political rights have gone together with marked inequality in economic results. This disjunction has created its own dynamic. The continuing relative economic disadvantages of the individuals and groups concerned have limited the extent to which formal political rights have been translated into full political power, which rests also on economic power. Pressure has grown for economic opportunity to be more evenly spread by means of political action, that is, in the demand for "equal economic opportunity"; and this pressure has expanded through its own force to impel political action for a more equal economic outcome.

In the traditional liberal analysis, a sharp distinction has been made between these two criteria of equality: equality of opportunity, denoting the commonly shared goal of an equal chance at the start of the race, and equality of outcome, denoting the much more controversial and radical notion of an equal finish. The distinction has dissolved under the ambiguity of what constitutes an equal start, or—what amounts to the same thing—what quality the competition is supposed to test.[2] Consequently, pursuit of a seemingly limited objective has automatically carried over into a virtually open-ended one.

This sequence was just what a long line of skeptics from Edmund Burke and Alexis de Tocqueville onward had feared. Political enfranchisement of property owners opened the breach to enfranchising those who owned nothing. The propertyless would be free of the restraining influence which is imposed by having one's own stake in existing society. In irresponsibility and ignorance, they would then demand from the state more than could be provided. They would seek through the state to redress a disadvantage whose origin was in nature. The populace would not remain content to leave political leadership and economic strength in the hands of those who understood these realities. It would be swayed by promises from demagogues of better things and, in the process, would threaten both the political and economic bases of prosperity.

---

[2] In the formal games from which the analogy is drawn the answer is clear enough: it is the ability to run 100 meters, and the like. But in the game of life? Which disabilities are to be removed? The early and fully bourgeois concept of equality of opportunity singled out ascriptive disabilities of birth—hereditary distinctions of status and role. But the other visible hereditary advantage, of wealth, soon appeared equally stark, as an arbitrary handicap to those who had little or none of it.

In contemporary times, research has made clear that further advantages are trans-

Such fears extended deep into the liberal camp.[3] They underlay the reservations of John Stuart Mill on a full extension of the franchise. They also lay behind Walter Bagehot's apprehension that the newly enfranchised working class would not follow the small shopkeepers in deferring to the superior wisdom of wealth and rank and that the way would be open to "a political combination of the lower classes, as such and for their own objects, [which] is an evil of the first magnitude."[4]

I

The deeper reason why the political apple cart was likely to be upset by the reality of universal political participation was exposed by Keynes almost as an aside, as a warm-up to his denunciation of the Versailles peace settlement. In a rare indulgence in neo-Marxist categorization, Keynes argued that the basis of the remarkable advances that the European economies had achieved in the golden period from 1870 to 1914 was to allow capitalists to appropriate the lion's share of the joint product and to compel, persuade, or cajole the laboring classes into claiming very little of it.[5] The social rationale and implicit condition of the arrangement was that the surplus appropriated by the capitalists was not consumed but was ploughed back in capital accumulation. To bluff the workers out of their full share, and the capitalists from realizing their swollen one,

---

mitted by parents in intelligence and family environment: neither in the cradle nor at the school gate do different children have an equal start in life. And then what of other differences in inherited or environmentally influenced characteristics which in individual cases may be of decisive importance for economic achievement—differences in health, in capacity for self-control and discipline, in physical strength? Can a competition that takes no account of these differences in initial capacities—as distinct from the use made of these capacities—be regarded as giving equal opportunity? Finally, if we could find a way of testing this utilization of personal capacity, or effort, what of capacity for effort itself? Is inherited lethargy a lesser handicap than inherited physical weakness? Clearly once the concept of economic opportunity is taken seriously, it expands without natural barrier toward equality of outcome. This is why those fearful of the implications of equality of outcome as a criterion are on solid ground in suspecting equality of opportunity as an economic concept and in confining their objectives to political concepts such as equality before the law and the opening of positions in public service and the professions to all who wish to compete for them. Not an equal start, but a universal chance to start: equality of access. See in particular Friedrich A. Hayek, *The Constitution of Liberty* (London: Routledge and Kegan Paul, 1970), pp. 91-95.

[3] "Inside and outside England, from Macaulay to Mises, from Spencer to Sumner, there was not a militant liberal who did not express his conviction that popular democracy was a danger to capitalism." Karl Polanyi, *The Great Transformation* (1944) (Boston: Beacon, 1970), p. 226.

[4] Walter Bagehot, *The English Constitution* (1867) (London: Collins Fontana, 1963), Introduction to 2d ed. (1872), p. 277.

[5] "The Economic Consequences of the Peace" (1919) *Collected Writings*, II, 11-13.

provided the only possible basis for growth in the national pie to a size at which all could in time secure a decent slice. But in the gloom of 1919, Keynes saw the double bluff exposed: "The war has disclosed the possibility of consumption to all and the vanity of abstinence to many." It also awakened attention to the aspect in which the implicit deal was less than evenhanded, an aspect Keynes did not mention: that the claims to ownership and control of the capital assets made available by the joint abstinence of workers and capitalists resided with capitalists alone.

The danger from the calling of the bluff was clear. Excessive claims on the fruits would jeopardize the life of the tree. Yet the earlier balance and restraint rested on nothing more than "unstable psychological conditions," which once unhinged might be impossible to re-create. The polemical purpose to which Keynes put this insight in his assault on the Carthaginian peace helped to obscure its significance, not least from himself. Capitalism, a rationalistic system living by its results, could not explicitly justify its most important result—who gets what.

In the frame of the previous discussion (Part III), the moral vacuum that eased the daily working of market capitalism undermined its long-term stability. To get by, the system depended on looking-glass logic. But in Keynes's conception, it could eventually come clean when its own success had provided enough worldly goods for all. Thus the close of the Keynesian system, no less than of the Marxian, depended on the end of economic scarcity.

Yet the dynamics of both capitalism and consumption-oriented socialism prevent economic scarcity from yielding to advancing material productivity. Competition for place is heightened and itself contributes to additional material needs. This malign interaction has been the recurring theme of this book. Certainly, claims on economic output have never lost their urgency in the past half century.

To return to the historical outline, economic demands appeared particularly urgent in the aftermath of World War I. The arithmetic of the matter was beginning to be shown in estimates of the distribution of national income. The distribution appeared pyramid-shaped, which meant that lopping off the pinnacle would do little to enlarge the base. "The pyramid creates an optical illusion, which causes the height of its apex to be exaggerated and the breadth of its base to be ignored." Thus R. H. Tawney (in 1931) citing the "venerable spectre" which makes such regular reappearances in our own day.[6] Economic advance raised the mass of working people from extreme poverty, leaving poverty in the sense of

[6] Tawney, *Equality*, p. 120. Tawney vigorously contested the associated assumption that redistribution of income would have a cost in foregone output; he expected the lessening of hostility and suspicion resulting from a more equitable distribution to remove existing impediments to increased output.

denial of primary biological wants as a minority condition suffered by people who were personally handicapped, or merely old. The breadth of the base shrank; the bulge moved upward; and the shape of the distribution in advanced economies took the form of a base-weighted diamond.

The political economy that was emerging as an outgrowth of the European mercantile and industrial revolutions was therefore developing a combination of conflicting characteristics:

(1) Its economic drive was essentially market capitalism.

(2) Its political legitimation was universal participation.

(3) Its economic constraint was the income distribution of pyramid shape, later molding into the form of a base-weighted diamond, in which the heights of consumption and civilized living are available only to a few.

Any two of these characteristics might be compatible: the three together were not. The twentieth century has seen a swaying struggle—in the marketplace, in the political arena, and among the wordsmiths and occasional fighting men locked in battle for hearts and minds—over which would be the incompatible element that would have to make way.

In some socialist thought—but specifically not in Marxist analysis— the extraneous element has been market capitalism. With distribution of income under some degree of state control and related to service rather than to market power, universal participation could be made compatible with economic scarcity. This would be done by scaling down the permitted possibilities of individual consumption—in a word, leveling down.[7] The pyramid or base weighted diamond would be flattened from the top. Marxists viewed with disdain the feasibility of dissociating income distribution, and the influence exerted by the state, from the social organization of production.[8] From the opposite end of the political spectrum, and as a specific counter to the prospect of leveling down, the cuckoo in the nest was rather the principle of full politico-economic democracy; at the least, the concept of universal participation needed to stop short of deliberate influence over the economic jurisdiction. Joseph Schumpeter and Friedrich Hayek were strong proponents of this view. These alternative resolutions of the excess of claims over availabilities— to get rid of capitalism or to get rid of universal participation in the above listing—were clearly in direct opposition. The remaining possible combination necessitated no such confrontation. This was to get rid of

[7] Tawney was the most eloquent and influential modern spokesman of this school. His key texts are *The Acquisitive Society* (1920) (New York: Harcourt, 1958) and *Equality* (1931).

[8] "Vulgar socialism (and from it in turn a section of democracy) has taken over from the bourgeois economists the consideration and treatment of distribution as independent of the mode of production." Karl Marx, *Critique of the Gotha Programme* (1875) (New York: International Publishers, 1966), p. 11.

the constraint itself. That, broadly, was the offering of economic growth, and so long as it appeared a credible solvent, it could hardly be resisted.

Arithmetic again spoke for itself. Compound growth rates provided the lift that the most severe income redistribution of a static total could not approach. At a rate of growth in gross national product per capita of 2 percent, which has been recorded for sustained periods by industrial economies in the past, and in the 1960s was widely regarded as modest, there is a doubling every generation. By this route—and by this route alone—the masses presently near the base of the distribution could be brought, over time, to its summit. The process of economic growth is itself stimulated by the transmission downward through the income distribution of new and urgently felt wants derived from observing the opportunities that first became available only at the top. The growth process has been seen as allowing these wants to be fulfilled over time. The luxury goods of one generation became the standard items of the next and the necessities of the third; as happened with motor cars, washing machines, television sets, and foreign travel, in this century, and in slower motion, with brick houses and glass windows in earlier ones.

In this way, an egalitarian tendency works with a time lag; and with great subtlety. For this "dynamic egalitarianism" results from the neglect of active egalitarian policies; in fact, it depends on such neglect. It is the natural outcome of market responses to uncoordinated individual actions, being powered by inequality in prevailing conditions at particular moments of time. These static inequalities provide the incentive as well as the means for general advance. The heights occupied by the well-off today will tomorrow be made over to us all. In the course of economic progress, on this view, the well-off form an advance guard, and the lead in income and consumption that they enjoy over others at any moment is an integral part of the dynamic of general advance.

The concept of the good things of life filtering or trickling down from the top is a very old one in growth economics; it was prominent in Smith's *The Wealth of Nations*. The specific image of economic growth as an egalitarian tendency proceeding over time is more recent. The connection between economic growth and income distribution has been the subject of much debate and dispute. There is some evidence of a widening of income disparities in the early stages of development, followed by a narrowing. But this equalizing tendency has been largely concentrated in the two world wars and periods of acute inflation,[9] such as experienced in the late 1960s and the first half of the 1970s.

[9] Simon Kuznets, "Economic Growth and Income Inequality," *American Economic Review* (March 1955); Lee Soltow, "Long Run Changes in British Income Inequality," *Economic History Review* (1968); U.S. Council of Economic Advisers, "Distribution of Income," *Annual Report 1974*, chap. 5; Atkinson, "Poverty and Income Inequality in Britain"; Royal Commission on the Distribution of Income and Wealth,

The most evocative rendering of the theme of growth as a dynamic equalizing agent has been offered by two British sociologists, Michael Young and Peter Willmott. Building on the analysis of Daniel Bell, in turn inspired by de Tocqueville, they represented the growth process as a marching column. The ranking of the column reflects the income distribution, which stays more or less unchanged over time, as the column as a whole advances. The people at the head are usually "the first to wheel in a new direction. The last rank keeps its distance from the first, and the distance between them does not lessen. But as the column advances, the last rank does eventually reach and pass the point which the first rank had passed some time before . . . The people in the rear cannot, without breaking rank and rushing ahead, reach where the van *is*, but, since the whole column is moving forward, they can hope in due course to reach where the van *was*."[10] Evidently, the vanguard is not the place for the proletariat: quite the contrary.

The weakness of this approach is its commodity fetishism in the sense discussed previously (Chapter 6). What is neglected is that by the time the sought-after ground is reached by the rear of the column, that ground will have been affected by the passage of the column itself. These effects are not only psychological, through the influence of expectations on the satisfaction derived from particular forms of consumption or other activity. More extensive proliferation of particular commodities or facilities also affects their characteristics in an objective, nonpsychological sense, by affecting the environment in which they are used. The ways in which this may happen have been extensively discussed. Here it may be recalled that for the family in the tail end of the Young-Willmott march that acquires its automobile after the luxury of pleasure driving has been qualified by congestion and parking restrictions—while the necessity of car ownership has been established by the decay of public transport and by the switching of the channels of physical communication between home, work, and social facilities—for this family passing the once-vaunted milestone of car ownership, the passage may appear less as a release from its old subordinate position than as a new facet of an unchanged subordinate reality. Or, as a middle-class professional remarked when cheap charter flights opened up a distant exotic country: "Now that I can afford to come here I know that it will be ruined."[11]

Report, Volume I, Cmnd 6171, 1975; J. D. Smith and S. D. Franklin, "The Concentration of Personal Wealth, 1922-1969," *American Economic Review*, Papers and Proceedings (May 1974).

[10] Young and Willmott, *The Symmetrical Family*, p. 20. The idea of autonomous equalization through time has also been powerfully stated by Hayek: "It is because scouts have found the goal that the road can be built for the less lucky or less energetic . . . Even the poorest today owe their relative material well-being to the results of past inequality." Hayek, *The Constitution of Liberty*, pp. 40-46.

[11] Nicholas Tomalin, *Sunday Times* (London), December 31, 1972.

The presumption that what the elite have today the mass will de-mand—and acquire—tomorrow has become deeply entrenched in west-ern society. It is the basic underlay of much social planning, and the gos-pel of the futurologist. Its attractions for both reside in its amenability to quantitative projection and apparently objective assessment. To project the future, one need merely observe the present in order to extrapolate the past. The cross section picture of how rich and poor live today traces the contour of future ascent for all below the summit, as the fruits of gen-eralized growth lift them to the economic position today occupied by the rich. Social planning for transport, housing, and education has, to a con-siderable extent, been grounded on this basic assumption.[12] The assump-tion, thereby, acquires an element of self-fulfillment.[13] Economic output in these conditions may be defensive in character—such as demand for personal car transport that is necessitated by the demise of public trans-port. An influence of this kind will exert pressure on the tail end of the column to catch up with the van, and this will be an important drive for increased economic activity, conventionally classified as economic growth. But in the conditions currently prevailing, the advance will be in economic output in the "gross" sense of bringing individual welfare to a higher level than would exist without the activity in question. To the extent that the growth in economic activity has an adverse effect on these conditions, that is, on city congestion in this example, the forward march

[12] Consider the following projection in a major work by Marion Clawson and Peter Hall, *Planning and Urban Growth: An Anglo-American Comparison* (Balti-more: Johns Hopkins University Press, 1973): "Many families or individuals will have a second, and some perhaps a third, or even a fourth home—for different seasons, for different purposes, in different locations. A downtown urban home for living while working, a suburban home for its spaciousness and privacy and for weekends, a mountain home for summer vacations, a beach home for winter vacations; housing standards or luxury now available only to the very rich may become available to a vastly larger fraction of the total population" (p. 273). The feasibility of this develop-ment is based on the expected doubling of real per capita income.

[13] This is illustrated in a major research survey of future transport needs in Lon-don, typical of its kind (Greater London Council, *Movement in London*, 1969). The survey took as its starting point the strong statistical association between income and car ownership shown in Britain and other countries; on the basis of the expected rise in incomes generated by economic growth, and of relative price movements, it fore-cast a doubling of the number of cars between 1961 and 1981, at which time 68 percent of households would have access to one. These trends are presented as the reflection of consumer demands. Since beyond some point the demand for car ownership feeds on itself—because its spread reduces the quality and increases the cost of public trans-port—an exercise of this kind incorporates on a grand scale the tyranny of small deci-sions with which the individual is faced at any moment of time. The large decision—cars with minimal public transport or no cars with lavish public transport—is in prin-ciple open to the social planner, but is undermined by a projection of individuals' responses to the small choices to which they are confined in market transactions.

of the column as a whole could be pictured as if occurring on a travellator moving in the reverse direction, and powered by the marching column itself.

The crude concept of economic growth neglects such complications and sees national growth as individual economic advance writ large. The limited extent to which such generalization from individual experience is admissible has been a major theme of this book. This is not to question that in past experience individuals as a whole have made real and substantial economic gains. Increased productivity based in part on technological advance has added to material availabilities throughout the income distribution. It also has added to social welfare, as measured by certain prime social indicators—expectation of life, access to medical attention, literacy. This material advance has been the result of two different processes of growth operating side by side. Their harmony can no longer be taken for granted.

III

The two processes of growth can be categorized as individualistic advance and collective advance. Individualistic advance has been the characteristic standard of the middle class; attainment depends on individual performance or position and is consequently open-ended. Collective advance has been the traditional standard of manual workers in Europe and of certain ethnic and low-income groups in the United States. Scope for individual advance has been limited by the absence of a career ladder to step up to higher job positions and/or by racial or ethnic discrimination; advance is achieved with and through the group; market power is in collective form rather than immanent in the individual. The appropriate norm is therefore fraternal loyalty within the group rather than competitive individualism. The horizon of personal expectations is limited; the reference group that forms the standard for the worker's own situation is restricted to a short distance within his own class.[14]

As long as the collective goals remain confined to acquisitions in the material sector (defined in Part I), comprising goods that can be made more widely available in the long term without reducing the quantity or quality available to others, advance can be achieved on this front without disturbing the middle-class growth process of individual competitiveness. That growth process essentially embraces the positional sector, which in its nature is the sphere of individual competition; it is occupied

---

[14] Ely Chinoy, *Automobile Workers and the American Dream* (New York: Doubleday, 1955); W. G. Runciman, *Relative Deprivation and Social Justice* (1966) (Harmondsworth, Eng.: Penguin, 1972); David Lockwood, *The Black Coated Worker* (London: Allen and Unwin, 1958); John Goldthorpe and David Lockwood, *The Affluent Worker*, vols. 1-3 (Cambridge, Eng.: Cambridge University Press, 1968 and 1969).

by the successful minority of winners. It is the sphere of the traditional bourgeois ethos, of boundless individual striving for rewards and prizes that only few can attain: of opportunities for distinction, for service, for leadership. Here it is possible only to rise above one's fellows, bourgeois style, rather than along with them, proletarian or communal style. Collective advance, the traditional growth process of the mass, has no place in this sector. Attempts to gain more for all merely intensify the struggle and add distance to the elimination race. For overall economic advance to remain pure, in the sense of avoiding the excrescences associated with excess demands on the positional sector, the two processes must remain in more or less separate compartments, avoiding interaction.

Yet it is characteristic of the growth process of market capitalism that it eventually breaks down these barriers. Extension of middle-class material and cultural values is itself an impetus to individual economic advance and is a natural consequence of the principle of universal participation to which the liberal order becomes increasingly wedded by the demands of political legitimation. *But while the spread of bourgeois objectives downward through the social scale strengthens the political legitimacy of liberal market capitalism, the same process proves ultimately disruptive for economic performance.* It spreads what are essentially minority facilities beyond the minority that can use them without mutual damage. The upshot is both frustration of individual demands and the sprouting of costly and haphazard side effects in the social infrastructure.

The progressive diffusion of middle-class standards to the mass of the population has long been seen as an integrative element in advanced societies. To make everyone middle class has appeared in prospect as the crowning achievement of liberal capitalism. Both John Stuart Mill and Alfred Marshall saw the discontent of the industrial working class as an understandable response to the coarseness of its work experience; the hope for the future lay in the opportunities that economic and educational advance would bring for "the official distinction between working men and gentlemen" to pass away, so that "by occupation at least, every man is a gentleman."[15]

In the 1950s, the same seam was intensively worked by one school of sociologists in the thesis of *embourgeoisement* or deproletarianization. Society was expected to extend progressively its adherence to middle-class norms and patterns of behavior, as an increasing sector attained

---

[15] Alfred Marshall, "The Future of the Working Classes" (1873), in A. C. Pigou, ed., *Memorials of Alfred Marshall* (London: Macmillan, 1925), pp. 101-118. A. H. Halsey sees this essay as "the locus classicus of liberal theories about the relation of education to social class," which he encapsules as follows: "economic growth will use education to abolish class by assimilating all men to the rank of gentlemen." A. H. Halsey, "Education and Social Class in 1972," in Kathleen Jones, ed., *Year Book of Social Policy in Britain, 1972* (London: Routledge and Kegan Paul, 1973).

traditional middle-class patterns of consumption (particularly in durable goods), residential location (in suburbs), and, to a lesser extent, character of work (in "service" occupations rather than in manual work). This thesis, with its emphasis upon the growth of individual opportunity and individual action, has had to be severely qualified. Investigations by John Goldthorpe and David Lockwood in Britain have stressed that substantial gains in income and consumption levels have not eroded collective orientation as a means to achievement in either the political or the industrial contexts. The effect of increased affluence has rather been to make support for the Labour party and participation in the works trade union more instrumental in character, a means to attainment of the *private* goal of increased individual real income. Manual workers have in fact become increasingly assimilated to the goals of the liberal market system. They have used their collective associations increasingly to pursue their individual demands. Their particular work situation—the absence of career ladders and of significant possibilities for individual advancement—has made collective action the natural vehicle for seeking such advance.[16]

Greater prosperity, together with the enormous increase in awareness and communication of different living standards and patterns of life throughout the population, in conjunction with other factors that are not understood, also seem to have broken through the remarkably restricted confines of the reference groups traditionally common to manual workers. The range of comparisons and expectations of production workers has increased; this seems to be a general phenomenon in the advanced economies (and not only in these). At the same time, both in Britain and in the United States, a growing cleavage has been developing in white-collar work, as increasing mechanization and the growing size of firms have curtailed the scope for both promotion and the exercise of personal initiative in clerical work. Particularly in Britain, bureaucratization has contributed to rapid growth in union activity in this sector, especially at the lower tiers of white-collar occupations. Bureaucratization and unionization have reinforced each other in clerical work.[17] Defensive unionization, to protect differentials vis-à-vis traditionally organized occupa-

[16] Goldthorpe and Lockwood, *The Affluent Worker*; Runciman, *Relative Deprivation and Social Justice*, chap. 6. The crude hypothesis of political *embourgeoisement* is also rejected in David Butler and Donald Stokes, *Political Change in Britain* (1969) (Harmondsworth, Eng.: Penguin, 1971), chap. 5. The more complex relationship between occupational status and party support which this study suggests, on the basis of survey findings, emphasizes the importance of parental party affiliation. It suggests this may explain why the Labour party's "loss" of working-class voters has become much smaller in the younger age cohorts than for their elders who grew up before Labour was entrenched as a major party.

[17] Lockwood notes that unionization in banking in Britain as long ago as 1919 was attributed as much to the bureaucratization that followed bank amalgamations as to salary demands. He quotes a contemporary union journal: "It is the grim factor of

tions, has been an additional factor, which has extended to professions such as teaching.

Competitive collective bargaining is one familiar result—wage struggles that are effectively between different groups of workers rather than between workers and employers. Such wage competition is itself a prime ingredient of inflation. The more that trade unions are oriented to meeting the immediate interests of their workers for more money, rather than oriented to wider political objectives, the greater the tendency toward leapfrogging wage claims. Each union then has the incentive to get ahead of others; and unions are then also more likely to be driven by their rank and file. Collective bargaining power is used more directly for maximization of group self-interest.

Paradoxically, therefore, the assimilation of manual workers to the goals of the market system poses threats to its economic stability, since the normal channel of self-improvement for workers in occupations with no career structures is through collective bargaining; and in conditions of full or near full employment, widespread and unrestrained collective bargaining destroys the harmony and anonymity of the market system, and perhaps also its stability and efficiency. To attain traditional individualistic middle-class objectives, only a minority of the population is in a position to employ traditional middle-class individualistic means.

The diffusion of middle-class modes to the mass of the population—which has always been regarded as the ultimate safeguard of bourgeois capitalism—is thus impeded by asymmetries in the structure of occupations in the modern division of labor. People in jobs with little career potential will be hard pressed to use individualistic means to achieve the goals of a middle-class society. But a latent process of *embourgeoisement* runs into a second snag, which has been my major theme in this book. It entices additional demands for goods and facilities that in their nature are attainable only by a minority.

In the early stages of the growth process, while demand of the mass of the population remains concentrated on material goods, its economic advance tends to outpace that of the existing middle-class elite,[18] which cannot increase its consumption of positional goods in the aggregate and faces progressively increasing competition for those scarce goods from below. Those already in the middle-class elite may in time lose out from economic growth in absolute terms even if they maintain their propor-

---

cold impersonal human treatment that hurts [the bankman] most of all. It cuts across his manhood, and he feels he is being ground down to a contemptible part in a soulless mechanism." Lockwood, *The Black Coated Worker*, p. 147.

[18] In the sense of those people, including the upper class, enjoying substantial access to positional goods.

tionate share of national income: the prices of the things they spend their money on rise disproportionately in price and/or deteriorate in quality. The ever-escalating cost of servants is the most prominent example of this development. Middle-class moans may rest on objective experience.

Yet, though the lead enjoyed by the winners in the economic race is diminished by the constraints of positional competition, these same constraints tend to preserve the lead itself. Additional competition for positional goods yields no additional product, and by lengthening the obstacle course that has to be run to acquire them, may be to the detriment of all—in effect, a negative-sum game. But the relative winners in that game will be those with the longest purses and with equity stakes in those aspects of positional competition that can be capitalized. Included in the latter category are not just ownership of scenic land and paintings by Old Masters but also the advantages—whether genetic or environmental—conferred by family background on individual life chances. When excess competition lengthens the obstacle course or raises the pass mark, the past winners retain the advantage, although their own position is less secure than when they had the field to themselves.

The newcomers to the competition for these minority goods therefore are generally the worst placed to attain them, because others have longer purses and established positions. Newly awakened demands by the mass of the population are likely to be frustrated: and the incentive to press for additional spending power will be heightened.

Thus the extension of middle-class objectives has outdistanced middle-class opportunities. The excess demand on middle-class life-styles reinforces the underlying inflationary thrust. To the extent that the demands for private consumption underlying the collective wage claims take the form of positional goods in restricted absolute supply—for education that provides better access to the more sought-after jobs, for housing in the more sought-after locations—such demands are doomed to eventual nonfulfillment. Through the process described in Part I, ever-increasing income in real terms ("real" by the measure of an index weighted by a typical current or past consumption pattern) will be found to be needed to secure specific facilities in the positional sector, as the level of general welfare rises. As a result, collective wage demands, besides being induced by inflation through the leapfrogging bargaining effects, as previously mentioned, are induced also by "real" growth, as increased competition for products in limited supply raises their relative prices or lowers their quality. Economic success on the conventional reckoning contributes in this way to frustration, tension, and inflation.

IV

Economic equality has been a compulsive political idea of the twentieth century. On the face of it, this has been very remarkable. The con-

cept of economic equality is not merely vague but fundamentally ambiv-
alent. Political equality, legal equality, and even social equality are
unambiguous by comparison. Economic equality for whom—individual
or family? And of what—of income, or income in relation to effort, or
income in relation to effort plus skill? Equality over what period—a
moment of time or a lifetime? Economic equality has been regularly exposed and denounced as a chimera. It is evidently a robust one. Frustration of a different kind emanates from those who persist in seeing economic equality as a meaningful objective and are accordingly chagrined
at the lack of evident progress made toward it.

The elusiveness of the objective of economic equality might be expected to diminish its salience over time. This has not happened. Its salience has receded for significant periods—broadly for those periods in
which economic growth has been seen as a feasible and effective alternative to redistribution of resources from the standpoint of those at the bottom of the pile. The growth alternative is inherently less divisive, as
noted earlier; it offers the possibility of consensus action, of a game with
winners but no absolute losers, of leveling up without leveling down:
limiting the political choice to distributing the increment, rather than
demanding the more fundamental political act of redistributing existing
resources.

Because of this immense political advantage in minimizing opposition, the growth objective is likely to dominate the distributional objective so long as its promise holds. This is broadly what happened in the
United States in the first decade after World War I, and more generally in
the United States and the advanced economies of western Europe in the
first two decades after World War II. But in the late 1960s the issue of
who gets what returned in new strength. This reemergence could not be
attributed to the collapse of economic growth—as had happened so
abruptly in 1929—or even to its decisive deceleration. The inflationary
crisis that pushed the western economies into their most severe postwar
recession in the mid-1970s can itself be seen as, in part, a result of the surfacing of political and economic pressures by the poor to get what they
saw as their fair share. In the quarter century following the end of World
War II, the leading economies showed an exceptional performance in
growth of national product. Why then did the intractable, divisive issue
of economic equality return to center stage?

The most common explanation is in the political dimension. Conservative critics have joined with radical advocates in locating the impetus of the drive for economic equality, not in economic criteria themselves but rather in a natural outgrowth of the more general egalitarian
tendency. The push for economic equality is seen as the continuation,
perhaps the culmination, of the egalitarian drive originating with Rousseau. This drive was from the beginning seen by Burke and a long line of

followers as a perilous misdirection of the modernistic rationalizing spirit of which it was a part. The fact that attempted moves toward economic equality have become embroiled in an economic impasse seems to confirm that the roots of these moves must be political.

This apparent absence of economic rationale for economic egalitarianism rests on the conventional view of the growth process, specifically on the view of growth as making available a continuous addition to undifferentiated consumable goods—that is, national product as malleable in whatever form we choose to use it. This growth process has the statistical property that a relatively short period of compounding would raise the consumption of the mass of lower income groups to levels higher than would result from redistribution of all the excess resources currently accruing to top income groups. That is the crude but classical case for giving priority to growth rather than to redistribution, a case that is regularly revived in popular discussion with an undiminished air of breathtaking novelty.

The themes developed in this book qualify both the priority and the promise of economic growth in two major ways. First—the paradox of affluence—economic growth in advanced societies carries some elements of built-in frustration: the growth process, when sustained and generalized, fails to deliver its full promise. The growth process runs into social scarcity. Second—the reluctant collectivism—continuation of the growth process itself rests on certain moral preconditions that its own success has jeopardized through its individualistic ethos. Economic growth undermines its social foundations. These then are the dual social limits to growth.

Social foundations of society rest on moral legitimation. A great strength of liberal capitalism has been its ability to dispense with an explicit ethical standard for distribution of rewards. Justification is provided by the benign outcome of autonomous unregulated processes. In its modern variant, this justification is no longer dependent on the assumption of natural harmony within all aspects of a market economy. It rests rather on the capacity of the system for sustained growth. The social harmony model reappears in the dynamic context: *through time,* all benefit. But moral legitimacy on this basis cannot attach to "socially limited" growth, which is prevented from achieving the validating equalization through time, which is the promise—and thereby the moral legitimacy—of unimpeded growth.

On this view, therefore, the otherwise missing economic impetus for the recurring salience of the distributional issue emerges from the shadows. Growth is a substitute for redistribution of resources for the worse off only in its early stages, for so long as unmet biological needs retain their primacy. Beyond that point, the potential consensus behind an a-distributional policy of economic expansion is weakened. In one key sector—the positional sector—there is no such thing as leveling up. One's reward is set by one's position on the slope, and the slope itself prevents a leveling, from below as well as from above.

This explains why the issue of distribution of welfare has obstinately kept its hold. It does not mean that actions to secure more equal distribution have become increasingly acceptable. The very nature of positional competition, of the struggle for precedence and priority in a closed system or sector, involves a "demand" for inequality of a more direct kind than is involved in claims for material output. For the material claims can be satisfied by expanding the size of the pie available to all. Admittedly, such expansion itself has certain consequential implications for income distribution, for example, in the presumed effects of a particular pattern of reward on incentives to work and save. Because of these consequential effects, certain inequalities or differences in rewards can properly and not merely apologistically be seen as "functional." To the extent that inequalities add to the size of the pie available for all, they operate to the benefit of all. There is then, in principle, an optimum degree of inequality; the problem is to find it.

Positional competition, as discussed in earlier chapters, demolishes this conceptual harmony. Inequalities are now more directly connected to what individuals seek: here, one man's gain is another's loss. Those who are at the winning end or who expect to get there may now be reinforced in their determination to maintain or widen differentials in income, wealth, and economic position. Those at the losing end will have equal reason to reduce their handicap in the positional race.

V

The liberal market economy in its heyday operated in the context of a dual, compartmentalized set of demands—for collective improvement in the basic means of life and for individual elevation into the higher planes. The full bourgeois ethos had only minority application and was supported by prebourgeois conventions and morality. As the ethos has spread in important components toward universal coverage; as the general level of productivity has risen, bringing increasing pressure on positional goods and facilities; and as the tradition of prebourgeois restraint of self-seeking has receded into a more distant past—as a result of each of these tendencies, the market system has become less efficient in delivery.

Together, these several strands in the earlier analysis suggest the following conclusions. The ability of market liberalism to transmit individual economic demands and to fulfill them faithfully, smoothly, and harmoniously cannot be seen as a general characteristic, even with the aid of specific correctives of state intervention. It appears rather as a special case, applying to the transitional period in which bourgeois aspirations were limited by political, and still more, by economic restraints to a small minority and in which the underlying ethos of market society remained heavily permeated by prebourgeois morality. The internal forces released by liberal capitalism have exerted pressure for conscious justification of the distribution of economic rewards, a pressure that undermines the system's drive and equipoise. That is the current crisis of the system.

13 Inferences for Policy

If the line of analysis developed in earlier chapters is correct and pertinent, the potential implications for public policy are obviously far-reaching. Nevertheless, there are two major considerations requiring that the immediate policy inferences be kept guarded and modest. The first cautionary consideration is that there is a restricted amount we can do. The second is that there is a restricted amount we know.

I

The general line of remedy for the ills that have been diagnosed in this book is as clear as it is immediately inaccessible. Over an increasing sphere of economic and social activity, action taken by individuals in response to their own preferences and needs in the situation they face has become an inefficient or ineffective way of achieving the objectives on which these actions rest. The social rationale of individual maximization weakens as the proportionate importance of public goods grows and social scarcity becomes more pressing. Within the realm of social scarcity, individuals can come closer to achieving their objectives if they cease, together, to pursue them outright. In this sense, a shift in the invisible hand from the private into the public or communal sector is needed. Rather than pursuit of self-interest contributing to the social good, pursuit of the social good contributes to the satisfaction of self-interest. The difficulty is that the latter pursuit needs to be deliberately organized under existing standards and instincts of personal behavior. So the invisible hand is presently unavailable where it is newly needed.

The harmony of an individualistic economy is in this general sense disrupted by a shift in economic conditions that narrows the sphere in which individualistic behavior yields the desired and attainable results. The clear policy implication of this shift is an associated change in the orientation of individual behavior. Individuals' motives—why people act—can remain self-interested, provided their actions within the relevant sphere are conditioned primarily by a social interest. The purpose is served if individuals act *as if* they put the social interest first, even if they do not, and merely follow convention or the social ethic that influences individual behavior. The key shift needed is therefore in that social ethic.

Can such a shift be expected? Conflicting forces are at work. The functional need for a change in the social ethic can be expected, over time, to promote it. Deliberate pursuit of the social good could be neglected in the earlier period of industrial development. During that phase, such neglect was generally benign. Since it is at the bottom a social rationale that must validate the pursuit of individual self-interest within a society, social pressures for a widening orientation of individual actions can be expected, in general and over time, to grow.

In general and over time. But some mechanism is needed through which the changed social need is transmitted to individual actions. The trouble is that such a mechanism cannot be expected to evolve through the independent responses of individuals. As was seen in Chapter 10, the essence of the problem is rather that the situation confronting individuals independently induces them to respond defensively in a way that worsens the situation for all. That is to say, when the invisible hand fails on the economic front, it cannot be expected to organize a social corrective.

The standard liberal faith that social needs will be most effectively met through a series of piecemeal responses to an evolving situation implicitly assumes that each action in the series takes account of the consequential effects, or at least sets corrective forces in train. A natural harmony is assumed, if not pervasively then at least cumulatively over time. Challenge is relied on to produce response. This assumes away the problem at issue, where interactions between social and individual needs are malign. Piecemeal responses then make things worse. It follows that just as centralized or coordinated action is needed to relate specific individual actions to the social interest in the presence of externalities, so some measure of deliberate direction is needed to encourage reorientation of individual action in general.

This is not to deny that changes in behavior can come about only when individuals perceive the need for them, whether consciously or subconsciously. It is not to take an organic view of society as existing apart from the individuals who compose it. Rather, it is to say that individuals can perceive a need for themselves and their fellows and yet have no rational basis to act on it in isolation. The socially concerned individual then faces a dilemma between social and individual needs.

In short, collective means may be necessary to implement individual ends. It may appear individualist to ignore the possibility of this awkward condition or to deny the validity of acting on it. But there is a deep sense in which this intended rearguard defense is anti-individualist. For it denies the fundamental distinction between what individuals generally and at large can do to change their situation, and the situation that confronts people personally in the situation that currently exists. It is to reduce the possibilities of individual redress of social ills in "dilemma" cases to the cavalier and the quixotic.

This is far from saying that either individual motives or behavior can be controlled, at least without abandonment of primary liberal values. Subjugation of individual judgment on moral issues and behavioral choices to the thought of some Chairman Mao would remove the heart of individualist autonomy. Thought control remains the most horrifying threat in the collectivist intrusion. Yet if individual orientation is outside our area of influence, we are left with an impasse. We know what needs to be done and cannot or dare not do it.

One slow way out of the impasse suggests itself. While deliberate action cannot or should not be used directly to legislate and enforce a change in individual motives and behavior, it can be applied effectively and legitimately to removing obstacles to such a change. It can reduce the cost incurred by the individual, in responding to his own instincts, to orient his behavior to a social need. It should therefore be amenable to the influence of public policy. But such influence is likely to remain slow and uncertain. The working of the available instruments is not well understood; their cost in terms of other objectives no more so. Above all, their efficacy is linked in a two-way connection with changes in the standards and instincts of personal behavior. They can help catalyze such changes in the springs of behavior, without which the instruments themselves may be ineffective or even perverse.

This mutual interdependence between the existent social morality and the means of adapting it impedes any speedy resolution of the tensions involved. It also drastically limits what can be expected from technical manipulation alone. Yet economic management, as it has been developed in the past generation, has relied wholly on such manipulation. The radical aspect of the appropriate solutions for the tensions diagnosed in this book may be precisely their imprecise, general, and evolving form. The prime need is not new instruments but a change in the climate of their use. The radical change needed is to accept that.

The first fundamental step therefore is diagnosis and recognition. This book has argued that the extension of welfare through economic growth is subject to social limits that are neglected in the standard analysis. In the long run, the challenge this presents is to surmount those limits. The immediate possibility and need is to lessen the damage caused by neglecting their existence. This damage takes the form of frustration of expectations, when the expected fruits of growth fail to appear. It also involves potential waste of resources devoted to competition that can yield no additional prizes. Neglect of social limits, therefore, has a cost separate from the constrictions imposed by the limits themselves. Not recognizing the barriers, we stumble into them. Removal or extension of the limits would solve both aspects of the problem, and this is, in principle, possible where organizational factors are at issue, such as the guidance of individual behavior to responses that take account of subsequent interactions. Other social limits, such as those deriving from pure scarcities of both physical and social kinds, have to be accepted as permanent fixtures. But here too recognition of the limits can help society to accommodate to them.

For the short or medium term, therefore, the policy issues are to accommodate policy to the social limits that currently exist and to reduce the cost that faces individuals in orienting their actions toward social objectives. Both of these courses are steps on a long march.

The second consideration requiring that policy inferences be kept guarded or modest is the restricted extent of the present analysis itself. The analysis of the preceding chapters, unfortunately, remains indeterminate at two key points. The first indeterminacy reflects the lack of a precise criterion for economic efficiency through use of collective action: we do not have a firm grasp on the full implications of collective action, so that the potential inefficiency that can be seen in its omission cannot be firmly categorized as actual inefficiency or waste. The second indeterminacy resides in the lack of a quantitative dimension of the critique: it has not been found possible to estimate over what proportion of economic activity social limits to growth are in play. Inferences for policy must be accordingly circumspect. The nature of the disease is known; its extent and the dangers of its antibody are not.

The disease, in brief, is the blight on individual action as an effective means to individually desired results. The antibody, collective action, has costs and adverse side effects of its own. Accordingly, there is a premium on any corrective that avoids or minimizes this countervailing damage.

II

Social limits to growth intensify the distributional struggle. They increase the importance of relative place. They intensify pressure for equalization of economic resources on the part of the worse off and stiffen resistance to equalization by the better off. They thereby reduce the chances of securing agreement to redistributive measures that add to the perceived welfare of all individuals because those on the paying end gain satisfaction of various kinds from the increased welfare of the recipients.[1] The sphere in which individual economic striving contributes to social welfare and social harmony is reduced. The distributional struggle acquires a dangerous rationale. It is increasingly pursued, not only individ-

[1] Known in the economic literature as "Pareto optimal" redistribution.

ualistically but through group action. Society is exposed to the struggles of competing groups seeking to increase their members' share of available economic rewards, legitimating their actions by the primacy of self-interest. The resulting divisive tensions have no obvious solution in an economy driven by an individualistic ethic, and therefore threaten to destroy it. How can these tensions be contained?

One broad solution which is propounded by the economic libertarian school of Hayek and Friedman is to deal with the distributional issue by taking it off the agenda.[2] Since no deliberate basis for distribution of economic rewards can be agreed upon, the arbitrary basis of the outcome of luck, personal effort, and heredity is the sole foundation for social stability. The liberal system in this approach provides open entry to the starting gate of the race: equal access as distinct from equal chance. It avoids the snare of equal opportunity and its corollary, a just outcome. The distributional conflict is depoliticized. This does not, of course, eliminate the conflict; the idea is that the conflict is suppressed and tamed by removing it from the sphere of policy action. The economic outcome is legitimized, not as just but as unjustifiable. Those who have drawn trumps in the existing allocation of economic endowments are merely fortunate, those who have drawn blanks unfortunate; all will be damaged by attempts to get a legitimated distribution by deliberate adjustment.

An alternative approach is open to those who consider the benign neglect of economic equity as impracticable, dangerous, or morally unacceptable but yet seek to maintain the benefits of a decentralized economy and of individual economic choice over a wide sphere. This alternative approach accepts the need to bring distributional issues into the turbulent political arena but seeks through policy action to reduce the turbulence. In Keynes's well-known characterization: the game can be played for smaller stakes. The crush on the positional sector has now added a new dimension to this issue. Smaller stakes in the outcome of the competition for place could help reduce the crush. At least up to a point, a reduction in positional competition has general benefits in reducing unnecessary obstacles that are a form of social waste. Here, therefore, smaller stakes offer a gain in equity of distribution, not at the expense of efficient allocation of resources, which is the traditional formulation of the choice, but with the potential for an improvement.

The further twist given by positional competition to the distributional struggle can be tackled at its source by seeking to reduce—but not eliminate—individual competition in the positional sector. Competition for place has a number of positive aspects. It contributes to internal efficiency in matching differing individual wants and capacities and in stim-

---

[2] Friedman, *Capitalism and Freedom*; Hayek, *The Constitution of Liberty*.

ulating improved performance; and the chase itself is a source of enjoyment for some. The negative aspects comprise the wasteful lengthening of the obstacle course that has to be run to fulfill individual wants, the frustration of reasonable expectations, and the destructive aspects of the chase. It is obvious that to some extent the benefits and drawbacks of competition for place are bound in the same package and have to be accepted or rejected together. But only to some extent. The benefits derive from the existence of some minimum of competition and of choice open to individuals, whereas the drawbacks derive from the false prospectus of the competition—from the false signals given to individuals seeking to optimize their own position. If the extent of individual striving for position can be curtailed in such a way as to preserve the beneficial minimum of competition and choice, an unqualified benefit should ensue.

This approach, together with the general benefits that accrue from reducing the stakes, suggests a broad guideline for policy. It is to reduce the incidental benefits from positional precedence. The operational objective should be to pare down the contestants to those who most value the benefits that cannot be obtained in other ways. Which benefits are incidental and which intrinsic will vary from case to case, and in some degree among differing potential contestants. But some broad inferences can be made on the direction that policy should take.

The most important positional sector, because of its major influence on the demand for education, is what we have termed positional jobs. These are the jobs at and near the pinnacle of professions and within business. These jobs, in all advanced societies, currently exert a double magnetism. They offer both relatively high pay and relatively large nonfinancial benefits—work satisfaction deriving from either the nature of the job or the status it carries in the community or both. This status may sometimes be partly linked to the relatively high pay itself, but there is now a good deal of evidence to indicate that this connection is a loose one; the high status of university professors compared with businessmen is perhaps the most prominent example. As long as the nonfinancial attractions of positional jobs are strong, the salaries attached to them can be regarded as incidental benefits. Money can be earned elsewhere; the attractions of the job can be gained only from doing it. A reduction in the monetary attraction can be expected to reduce total demand for such jobs by shedding potential applicants for whom the pay advantage is dominant.

A relative pay reduction of this kind would therefore tend to reduce the extent of competition for the limited number of top jobs and also to alter the composition of the contestants. These would now consist, to a greater extent, of people predominantly attracted to the job itself. Whether this shift would involve deterioration in the quality of applicants, in the sense of capacity to do the job, would depend in important degree on the range of occupations over which the policy-induced reduction in pay was spread. A reduction applied to a single profession or industry would be most exposed to such loss, as the most competent contestants could then easily find alternative employment, perhaps intensifying positional competition where they were successful. A reduction in relative pay of positional jobs would be far more effective if applied on a national basis, and still more so if put in practice internationally.

The means of such a reduction could take a variety of forms. One possibility is a payroll tax related to the size of differentials in pay within the firm, combined with direct action by government and other public sector employers to reduce differentials applying to executive and high professional positions. The effectiveness of such measures would depend in important degree on their acceptance by the public. Deliberately contrived avoidance of these and related taxes would have to be considered antisocial in the same vein as legal embezzlement. To this extent, implementation of such measures would need to go hand in hand with public understanding of the social need for them.

The required fiscal action would, in part, be merely a substitute for the response that might be expected from market forces to the expansion in the availability of competent personnel. This market response is inhibited by imperfect information and other market impairments. Because of these influences, an increase in the potential supply of members for top jobs lengthens the obstacle course and the labor line required to attain them, instead of reducing wage and salary differentials. As a result, economic advantages in various dimensions, notably financial remuneration and work satisfaction, continue to be often cumulative rather than offsetting. Pleasant or stimulating work goes along with high pay rather than taking its place.

The case for a reduction of income differentials in this and other ways has traditionally been argued on the basis of society's presumed "taste" for greater equality. The phenomenon of positional competition provides two additional arguments. The first, referred to earlier, relates to improved allocation of resources rather than their redistribution. Reducing the financial return from top jobs will reduce the monetary value of educational credentials that are sought to gain access to these jobs. This should help to counter excess investment in acquisition of educational credentials. It should also improve the efficiency and consumption benefits of education itself, as it would help sort entrants to higher education increasingly in favor of those who enjoyed the education itself and/ or the job to which it led. Turning education into a vocational test has involved a double loss, to education as well as to its unprofiting victims. It is another facet of the modern affliction of doing even luxury things not for their own sake but as a means to something else.

The second additional argument for a squeezing of top salaries that follows from the analysis of positional competition is a new distributional consideration, derived from the heightened significance of relative income and the "connectedness" of the income distribution throughout the range. To the extent that we do not merely feel worse off but are worse off when people ahead of us have more income, differentials are a larger provocation and source of potential financial and social instability than they are under even-handed growth.

Admittedly, the same influence makes people enjoying the positive differentials more reluctant to see them reduced. They, however, will generally have a relatively larger stake in preservation of social stability, if only because the market exploitation of their special skills depends on a degree of division of labor which is possible only in a highly complex society. The airline pilot, the industrial manager, and the administrator are much farther from the incomes they could rely on if society broke down than are the laborer and the craftsman.

But this negative consideration is likely to be compelling only in situations of extreme stress, and then only when social cohesion persists among the group for which collective sacrifice offers individual gain. A positive supporting influence, operating directly on individuals, would be a reduction in the significance of relative income in its command over other positional goods, that is, besides the top jobs themselves. This would be achieved by making access to such goods less attainable with money and more available without it—that is to say, by partially removing positional goods from the commercial sector and making them more available through public access or public allocation on a nonmarket basis. Education or pleasant environment financed from general taxation rather than from charges to users are prominent examples. Provision of public access to scarce facilities in such ways would be one important means of reducing the cost to the individual of socially oriented action. Relinquishment of some positional advantage would then involve a smaller disproportionate burden to the individual who volunteered it. The same influence is achieved if the goods or facilities involved have no element of specifically social scarcity; health services are the most prominent examples.

Positional competition has hidden costs for others, and over time for the individual involved; and it intensifies the distributional struggle to a potentially dangerous point. In short, it threatens to displace Smithian harmony by Hobbesian strife and is thereby a dangerous element to leave in the Smithian sector of individualistic optimization.

III

The principle of restricting certain goods and facilities from private appropriation has long been accepted in liberal societies. In the developed urbanized society, private property is validated not as a natural right, but for its contribution to social efficiency and social harmony. The form and extent of property rights have undergone long and continuous modification on this count. Thus effective rights over ownership and the use of capital have been severely qualified by taxation and by direct restrictions on what owners of capital assets may do with them, for example, through limitations on the right to hire and fire.

Even under the most favorable conditions for market society, certain things have to be kept off the market. The most important items not for sale are key elements in the constitutional fabric, such as judicial and political decisions. But to these are added some of the scarcest positional goods: historical monuments, outstanding natural scenery, the foreshore that provides access to the sea. More generally, the rights pertaining to private property in socially scarce or otherwise sensitive facilities are in a continuous process of evolution, with a clear recent tendency toward greater restriction. The major example is the need for public approval of new building through zoning regulations and planning procedures. The recent establishment in the United States of public rights of way over privately owned land giving access to the foreshore in a number of states is another significant example.

Less obviously in the same category have been the series of measures, part legislative and part judicial, that have attempted to achieve both racial and social integration in the public school system in the United States, and the parallel efforts in Britain to establish state schooling on a basis of comprehensive rather than selective schools. Although these measures have had widely varying success and have left the major escape hatch of the private school sector intact, and at points strengthened, they probably have reduced the extent to which advantage in schooling is associated with parents' income and wealth. In this sense, these measures can be considered, by their proponents as well as by their critics, as setting a precedent for a wider insulation of educational competition from the power of the purse.

The main objection to more extensive measures in this area is the damage this would entail for educational diversity and individual choice. These have a value of their own in providing alternative approaches to education and catering to differing individual needs. But, as is well established, an additional effect of educational diversity and local choice is to provide faster tracks for those enjoying advantages of economic resources and social background. Such effects may be deliberate or incidental, but they will tend to flow from the opportunity afforded to parents and students seeking to make the best of their own situation—an opportunity that will be more costly to forego if offered to others than if available to only oneself. (Compare the relative benefit and burden incurred by the first and last middle-class student to exit from a city to a suburban school.) So diversity and individual choice in education are in present conditions attained at the cost of a widening of economic and social inequalities.

Here again, the conflict could be lessened if the ultimate stakes were made smaller. If education were made a less sure means to acquisition or perpetuation of financial advantages, there would be less reason to restrict competition and diversity within education on distributional grounds. People would then be more likely to choose a particular school or course of education because it fitted their individual needs, rather than as a fast track to high-paying jobs.

In this way, measures to reduce the financial attractions of the most sought-after jobs, that is, to loosen the connection between education and wealth, would avoid some of the conflicts involved in present-day measures to loosen the connection between wealth and education. Attaching less cream to scarce positions should make them less sought after and thereby relieve the crush to acquire them. The more this is done, the less the disadvantage to society of leaving individual striving and competition to follow their own course.

The conclusions for policy of this range of considerations may be summed up as follows. Excess competition in the positional sector has been seen to involve important external costs. If these costs are allowed to become large, a point will come where the damage to society appears too great to justify the individual freedom of action that results in such damage. The individual freedom will then be seen to be socially destructive and ultimately self-destructive, and pressure to restrict such freedom will become irresistible.

The development of the managed liberal economy contains a long line of precedents for such action, as previously mentioned. Freedom to undertake economic transactions can serve its purpose and retain its social rationale only where the interaction of individual transactions operates in a benign way, or is made to do so by a guided invisible hand. Reducing the stakes for which the positional competition is played is probably the most promising available means of such guidance here. It may be the only means of ensuring the continuance of individual competition in this sphere. Alternative methods of allocation are already in place. Restrictions on educational choice available to the individual provide one example. Another, more drastic device is use of quotas to preassign a certain number or proportion of valued positions to members of a given race or otherwise defined group. Ethnic or class "quotas" should be seen as a sharp advance warning of the illiberal pressures that must be expected when individual competition for limited opportunities produces strongly skewed results.

More generally, the fact of social scarcity gives individual appropriation in the positional sector an insecure social rationale. The ultimate justification of the pursuit of individual economic interests and the establishment of rights in private property is that the resources available to all are thereby increased. This connection is missing in the positional sector. It is true that current alternatives to individual maximization are subject to social costs of their own. Collective provision under an individualistic ethos has its own contradictions. Structural shifts in the economy have induced progressive and cumulatively very large increases in public expenditures; but the persistence of individualistic economic orientation has eroded the intended results. This lack or unreadiness of satisfactory alternatives, as has been seen, limits the implications that the weakening of social rationale for individual maximization in the positional sector has for immediate policy. Material growth under the drive of liberal capitalism leads to this impasse. But the pressure of circumstances creates its own opening, and policy actions at selected points can help break the stalemate.

IV

A major adjustment needs to be made in the legitimate scope for individual economic striving. Individual economic freedom still has to be adjusted to the demands of majority participation. The traditional availabilities, grounded by circumstances in minority status, now represent an overload. In this sense, the excess expectations in modern economies are the traditional expectations of the occupants of their highest echelons. For these have set an unattainable general standard. It is the haves who expect too much.

The liberal opportunity state now appears in much diminished prospect. Its attractions in themselves are undiminished. What has to be scaled down is the possibility of extending them to the populace as a whole. Capitalism has indeed brought the silk stockings that were the privilege of queens to every factory girl; in this sphere and in this phase it has been a great leveler, as Schumpeter so evocatively showed.[3] The achievement unfortunately does not enable it to repeat the performance with nonmaterial aspects of privilege, past or present.

This in effect returns the political choice to the issue that nineteenth-century liberals mostly ducked: the choice between preserving the full fruits of individual opportunity and unrestricted individual choice available to a minority, as against making the adaptations necessary to extend these fruits to the majority. Liberal-conservatives, from Burke to Hayek, have always drawn the limits around the liberal offering and warned of the dangers of dilution from its unnatural extension. This conservative strand of liberalism has implicitly acknowledged the social limits to growth. What is here offered to the majority is not validation of its condition but a chance to rise from it. In the imagery of R. H. Tawney, the consolation for the tadpoles is that a few of them, too, may elevate them-

---

[3] Schumpeter, *Capitalism, Socialism and Democracy*, p. 67.

selves into frogs.[4] If a reversion to this approach is now morally and politically unthinkable, it can yet be seen to incorporate an economic realism that is lacking in the more sanguine faith that all should eventually make the ascent.

If the objective of universal participation is not abandoned, the constraints set by social limits will inexorably make society more dependent on collective provision and collective orientation. This in turn demands some adjustment in perceptions. What is involved here is not a revolutionary change in attitudes, the visionary "change in human nature," but an adjustment of degree. Individual behavior in liberal societies has always been oriented to social needs in certain sectors of behavior. The supposition that individual behavior in our present societies is oriented exclusively to private objectives has been seen to be refuted by the working of our political institutions. The issue has been well put by an economist who is himself within the orthodox classical tradition.

> In any actual world there will be, for the individual, cases in which he can give free rein to his personal predilections, and others in which it will be hoped that he will draw upon his moral resources and act in accordance with ultimate ethical values rather than indulge his own preferences. The initial problem, for the individual, will be one of learning how to distinguish readily between these two cases; the subsequent problem will be of finding out what decision to make where it has been determined that self-interest is not to be allowed free rein. One of the sins committed by the glorification of economic freedom has been precisely that it has tended to confuse individuals as to where the boundary between the two cases lies.[5]

Social scarcity shifts the boundary, annexing a part of the sphere of legitimate self-interest to the sphere of social obligation. And it increases the danger that neglect of this social sphere will corrode the basis necessary for pursuit of private objectives in a market economy. The glorification of economic freedom thereby threatens to destroy it, much as breast-beating patriotism all but destroyed the nation state.

V

The analysis presented here has been seen to have definite but restricted implications for policy. It points to dangers in the current line of advance and suggests a direction that looks more promising. It does not offer an operational blueprint for such advance. Faith that such a blueprint must be available—that specific operational solutions for social

---

[4] Tawney, *Equality*, p. 105.

[5] William S. Vickrey, "The Goals of Economic Life," in A. D. Ward, ed., *Goals of Economic Life* (New York: Harper, 1953), reprinted as "An Exchange of Questions between Economics and Philosophy," in E. S. Phelps, ed., *Economic Justice* (Harmondsworth, Eng.: Penguin Education, 1973), p. 60.

problems must be there to be found—is an obstinate and probably fortunate remnant of the belief in progress: it has been called the nonfiction version of the happy ending. This is a part of the pragmatic faith in piecemeal incrementalism, a faith that is as Utopian as the Utopianism it seeks to replace. The latter conception rests on a benign implementation of a planned order of society; the former rests on the benign interaction of spontaneous actions and piecemeal tinkering with their results. The hidden Utopian assumption is that progressive evolution will look after us and meanwhile there is always some way of tinkering that will plug the holes.

This book has suggested that the prime economic problem now facing the economically advanced societies is a structural need to pull back the bounds of economic self-advancement. That in turn requires a deliberate validation of the basis of income and wealth distribution that these economies have managed to do without in a transition period that is ending. Piecemeal expedients now have little to offer by themselves. This does not deny them their place but makes them secondary to a shift of view and of understanding. We may be near the limit of explicit social organization possible without a supporting social morality. Additional correctives in its absence simply do not take. That is the decisive weakness of the purely technocratic approach to keeping the market economy to its social purpose.

Society is in turmoil because the only legitimacy it has is social justice; and the transition to a just society is an uncertain road strewn with injustice. This is the awkward stage that has been reached through the working out of the modern western enlightenment. The central fact of the modern situation is the need to justify. That is its moral triumph and its unsolved technical problem. The need to justify imposes drastic limits on the set of feasible solutions. Solutions that work have traditionally dominated solutions that have ethical appeal. The distinction is now blurred: to work it must be ethically defensible. Who were the realists in Vietnam? For the overriding economic problem discussed in this book, the first necessity is not technical devices but the public acceptance necessary to make them work.

References

Index

References

Aaron, Henry, and McGuire, Martin. "Public Goods and Income Distribution," *Econometrica* (November 1970).

Abrams, Mark. "Subjective Social Indicators," *Social Trends*, no. 4 (1973).

Akerlof, G. A. "The Market for 'Lemons': Qualitative Uncertainty and the Market Mechanism," *Quarterly Journal of Economics* (August 1970).

Aronson, J. Richard. "Voting with Your Feet," *New Society* (August 29, 1974).

Arrow, Kenneth J. "Gifts and Exchanges," *Philosophy and Public Affairs* (Summer 1972).

_____ "Higher Education as a Filter," *Journal of Public Economics* (July 1973).

_____ "Some Ordinalist-Utilitarian Notes on Rawls's Theory of Justice," *Journal of Philosophy* (May 1973).

_____ "Uncertainty and the Welfare Economics of Medical Care," *American Economic Review* (December 1962).

Atkinson, A. B. "Poverty and Income Inequality in Britain," in Dorothy Wedderburn, ed., *Poverty, Inequality and Class Structure* (Cambridge, Eng.: Cambridge University Press, 1974).

Bachrach, Peter. *The Theory of Democratic Elitism* (1967) (London: University of London Press, 1969).

Bagehot, Walter. *The English Constitution* (1867) (London: Collins Fontana, 1963).

Balassa, Bela. "The Purchasing Power Parity Doctrine: A Reappraisal," *Journal of Political Economy* (December 1964).

Baran, Paul A., and Sweezy, Paul M. *Monopoly Capital* (New York: Monthly Review Press, 1966).

Barry, Brian. *The Liberal Theory of Justice* (Oxford: Clarendon, 1973).

_____ *Sociologists, Economists, and Democracy* (New York: Collier-Macmillan, 1970).

Baumol, William J. "The Dynamics of Urban Problems and Its Policy Implications," in Maurice Peston and Bernard Corry, eds., *Essays in Honour of Lord Robbins* (London: Weidenfeld and Nicolson, 1972).

_____ "Environmental Protection and Income Distribution," in Harold M. Hochman and George E. Peterson, eds., *Redistribution Through Public Choice* (New York: Columbia University Press, 1974).

_____ and Bowen, William G. *Performing Arts: The Economic Dilemma* (New York: Twentieth Century Fund, 1966; Cambridge, Mass.: MIT Press, 1968).

Becker, Gary S. "A Theory of Marriage," *Journal of Political Economy* (July/August 1973 and March/April 1974).

_____ "A Theory of the Allocation of Time," *Economic Journal* (September 1965).

Beckerman, Wilfred. *In Defence of Economic Growth* (London: Cape, 1974).

_____ " 'Environment', 'Needs' and Real Income Comparisons," *Review of Income and Wealth* (December 1972).

_____ "Sex and the Falling Rate of Profit," *New Statesman* (July 20, 1973).

Beigel, Hugo G. "Romantic Love," *American Sociological Review* (June 1951).

Bell, Daniel. *The Coming of Post-Industrial Society* (London: Heinemann, 1974).

Bellah, Robert N. "The Sociology of Religion," *International Encyclopaedia of the Social Sciences*, vol. 13 (London: Macmillan, 1968).

Beveridge, William, ed., *Tariffs: The Case Examined* (London: Longmans Green, 1932).

Bielckus, C. L. and others. *Second Homes in England and Wales* (Ashford, Eng.: Wye College School of Rural Economics and Related Studies, 1972).

Blaug, M., ed. *Economics of Education*, vol. I (Harmondsworth, Eng.: Penguin, 1968).

Bliss, C. J. "R. M. Titmuss, The Gift Relationship: from Human Blood to Social Policy," book review in *Journal of Public Economics* (April 1972).

Bottomore, T. B. *Elites and Society* (1964) (Harmondsworth, Eng.: Penguin, 1966).

Boulding, Kenneth E. "Economics as a Moral Science," *American Economic Review* (March 1969).

_____ *The Economy of Love and Fear* (Belmont, Calif.: Wadsworth Publishing Co., 1973).

_____ "Notes on a Theory of Philanthropy," in Frank G. Dickinson, ed., *Philanthropy and Public Policy* (New York: National Bureau of Economic Research, 1962).

_____ and Pfaff, Martin, eds. *Redistribution to the Rich and the Poor* (Belmont, Calif.: Wadsworth Publishing Co., 1972).

Bowen, William G. "Assessing the Economic Contribution of Education" (1963), in M. Blaug, ed., *Economics of Education*, vol. I (Harmondsworth, Eng.: Penguin, 1968).

Bowles, Samuel. "Understanding Unequal Economic Opportunity," *American Economic Review* (May 1973).

Bowley, Arthur. *Three Studies on the National Income* (London School of Economics [1919-1927], 1938).

Boyd, David. *Elites and Their Education* (Windsor, Eng.: NFER Publishing, 1973).

Bradford, D. F., and Kelejian, H. H. "An Econometric Model of the Flight to the Suburbs," *Journal of Political Economy* (May/June 1973).

Brittan, Samuel. *Capitalism and the Permissive Society* (London: Macmillan, 1973).

_____ *The Treasury under the Tories* (Harmondsworth, Eng.: Penguin, 1964).

Buchanan, James M. *Costs and Choice* (Chicago: Markham Publishing Co., 1969).

_____ The Demand and Supply of Public Goods (Chicago: Rand McNally, 1968).

_____ "An Economic Theory of Clubs," Economica (February 1965).

_____ and Tullock, Gordon. The Calculus of Consent (Ann Arbor: University of Michigan Press, 1962).

Butler, David, and Stokes, Donald. Political Change in Britain (1969) (Harmondsworth, Eng.: Penguin, 1971).

Chinoy, Ely. Automobile Workers and the American Dream (New York: Doubleday, 1955).

Clawson, Marion, and Hall, Peter. Planning and Urban Growth: An Anglo-American Comparison (Baltimore: Johns Hopkins University Press, 1973).

Clout, H. D. "Second Homes in France," Journal of the Town Planning Institute (December 1969).

Coats, A. W., ed. The Classical Economists and Economic Policy (London: Methuen, 1971).

Cole, H. S. D. and others. Thinking About the Future (London: Chatto and Windus for Sussex University Press, 1973).

Comte, Auguste. System of Positive Policy, vol. 2 (1851) (New York: Franklin, 1875).

Cooper, Michael H., and Culyer, Anthony J. "The Economics of Giving and Selling Blood," in Armen A. Alchian and others, The Economics of Charity (London: Institute of Economic Affairs, 1973).

Crean, John F. "Foregone Earnings and the Demand for Education: Some Empirical Evidence," Canadian Journal of Economics (February 1973).

Crosland, Anthony. The Future of Socialism (London: Cape, 1956; rev. ed., 1964).

_____ "A Social Democratic Britain," in his Socialism Now (London: Cape, 1974).

Crowther, Geoffrey. Economics for Democrats (London: Thomas Nelson, 1939).

Dahl, Robert A., and Lindblom, Charles E. Politics, Economics, and Welfare (New York: Harper and Row, 1953; Torchbook ed., 1963).

David, E. J. "The Exploding Demand for Recreational Property," Land Economics (May 1969).

Denison, E. F. Why Growth Rates Differ (Washington, D.C.: The Brookings Institution, 1967).

Diamond, Robert S. "A Self-Portrait of the Chief Executive," Fortune (May 1970).

Downing, Peter, and Dower, Michael. Second Homes in England and Wales (London: Countryside Commission, 1974).

Downs, Anthony. An Economic Theory of Democracy (New York: Harper and Row, 1957).

Duesenberry, James S. Income, Saving and the Theory of Consumer Behavior (Cambridge, Mass.: Harvard University Press, 1949).

Duncan, Graeme. Marx and Mill: Two Views of Social Conflict and Social Harmony (Cambridge, Eng.: Cambridge University Press, 1973).

Durbin, Evan. The Politics of Democratic Socialism (London: Routledge, 1940).

Durkheim, Emile. The Elementary Forms of the Religious Life (1915) (London: Allen and Unwin, 1971).

Easterlin, Richard A. "Does Economic Growth Improve the Human Lot?" in Paul A. David and Melvin W. Reder, eds., *Nations and Households in Economic Growth: Essays in Honor of Moses Abramovitz* (Stanford, Calif.: Stanford University Press, 1972).

Frankel, S. Herbert. " 'Psychic' and 'Accounting' Concepts of Income and Welfare" (1953), in R. H. Parker and G. C. Harcourt, eds., *Readings in the Concept and Measurement of Income* (Cambridge, Eng.: Cambridge University Press, 1969).

Freeman, Richard B. "Overinvestment in College Training?" *Journal of Human Resources*, 10 (Summer 1975).

_____ "Supply and Salary Adjustments to the Science Manpower Market: Physics, 1948-1973," Harvard Institute of Economic Research Discussion Paper 318, September 1973.

Friedman, Milton. *Capitalism and Freedom* (Chicago: University of Chicago Press, 1962).

Gagnon, John H. "Prostitution," *International Encyclopaedia of the Social Sciences*, vol. 12 (London: Macmillan, 1968).

Galbraith, John Kenneth. *The Affluent Society* (London: Hamish Hamilton, 1958).

_____ *Economics and the Public Purpose* (London: Andre Deutsch, 1974).

_____ *The New Industrial State* (Boston: Houghton Mifflin, 1967).

Giddens, Anthony. *The Class Structure of the Advanced Societies* (London: Hutchinson University Library, 1973).

Gintis, Herbert. "A Radical Analysis of Welfare Economics and Individual Development," *Quarterly Journal of Economics* (November 1972).

Goldthorpe, John. "Industrial Relations in Great Britain: A Critique of Reformism," Columbia University Conference, March 1974.

_____ and Lockwood, David. *The Affluent Worker*, vols. 1-3 (Cambridge, Eng.: Cambridge University Press, 1968 and 1969).

Goode, William J. "The Economics of Non-monetary Variables," *Journal of Political Economy* (March/April 1974).

Gordon, Scott. "The Close of the Galbraithian System," *Journal of Political Economy* (July/August 1968).

_____ "The Ideology of Laissez-Faire," in A. W. Coats, ed., *The Classical Economists and Economic Policy* (London: Methuen, 1971).

_____ "The London *Economist* and the High Tide of Laissez-Faire," *Journal of Political Economy* (December 1955).

Gramlich, E., and Kushel, Patricia. *Educational Performance Contracting* (Washington, D.C.: The Brookings Institution, 1975).

Greater London Council. *Movement in London* (1969).

Haavelmo, Trygve. "Some Observations on Welfare and Economic Growth," in W. A. Eltis and others, eds., *Induction, Growth and Trade* (Oxford: Clarendon Press, 1970).

_____ "Time in Economic Life," *Quarterly Journal of Economics* (November 1973).

Halsey, A. H. "Education and Social Class in 1972," in Kathleen Jones, ed., *Year Book of Social Policy in Britain, 1972* (London: Routledge and Kegan Paul, 1973).

Hardin, G. "The Tragedy of the Commons," *Science* (1968).

Harrod, Roy Forbes. *The Life of John Maynard Keynes* (1951) (London: Macmillan, 1963).

_____ "The Possibility of Economic Satiety—Use of Economic Growth for Improving the Quality of Education and Leisure," in *Problems of United States Economic Development* (New York: Committee for Economic Development, 1958), I, 207-213.

Hayek, Friedrich A. *The Constitution of Liberty* (London: Routledge and Kegan Paul, 1960).

_____ "The Price System as a Mechanism for Using Knowledge," *American Economic Review* (September 1945), in Morris Bornstein, ed., *Comparative Economic Systems* (Chicago: Richard D. Irwin, 1965).

Heller, Joseph. *Catch-22* (1955) (New York: Dell, 1970).

Heller, Walter W. "Economic Growth and Ecology— An Economist's View," *Monthly Labor Review* (November 1971).

Hirsch, Fred. "Empty Shelves on the Market Counter," *The Banker* (June 1973).

Hollander, Samuel. *The Economics of Adam Smith* (London: Heinemann, 1973).

Jencks, Christopher. *Inequality* (New York: Basic Books, 1973).

Jenkins, Roy. *Asquith* (London: Collins, 1964).

Johnson, Elizabeth. "The Collected Writings of John Maynard Keynes: Some Visceral Reactions," in Michael Parkin and A. R. Nobay, eds., *Essays in Modern Economics* (London: Longman, 1975).

Johnson, Harry G. "Cambridge in the 1950s," *Encounter* (January 1974).

_____ "The Economic Approach to Social Questions," *Economica* (February 1968).

_____ "The Keynesian Revolution and the Monetarist Counter-Revolution," *American Economic Review* (May 1971).

_____ "The Political Economy of Opulence," in his *Money, Trade and Economic Growth* (Cambridge, Mass.: Harvard University Press, 1967).

_____ *The Theory of Income Distribution* (London: Gray-Mills, 1973).

Johnson, Samuel. *A Journey to the Western Islands of Scotland* (New Haven: Yale University Press, 1971).

Jouvenel, Bertrand de. "Organisation du travail et l'amenagement de l'existence," *Free University Quarterly*, 7 (August 1959).

Juster, Thomas. "A Framework for the Measurement of Economic and Social Performance," in Milton Moss, ed., *The Measurement of Economic and Social Performance* (New York: National Bureau of Economic Research, 1973).

Kahn, Alfred E. "The Tyranny of Small Decisions: Market Failures, Imperfections, and the Limits of Economics," *Kyklos* (1966).

Kahn, Herman, and Wiener, Anthony. *The Year 2000* (New York: Macmillan, 1967).

Katona, George, Strumpel, Burkhard, and Zahn, Ernest. *Aspirations and Affluence* (New York: McGraw-Hill, 1971).

Keynes, John Maynard. *Collected Writings*, 16 vols. (London: St. Martin, 1971-1973).

Knight, Frank H. "Ethics and the Economic Interpretation," in *The Ethics of Competition* (London: Allen and Unwin, 1951).

_____ "Some Fallacies in the Interpretation of Social Cost," *Quarterly Journal of Economics* (1924).

Kristol, Irving. "Capitalism, Socialism and Nihilism," *The Public Interest* (Spring 1973).

Kropotkin, P. *Mutual Aid* (London: Heinemann, 1904).

Kuznets, Simon. "Economic Growth and Income Inequality," *American Economic Review* (March 1955), in his *Economic Growth and Structure* (London: Heinemann, 1966).

_____ *Modern Economic Growth* (New Haven: Yale University Press, 1966).

_____ "The Share and Structure of Consumption," *Economic Development and Cultural Change*, 10 (January 1962), Part II.

Lancaster, Kelvin J. "A New Approach to Consumer Theory," *Journal of Political Economy*, 74 (1966), 132-157, reprinted as "Goods Aren't Goods," in A. S. C. Ehrenberg and F. G. Pyatt, eds., *Consumer Behavior* (Harmondsworth, Eng.: Penguin, 1971).

Leibenstein, Harvey. "Toward a Significantly (But Not Radically) New Theory of Consumption," Harvard Institute of Economic Research Discussion Paper 343, February 1974.

Levitt, Theodore. "The Lonely Crowd and the Economic Man," *Quarterly Journal of Economics* (February 1956).

Linder, Staffan B. *The Harried Leisure Class* (New York: Columbia University Press, 1970).

Lockwood, David. *The Black Coated Worker* (London: Allen and Unwin, 1958).

Macfie, A. L. "The Invisible Hand in the 'Theory of Moral Sentiments,' " in *The Individual in Society* (London: Allen and Unwin, 1967).

MacIntyre, Alasdair. *Marxism and Christianity* (1953) (Harmondsworth, Eng.: Penguin, 1971).

McKean, Roland N. "Growth vs. No-Growth: An Evaluation," in Mancur Olson and Hans H. Landsberg, eds., *The No-Growth Society* (London: Woburn Press, 1975).

_____ "Time in Economic Life: Comment," *Quarterly Journal of Economics* (November 1973).

Mackenzie, Gavin. *The Aristocracy of Labor* (Cambridge, Eng.: Cambridge University Press, 1973).

Macmillan, Harold. *The Middle Way* (London: Macmillan, 1938).

Macpherson, C. B. *The Political Theory of Possessive Individualism* (Oxford: Clarendon, 1962).

Macrae, Norman. "The Future of International Business," *The Economist* (January 22, 1972).

_____ *Sunshades in October* (London: Allen and Unwin, 1963).

Maine, Sir Henry. *Ancient Law* (1861) (London: Murray, 1894).

Malthus, Thomas. *An Essay on Population* (1798) (London: Dent, 1914 and 1960).

Marris, Robin. *The Economic Theory of Managerial Capitalism* (London: Macmillan, 1964).

_____ ed. *The Corporate Society* (London: Macmillan, 1974).

Marshall, Alfred. "The Future of the Working Classes" (1873), in A. C. Pigou, ed., *Memorials of Alfred Marshall* (London: Macmillan, 1925).

_____ *Principles of Economics* (1920), 8th ed. (London: Macmillan, 1969).

Marwick, Arthur. *Britain in the Century of Total War, 1900-60* (London: Bodley Head, 1968).

Marx, Karl. *Capital,* vol. I (London: Dent, 1951).

_____ *Critique of the Gotha Programme* (1875) (New York: International Publishers, 1966).

_____ *Early Writings,* ed. T. B. Bottomore (New York: McGraw-Hill, 1964).

_____ *Grundrisse* (London: Pelican Marx Library, 1973).

_____ *The Poverty of Philosophy* (London: Lawrence and Wishart, 1955).

Matthews, Robin. "Comment," in *Economic Growth* (New York: National Bureau of Economic Research, 1972), pp. 87-92.

Meade, James E. *The Intelligent Radical's Guide to Economic Policy: The Mixed Economy* (London: Allen and Unwin, 1975).

_____ "Is 'The New Industrial State' Inevitable?" *Economic Journal* (June 1968).

_____ *Planning and the Price Mechanism* (London: Allen and Unwin, 1948).

Michael, Robert T. *The Effect of Education on Efficiency in Consumption* (New York: National Bureau of Economic Research, 1972).

Mill, John Stuart. "Utility of Religion" (1874), *Collected Works,* X (Toronto: University of Toronto Press, 1969).

_____ *Principles of Political Economy,* Book IV, Chapter VI (1848) (Harmondsworth, Eng.: Penguin, 1970).

Mishan, E. J. *The Costs of Economic Growth* (London: Staples Press, 1967).

_____ "On the Economics of Disamenity," in Robin Marris, ed., *The Corporate Society* (London: Macmillan, 1974).

Moore, Geoffrey H., and Hedges, Janice N. "Trends in Labor and Leisure," *Monthly Labor Review* (February 1971).

Myrdal, Gunnar. *The Political Element in the Development of Economic Theory* (New York: Simon and Schuster, 1969).

Nerlove, Marc. "Household and Economy: Toward a New Theory of Population and Economic Growth," *Journal of Political Economy* (March/April 1974).

Niskanen, William A. *Bureaucracy: Servant or Master?* (London: Institute of Economic Affairs, 1973).

Nordhaus, William D. "World Dynamics: Measurement without Data," *Economic Journal* (December 1973).

_____ and Tobin, James. "Is Growth Obsolete?" in *Economic Growth* (New York: National Bureau of Economic Research, 1972).

Nozick, Robert. *Anarchy, State and Utopia* (New York: Basic Books, 1974).

Olson, Mancur. *The Logic of Collective Action* (1965) (New York: Schocken, 1971).

_____ and Landsberg, Hans H., eds., *The No-Growth Society* (London: Woburn Press, 1975).

Owen, John D. *The Price of Leisure* (Rotterdam: Rotterdam University Press, 1969).

Pechman, Joseph A., and Okner, Benjamin A. *Who Bears the Tax Burden?* (Washington, D.C.: The Brookings Institution, 1974).

Peterson, George E. "The Distributional Impact of Performance Contracting in Schools," in Harold M. Hochman and George E. Peterson, eds., *Redistribution Through Public Choice* (New York: Columbia University Press, 1974).

Plamenatz, John. *Democracy and Illusion* (London: Longman, 1973).

Polanyi, Karl. *The Great Transformation* (1944) (Boston: Beacon, 1970).

Potomac Associates. *Survey of National Concerns* (1970).

Rainwater, Lee. *What Money Buys: Inequality and the Social Meaning of Income* (New York: Basic Books, 1974).

Rawls, John. *A Theory of Justice* (Cambridge, Mass.: Harvard University Press, 1971).

Ricardo, David. *The Principles of Political Economy and Taxation* (1798), in P. Straffa, ed., *Works of David Ricardo*, vol. I (Cambridge, Eng.: Cambridge University Press, 1962).

Roberts, David. *Victorian Origins of the British Welfare State* (New Haven: Yale University Press, 1960).

Robertson, D. H. "What Does the Economist Economize?" in his *Economic Commentaries* (London: Staples, 1956)

Robinson, Joan. *Economic Philosophy* (1962) (Harmondsworth, Eng.: Penguin, 1964).

Runciman, W. G. *Relative Deprivation and Social Justice* (1966) (Harmondsworth, Eng.: Penguin, 1972).

Russell, Bertrand. "In Praise of Idleness," in Eric Larrabee and Rolf Meyersohn, eds., *Mass Leisure* (New York: Free Press, 1958).

Samuelson, Paul A. *Economics*, 9th ed. (New York: McGraw-Hill, 1973).

_____ "The Pure Theory of Public Expenditure," *Review of Economics and Statistics* (1954), in R. W. Houghton, ed., *Public Finance* (Harmondsworth, Eng.: Penguin, 1970).

_____ "Social Indifference Curves," *Quarterly Journal of Economics* (February 1956).

Schelling, Thomas. "On the Ecology of Micromotives," in Robin Marris, ed., *The Corporate Society* (London: Macmillan, 1974).

Schultz, T. W. "Investment in Human Capital" (1961), in M. Blaug, ed., *Economics of Education*, vol. I (Harmondsworth, Eng.: Penguin, 1968).

Schumpeter, Joseph A. *Capitalism, Socialism and Democracy* (New York: Harper, 1942).

Scitovsky, Tibor. "Inequalities—Open and Hidden, Measured and Immeasurable," American Academy of Political and Social Science, *Annals* (September 1973).

_____ *The Joyless Economy* (New York: Oxford University Press, 1976).

_____ "What Price Economic Progress?" (1959), in his *Papers on Welfare and Growth* (London: Allen and Unwin, 1964).

Scott, Robert H. "Avarice, Altruism, and Second Party Preferences," *Quarterly Journal of Economics* (February 1972).

Sen, Amartya. "Behaviour and the Concept of Preference," *Economica* (August 1973).

_____ *On Economic Inequality* (Oxford: Clarendon Press, 1973).

Shanks, Michael. *The Stagnant Society* (Harmondsworth, Eng.: Penguin, 1961).

Shonfield, Andrew. *British Economic Policy Since the War* (Harmondsworth, Eng.: Penguin, 1958).

Simon, H. "The Compensation of Executives," *Sociometry* (1957), in A. B. Atkinson, ed., *Wealth, Income and Inequality* (Harmondsworth, Eng.: Penguin Education, 1973), pp. 199-202.

Simon, Julian L. "Interpersonal Welfare Comparisons Can Be Made—And Used for Redistribution Decisions," *Kyklos* (1974).

Smith, Adam. *The Theory of Moral Sentiments* (1759) (London: Bell, 1907).

_____ *The Wealth of Nations* (1776) (London: Dent, 1960).

Smith, J. D., and Franklin, S. D. "The Concentration of Personal Wealth, 1922-1969," *American Economic Review*, Papers and Proceedings (May 1974).

Solow, Robert M. "The Economics of Resources or the Resources of Economics," *American Economic Review*, Papers and Proceedings (May 1974).

_____ "Is the End of the World at Hand?" *Challenge* (March/April 1973).

_____ "The New Industrial State: A Discussion," *Public Interest*, no. 9 (Fall 1967).

Soltow, Lee. "Long-Run Changes in British Income Inequality," *Economic History Review* (1968).

Spence, A. Michael. *Market Signaling: The Informational Structure of Hiring and Related Processes* (Cambridge, Mass.: Harvard University Press, 1974).

Stein, Herbert. *The Fiscal Revolution in America* (Chicago: University of Chicago Press, 1969).

Stephen, James Fitzjames. *Liberty, Equality, Fraternity* (1873) (Cambridge, Eng.: Cambridge University Press, 1967).

Taubman, Paul, and Wales, Terence. *Higher Education and Earnings* (New York: McGraw-Hill, 1974).

Tawney, R. H. *The Acquisitive Society* (1920) (New York: Harcourt, 1958).

_____ *Equality* (1931) (London: Allen and Unwin, 1952).

_____ *Religion and the Rise of Capitalism* (1926) (London: Murray, 1964).

Taylor, Arthur J. *Laissez-Faire and State Intervention in Nineteenth-Century Britain* (London: Macmillan, 1972).

Thompson, Edward P. *The Making of the English Working Class* (Harmondsworth, Eng.: Penguin, 1968).

Thurow, Lester C. *Generating Inequality* (New York: Basic Books, 1975).

_____ *Investment in Human Capital* (Belmont, Calif.: Wadsworth Publishing Co., 1970).

_____ and Lucas, Robert E. B. "The American Distribution of Income: A Structural Problem," U.S. Congress, Joint Economic Committee, March 17, 1972.

Tinbergen, Jan. *An Interdisciplinary Approach to the Measurement of Utility or Welfare* (Dublin: Economic and Social Research Institute, 5th Geary Lecture, 1972).

Titmuss, Richard M. *The Gift Relationship* (London: Allen and Unwin, 1970).

_____ *Social Policy, 1939-45* (London: Allen and Unwin, 1974).

Tullock, Gordon. "The Charity of the Uncharitable," in Armen A. Alchian and others, *The Economics of Charity* (London: Institute of Economic Affairs, 1973), pp. 16-32.

_____ *The Politics of Bureaucracy* (Washington, D.C.: Public Affairs Press, 1965).

United States, Council of Economic Advisers. "Distribution of Income," *Annual Report 1974*, chap. 5.

_____ Department of Commerce, Bureau of Census. *Characteristics of Second Home Owners for the United States, 1970,* Census of Housing, HC 51 (13).

_____ _____ _____ *Current Housing Reports,* Series H-121, no. 16.

_____ Department of Housing and Urban Development. *Third Annual Report* (1967).

Usher, Dan. *The Price Mechanism and the Meaning of National Income Statistics* (Oxford: Clarendon Press, 1968).

Vickrey, William S. "The Goals of Economic Life," in A. D. Ward, ed., *Goals of Economic Life* (New York: Harper, 1953), reprinted as "An Exchange of Questions between Economics and Philosophy," in E. S. Phelps, ed., *Economic Justice* (Harmondsworth, Eng.: Penguin Education, 1973).

_____ "One Economist's View of Philanthropy," in Frank G. Dickinson, ed., *Philanthropy and Public Policy* (New York: National Bureau of Economic Research, 1962).

Vilander, Kathleen. "Outer-City: Suburbia Seeks New Solutions," *Real Estate Review* (Summer 1973).

Weber, Max. *The Protestant Ethic and the Spirit of Capitalism* (1904) (New York: Scribner's Sons, 1958).

Weisbrod, Burton A. "Collective-Consumption Services of Individual-Consumption Goods," *Quarterly Journal of Economics* (August 1964).

Westergaard, J. H. "Sociology: The Myth of Classlessness," in Robin Blackburn, ed., *Ideology in Social Science* (London: Collins Fontana, 1972).

Wicksteed, Philip H. *The Common Sense of Political Economy* (1910), vol. II (London: Routledge and Kegan Paul, 1933).

Winch, Donald. *Economics and Policy* (London: Hodder and Stoughton, 1969).

Young, George. *Tourism, Blessing or Blight?* (Harmondsworth, Eng.: Penguin, 1973).

Young, Michael. *The Rise of the Meritocracy 1870-2033* (1958) (Harmondsworth, Eng.: Penguin, 1961).

_____ and Willmott, Peter. *Family and Kinship in East London* (London: Routledge and Kegan Paul, 1957).

_____ *The Symmetrical Family* (London: Routledge and Kegan Paul, 1973).

Index

Aaron, Henry, 104
Abrams, Mark, 111
Adding-up problem, 4, 7
Advertising, 82-83
Affluence: frustrations of, 7, 67, 73, 107-110, 113-114; paradox of, 1, 7, 26, 175. *See also* Economic growth
Akerlof, G. A., 97
Altruism, 78-82, 94-96, 104, 139, 142, 146-147
American Medical Association, 86
Antigrowth school, 4, 19, 37-38
Arrow, Kenneth, 47, 95, 100, 105, 134, 143
Asquith, H. H., 133
Auction process, 28-30, 31-36, 40, 42, 45, 52, 102, 150

Bachrach, Peter, 94
Bagehot, Walter, 163
Balassa, Bela, 28
Barry, Brian, 134, 136, 140, 155
Baumol, William J., 25, 28
Becker, Gary S., 47, 73, 93
Beckerman, Wilfred, 17, 38, 57, 62, 72, 98
Behavioral standard, distinguished from preferences, 146-147, 157
Beigel, Hugo G., 99
Bell, Daniel, 43, 44, 167
Bellah, Robert N., 138
Bentham, Jeremy, 133
Benthamite calculus, 60-61, 125

Bielckus, C. L., 33
Blaug, M., 46
Bookshops, neglect of option demand, 40
Boulding, Kenneth E., 93, 104, 147
Bourgeois virtue, 137
Bowen, William G., 25, 28, 46, 49
Bowley, Arthur, 15
Brittan, Samuel, 72, 127, 135
Buchanan, James M., 89, 93, 131
Bureaucracy, individual maximization in, 129-130, 144
Burke, Edmund, 162, 174, 188
Butler, David, 171

Capitalism: its dynamics, 110, 120, 164-165, 170; favorable inaugural conditions, 11, 117, 176-177; its institutional bias, 105-106; and moral values, 117-118, 133-134, 157, 175; related to market bias, 91
Carefree society, 26, 72, 164
Catch-22, 136, 143-144
Chicago approach: to economic liberalism, 122, 128, 137, 182; to political action, 93-94, 146; to sexual pairing, 87, 96-98; to unification of social sciences, 46, 92-93
Chinoy, Ely, 169
Choice, *see* Economic allocation; Freedom of choice
Civilisation de toujours plus, la, 62
Clark, J. B., 153

Clawson, Marion, 168
Clout, H. D., 34
Club of Rome, 4
Collective action, 4, 5, 10, 118, 146,
  171, 179, 181; in *Catch-22*, 143-144;
  its rationale, 135-136
Collective advance, 169-170
Collective bargaining, 9, 118, 132,
  145, 153-156, 171-173
Collective goods, 3-5, 17, 89-90, 99,
  145, 157
Collective objectives and individual
  maximization, 146-147, 157, 188
Collectivism, reluctant, 1, 7, 175
Commercialization effect, 84, 89, 94,
  105, 130; in education, 129-130; in
  leisure, 89-91; in medicine, 86, 94; in
  sex, 87, 95, 101
Commodity approach to politics, 94
Commodity bias, 84-94, 105, 129, 167
Common property, 92, 186
Comte, Auguste, 141
Congestion, physical and social, 3-5,
  22, 27-31, 36-41, 85, 167-168
Consumer sovereignty, 61, 108-109
Consumerism, 82-84, 109; in sex, 100-
  101
Consumption: defensive or intermedi-
  ate, 57, 59, 62, 64, 113, 168; as the
  economic objective, 16-18, 61, 93,
  123-124; as a malleable aggregate,
  17, 175; public, 57, 106-107, 132,
  148; service-intensive, 24; social
  pressures, 112-113; time-absorbing,
  72-77, 81
Cooper, Michael H., 94
Cosgrove, Isobel, 37
Crean, John F., 50
Credentials, educational, 47-51
Crosland, Anthony, 17, 72
Cross-section fallacy, 168
Crowding, *see* Congestion
Crowther, Geoffrey, 126

Dahl, Robert A., 93
David, E. J., 35
De Jouvenel, Bertrand, 62
De Toqueville, Alexis, 162, 167

Democracy: dependence on participa-
  tion, 94; economic consequences of,
  162-165; economic theory of, 93-94,
  146
Denison, E. F., 47, 77
Deprivation, relative, 111, 113, 151
Diamond, Robert S., 33
Distributional compulsion, 1, 2, 7,
  152-158
Distributional struggle, 6, 15, 32, 38,
  118, 172, 174, 181-182, 185
Downs, Anthony, 93, 94
Duesenberry, James, 111
Durbin, Evan, 126, 157
Durkheim, Emile, 141

Easterlin, Richard, 111, 112
Economic advance: collective, 169-
  172; individual, 5, 9, 10, 169-170;
  opportunities for, 4-5, 35, 162-165
Economic allocation, market and political mechanisms for, 4, 18, 81, 90-
  91, 148, 157, 187
Economic growth, 1, 6-10, 15-20, 24,
  32, 104, 112, 163-164, 166, 169, 174;
  limits to, 4, 19-20, 175, 180-181,
  188; process of, 44, 166-172, 175;
  theory of, 16-17. *See also* Scarcity
Economic input, 16, 58, 67
Economic output, 7-8, 16, 45, 55-67,
  118, 141, 164, 176; defensive or intermediate, 44, 55-57; pattern of, 108
Economics: classical, 19, 61, 118-121,
  153; neoclassical, 45, 60-62, 110
"Economics imperialism," 93
Education, 5-6, 30-31, 45-51, 57, 103,
  151, 183-187; commercialization effect, 129-130; as a positional good,
  48-51, 53, 149; and suicide, 112
Egalitarianism, dynamic of, 166, 174,
  175, 188
Elitism in the liberal tradition: British,
  24, 122, 125-127; neoclassical and
  American, 61, 128
Embourgeoisement, 170, 172
Equality, economic, 173-175. *See also*
  Distributional compulsion; Distri-
  butional struggle

Equality of opportunity, 5-6, 162-163. *See also* Distributional compulsion; Distributional struggle

Ethos: bourgeois, 170, 176; individual, 132, 144, 188; market, 143; social, 12, 86, 151

"Excessive expectations," 8-9, 188

Expenditure, *see* Consumption

Externalities, 52-53, 86, 187; in friendship, 80-81

Frankel, S. Herbert, 63

Freedom of choice, 4, 18, 92, 187-189

Freeman, Richard B., 43, 50, 51

Friedman, Milton, 122, 137, 182

Friendliness, 77-81

Gagnon, John H., 100

Galbraith, John Kenneth, 17, 62, 107-110, 127

Game theory, 52, 66, 136, 173

Giddens, Anthony, 43

Gintis, Herbert, 86

Goldthorpe, John, 145, 169, 171

Good Samaritan, 79-80

"Goods aren't goods," 85

Gordon, Scott, 126

Gross national product, 8, 15-17, 55-59, 63-64, 73-75

Growth as substitute for redistribution, 7, 66-67, 174. *See also* Economic growth

Haavelmo, Trygve, 80

Halsey, A. H., 170

Happiness, relation to income, 111-114

Hardin, G., 92

Harmony of interests, dynamic model, 164, 166-167, 175

Harrod, Roy, 23-27, 127

Hayek, Friedrich, 131, 165, 188

Hayek-Friedman school, 132, 182

Heller, Joseph, 136, 143-144

Hirsch, Fred, 92

Hobbesian conflict, 65, 185

Human capital, *see* Education

Idiotariat, 126

Income distribution, *see* Distributional compulsion; Distributional struggle; Relative income

Individualism: contrasted with collective advance, 169-173; liberal fallacy, 135, 140; misapplied aggregation, 6-10; in Adam Smith and in Chicago, 12, 137; social rationale, 178-180, 190. *See also* Private interests

Inflation, 9, 118, 172-174

Invisible hand, 11; guided invisible hand, 119, 131, 146-147 (*see also* Managed capitalism); original moral context, 65; and social scarcity, 178-179

Jencks, Christopher, 149

Job satisfaction, 16, 41-42, 44, 51, 71-72, 113, 183, 184

Johnson, Harry G., 46, 93, 110, 123, 126

Johnson, Samuel, 48, 133

Juster, Thomas, 57, 58

Justice, functional role in capitalism, 132-134, 144-145, 152-153, 182, 190

Kahn, Alfred E., 40

Kahn, Herman, 25, 44

Kennedy administration, 127

Keynes, John Maynard, 24-26, 72, 119-128, 133-135, 156, 157, 163, 164, 182

Keynesianism, political, 123-134; and economic journalists, 127

Keynesian system, 15, 119, 122, 164

Knight, Frank, 31, 61

Kristol, Irving, 137

Kropotkin, P., 77

Kuznets, Simon, 44, 58, 77, 166

Laissez-faire, 11, 12, 121, 124-126

Lancaster, Kelvin, 85

Levitt, Theodore, 137

Liberal opportunity state, 11, 188

Liberalism: Keynes and ultras, 123-125; political and economic, 161-162; pragmatic approach, 179, 189-

190; role of self-interest, 137. *See also* Elitism
Libertarianism, economic, 182
Linder, Staffan, 23, 24, 72-73, 77, 98
Lockwood, David, 169, 171, 172
Love, as economic maximand, 95. *See also* Altruism; Friendliness; Sex
Luxuries, changing function, 65-67

Macfie, A. L., 65
MacIntyre, Alasdair, 138
Macmillan, Harold, 126, 134
Macrae, Norman, 25, 127
Macromorality, 133, 175
Maine, Henry, 121
Malthus, Thomas, 19
Managed capitalism, 118, 123-132; intellectual foundations, 119, 133-134
Market failure, 52, 108
Market mechanism: for positional goods, 28-31; social foundations of, 12, 117, 120-122, 141
Marriage, economics of, 96-101
Marriage contract, 87, 99, 101
Marris, Robin, 37, 41
Marshall, Alfred, 60-61, 119, 157-158, 170
Marwick, Arthur, 161
Marx, Karl, 26, 60, 62, 84, 105, 123, 133, 138, 165
Marxism: carefree society, 26; end of scarcity, 164; on commercialization bias, 86, 105; on role of interests, 127-128, 165; on wants as objects, 61
Matthews, Robin, 63
McKean, Roland N., 80
Meade, J. E., 108, 126
Meadows, Dennis L., 4
Mercantile populism, 61
Merit and meritocracy, 50, 126, 149, 162-163
Micromorality, 132-134
Mill, John Stuart: on market correctives, 119; on self-interest and altruism, 12, 95, 133, 137, 142; "small numbers" state, 142; on working class, 163, 170

Mishan, E. J., 37, 38
Mobility, 80, 81
Moore, Geoffrey H., 72
Morality: capitalism's legacy, 11-12, 117, 177; as a collective good, 138, 141-142, 145; in managed capitalism, 119, 126-129, 132-134, 180
Museum charges, 91
Myrdal, Gunnar, 123

Nader, Ralph, 82, 109
National accounts, *see* Gross national product
"Needs," 44, 57-58, 61, 102, 113
Niskanen, William A., 144
Nordhaus, William D., 19, 63
Norman, Montagu, 126
Nozick, Robert, 134

Olson, Mancur, 136, 144

Paternalism, 122, 124
Pechman, Joseph A., 104
Performance contracting, 129-130
Peterson, George E., 129
Pigou, A. C., 119, 135
Plamenatz, John, 147
Polanyi, Karl, 163
Politics, commodity approach to, 93, 94, 147
Pollution, 57, 64, 106
Positional competition, 5, 52-54, 64, 66-67, 71, 75, 102-105, 176, 185; and time pressure, 75
Positional goods, 11, 27-31, 36, 38-39, 60; capitalization, 35-36, 173
Positional jobs, 41, 183-184
Power, 134, 152-153; acquisitive, 154-155, 162; disruptive, 155-156; political, 134, 155, 161-162
Prices, *see* Market mechanism
Prisoner's dilemma, 136
Private interests, maximization of: in bureaucracy, 129-130, 144; with collective goods, 136, 144, 146-148, 150-151, 157, 178, 188; as constraint or desideratum, 121-122, 137; under managed capitalism, 124, 130-132;

in personal relations, 81, 99; and social ethic, 11-12, 82-83. *See also* Individualism

Privatization, 88, 90, 92; cumulative effects, 104, 109

Productivity: in education, 47, 49; in material and positional sectors, 27-28; and pay, 43, 153; and valuation of leisure, 72, 74, 98

Property rights, 91-92, 186

Prostitution as commercialization effect, 87, 100

Public expenditure, 103-104, 107, 168

Public goods, *see* Collective goods

Quotas, ethnic, 187

Rainwater, Lee, 112-113

Rawls, John, 134, 140, 152, 156

Reference groups, 112, 171

Relative income: and happiness, 111-113; and positional goods, 6, 36, 113, 185

Religion, economic role of, 138-143

Ricardo, David, 17, 19, 60

Roberts, David, 126

Robertson, D. H., 95

Robinson, Joan, 139

Rousseau, Jean Jacques, 174

Runciman, W. G., 169

Russell, Bertrand, 44, 135

Samuelson, Paul A., 96, 120, 133-134, 148

Scarcity: dynamics of social scarcity, 25-26, 67; economic, 22, 95, 164; physical, 4, 19, 20, 21; social, 3, 7, 20-21, 28-30, 65, 102, 107, 111, 150, 175, 178, 181, 185, 187

Scenic land, 32-36, 91, 186

Schelling, Thomas, 37, 89, 150

Schultz, T. W., 46

Schumpeter, Joseph, 93, 165, 188

Scitovsky, Tibor, 23, 28, 80, 113

Scott, Robert H., 78

Segmentation, social, 149

Self-interest and social norm, 88, 99-100, 130, 146-147. *See also* Individualism; Private interests

Sen, Amartya, 50, 99, 139, 146, 147

Service industries, 42-44, 171-172

Services, personal, 23, 24, 28, 56, 75

Sex: limits of individual optimization, 98-101; open or implicit commercialization, 87, 98, 100

Shanks, Michael, 127

Shonfield, Andrew, 127

Simon, H., 41

Simon, Julian L., 112

Smith, Adam: on consumption as the economic objective, 123; his invisible hand, 2, 119—in *Moral Sentiments*, 65-66, 137—supporting social principle, 11-12; on trickling down, 166-168

Sociability, and economic basis of its decline, 77-82, 89

Social indicators, 8, 55, 63-64, 112

Social norms, *see* Morality; Self-interest

Social restraints, economic rationale, 99-100, 147

Socialism, consumption oriented, 106, 164

Solow, Robert M., 19, 27, 108

Soltow, Lee, 166

Speculation, morality of, 133

Spence, A. Michael, 32

Standard of living, 1, 8, 9, 24-25, 66, 72, 172-173

Stein, Herbert, 127

Stephen, James Fitzjames, 141, 143

Strachey, John, 126

Substitution: in positional goods, 66; in production and consumption, 18-20, 109

Suburbs, 36-41, 90-91

Suicide, 112

Taubman, Paul, 47-48

Tawney, R. H., 138, 164, 165, 188, 189

Taylor, Arthur J., 125

Technocratic approach, 125, 127, 190

Thompson, Edward P., 138

Thurow, Lester C., 43, 47, 49, 51

Time, scarcity of, 72-81, 84; effects on

friendliness and sex, 80, 98
Tinbergen, Jan, 51
Titmuss, Richard, 86, 94, 105, 141, 161
Tourism, 37-38, 167
Trickling down, 166-168
Trinkets, contrasted with positional
  goods, 65-66
Trust, 86, 88, 97, 99, 141
Tullock, Gordon, 93, 104, 144
Tyranny of small decisions, 40, 79,
  106, 168

Unemployment, 58, 118, 135
Usher, Dan, 63
Utilitarianism, 140, 141, 147
Utopianism, 190

Vacation homes, 33-34, 168
Vickrey, William S., 189
Vietnam war, 127, 129, 144, 190

Vilander, Kathleen, 40
Virginia school, 146

Wales, Terence, 47-48
Wants: hierarchy, 58-59; relation to
  welfare, 60-62
Wealth, democratic and oligarchic, 23-
  27
Weber, Max, 138
Weisbrod, Burton A., 40
Welfare, see Economic output; Gross
  national product
Westergaard, J. H., 110
Wicksteed, Philip H., 23, 66, 81
Willmott, Peter, 34, 91, 167
Winch, Donald, 126

Young, Michael, 34, 91, 149, 167

Zoning, 41